SPEED-READING

The Easy Way

Howard Stephen Berg

and

Marcus Conyers

BARRON'S

The reading selections in this book were printed with permission as follows: pages 27–30 (P. Dutwin and H. Diamond, *Writing the Easy Way, 2nd ed.*, Barron's Educational Series, Inc., 1991); pages 120–143 (J. Snyder and C. L. Rogers, *Barron's College Review Series: Biology, 3rd ed.*, Barron's Educational Series, Inc., 1995); pages 144–147 (E. Kostiner, *Barron's EZ-101 Study Keys: Chemistry*, Barron's Educational Series, Inc., 1992); pages 148–154 (J.S. Wolf, *Barron's College Review Series: Physics*, Barron's Educational Series, Inc., 1996); pages 155–166 (D. Baucum, *Barron's EZ-101 Study Keys: Psychology*, Barron's Educational Series, Inc., 1996); pages 167–183 (P.J. Eisen, *Accounting the Easy Way, 3rd ed.*, Barron's Educational Series, Inc., 1995); pages 184–189 (M. Rockowitz, *et al., How to Prepare for the GED, 9th ed.*, Barron's Educational Series, Inc., 1995); pages 190–207 (W.O Kellogg, *American History the Easy Way, 2nd ed.*, Barron's Educational Series, Inc., 1995); pages 208–233 (A. H. Bell, *et al., Barron's College Review Series: World Literature: Early Origins to 1800*, Barron's Educational Series, Inc., 1994); pages 234–248 (C. Goozner, *Business Mathematics the Easy Way, 2nd ed.*, Barron's Educational Series, Inc., 1991); pages 249–267 (R.W. Emerson, *Business Law the Easy Way*, Barron's Educational Series, Inc., 1994); pages 268–293 (R. Miller and M.R. Miller, *Electronics the Easy Way, 3rd ed.*, Barron's Educational Series, Inc., 1995); pages 294–317 (I.E. Alcamo, *Anatomy and Physiology the Easy Way*, Barron's Educational Series, Inc., 1996); pages 318–333 (W.S. Bainbridge, *Barron's College Review Series: Sociology*, Barron's Educational Series, Inc., 1997)

All inquiries should be addressed to:
Barron's Educational Series, Inc.
250 Wireless Boulevard
Hauppauge, New York 11788
http://www.barronseduc.com

International Standard Book No. 0-8120-9852-8

Library of Congress Catalog Card No. 98-72163

Printed in the United States of America

Dedicated to Marcy, Alex, and Vicki—for giving my life special meaning
...Howard Stephen Berg

Dedicated to my mother Hazel Powell and my stepfather Bryan for
their boundless belief in me and to my nieces Camellia Rose and Anna
for teaching me how learning really happens.
...Marcus Conyers

Unit 3
Practicing Your Speed-Reading the Easy Way
Skills in Different Types of Materials

How to Use This Book

EVER NOTICE HOW some books seem easy to use, while others are puzzling and difficult from the first page? Easy-to-read books are "designed with your brain in mind." These easy books contain features that work in harmony with how your brain likes to learn. With the help of subtle clues, difficult information becomes easy to learn. *Speed-Reading the Easy Way* contains many useful tools to make mastering speed-reading a snap. Use the following information to effortlessly get the most from this book:

- Each chapter begins with a brief listing of the topics it contains. Briefly scan this listing to develop an awareness of the chapter's focus and the sequence of its topics.

- Before reading each chapter, quickly scan the pages to see the charts, diagrams, subheadings, and other visual aids that you can put to use when reading. Do not attempt to learn the material contained in the chapter at this point, simply become aware that it is available for you should you require it when reading the chapter.

- Scan the Bookmap at the end of each chapter, which summarizes all the chapter's information.

Introduction

IN THE PAST TEN YEARS our knowledge of the world has doubled, and information continues to grow at an unprecedented pace. This information explosion challenges even the most gifted student to stay abreast of the latest developments. Yet, of the over 15,000 hours you spend in school and doing homework, how much time is actually spent teaching you how to learn? Think about this question for a moment. Virtually no time is spent showing you how to unleash the incredible power of your mind to master the information glut that every student faces. Yet educators are puzzled when students have difficulty learning in school.

Howard Stephen Berg
Marcus Conyers

Consider the following puzzling event. You turn on the radio, hear a few notes, then immediately recognize a familiar song you haven't heard in a long time. Effortlessly you begin singing the words to this song, just as you could for many other songs you've heard in the past. You can remember irrelevant songs like the theme to Gilligan's Island, or the jingle "you've got the right one baby, u-huh." Think about this. How can you remember the details to song lyrics you never read, accurately and completely within an instant; yet, frequently forget the title and author of a book, let alone the details of the text, after studying it for several hours? Doesn't it make sense that the same brain that can effortlessly retain meaningless details can also learn to remember information necessary for school and success? Congratulate yourself for purchasing this book for it contains the solution to this puzzle. *Speed-Reading the Easy Way* is actually a complete accelerated learning system designed to release the power of your mind for learning the things you need with little effort. Your brain's unlimited learning power is about to be released. So relax, follow the easy instructions contained in this book, and prepare to amaze yourself as you unleash the full learning potential of your mind.

The Seven Deadly Myths That Reduce Your Reading Speed

RESEARCH AT NORTHWESTERN University clearly demonstrates that right now you have the ability to read at least 1,800–2,000 words per minute. Yet it is likely that your current reading speed is around 200–250 words per minute. Why? The answer is simple. The way you were taught to read was based upon some assumptions, or myths. When you learn to let go of these myths, you will be able to rapidly increase your reading speed.

Imagine a beautiful, brightly colored hot air balloon that is able to soar effortlessly up to 2,000 feet. But right now it has seven heavy sandbags weighing it down. When these sandbags are released, the balloon will soar. The same is true about your reading speed: right now you are weighed down by seven erroneous assumptions, but once you let go of them, you'll soar, too.

1. **You need to read one word at a time.** When you were reading aloud in class, your teacher would make sure that you got each word absolutely perfect. If not, you would be corrected. Speed-readers read whole chunks of text at once rather than one single word. In fact, it has been discovered that 90% of your reading time is spent pausing between individual words. Research at the University of Minnesota has found that the average person pauses for one quarter of a second after each word. This reduces your speed to around 240 words per minute. The fact is you can read much faster by taking in whole chunks of data at one time.

2. **You need to read everything at the same speed.** Speed-readers have the ability to slow down or accelerate depending on the complexity of the material. Just as a race car driver slows his vehicle down when it approaches a curve, the speed reader slows down when there is new information that needs maximum comprehension and retention. But what happens when they reach an easy stretch? That's right. They accelerate. Research shows us that only 11 to 40 percent of a book contains the vital meaning of that book. The rest of the book contains examples and reinforcements. By reading the book at different speeds you can get through the whole text in a fraction of the time it would take to read it at "normal" speed.

3. **Slower reading speeds improve comprehension.** Has this ever happened to you? You pick up a book and begin to read. Suddenly you find that five minutes have passed and you don't even remember the name of the book. Why? You were going too slowly for your brilliant brain. When you read slowly, you are accessing the auditory front left portion of your brain. This section is one of the least efficient at storing information into long-term memory, and therefore, your comprehension actually drops. Consider the following example. Marcus once gave a seminar to celebrate the success of firefighters in Toronto. He wanted to speak about Olympic Gold Medalist Mark Tewksbury, whom he had met before. He picked up a biography on Tewksbury at the bookstore and read it in twelve minutes during the taxi ride to the seminar room. He then began to speak at the conference. Suddenly he could see the whole book like a movie in his mind's eye. At the end of the seminar a man walked up to Marcus and said, "How well did you know my brother?" Mark Tewksbury's brother had been sitting in the front row. Comprehension and recall actually increases when you read at an accelerated rate because it switches on the powerful visual area of the brain.

4. **You must read the whole book in sequence to understand it.** In school we were told that the only way to read a book is to start at the beginning, and read through to the end. Even if you don't like it. As we said earlier, only 11 to 40 percent of the book contains the real information. Speed-readers will often begin with a completely different sequence, one that maximizes comprehension and recall.

For example, much of the information in the book is contained in the final chapter—which is a summary—and in the introduction, which often paints the big picture of the book just as the picture on the box of a jigsaw puzzle shows what the completed puzzle looks like. Speed-readers can learn the key elements of a book at an accelerated rate by reading the book in a different sequence.

5. **You must stop to look up a word if you don't understand it.** Slow to average readers have been trained to stop and look up a word if they don't understand it. The simple act of stopping, going to a dictionary, looking up a definition, can take minutes out of your reading time. Often it leaves you vulnerable to distractions. For example, you might read another interesting word right next to the one you've looked up. This breaks your flow and concentration. Since books are designed to enhance comprehension, you may find that when you've gone through the entire book the word's meaning will become clear to you. So speed-readers do not stop to look up individual words. They simply mark them in the margin and look it up later if still necessary. This one step will boost your reading speed and recall tremendously.

6. **You should never use a pen or your finger as a guide during reading.** Many readers were taught specifically by their teachers not to use their finger or their pen as a reading guide. Speed-readers know that eye and hand coordination allow you to accelerate your reading speed tremendously. Marcus prefers to use a pen as a guide, and rips through pages at a high speed simply marking the bits he needs to recall. Howard, who reads at 80-pages-per-minute, simply runs his hand down the page. This simple trigger promotes accelerated reading speed.

7. **Reading a book is the same as learning the material in that book.** Reading is not the same as learning; they are two separate stages. Speed-readers know that the key to effectively acquiring information at an accelerated rate is to use the following sequence. First explore and examine the book at a high speed, second identify the key data that needs to be remembered. Third, to use specific memory tools to load this information into long term memory.

Once you understand these seven deadly myths and how they can slow your speed, you can turn these myths into factual information you can use. The sandbags that are holding back your reading speed will fall away and your reading speed will soar to new heights naturally.

Unit 1

Triggering the Peak Learning State

Chapter 1

Creating Your Peak Learning Environment

Chapter Preview

- Using various props to induce a learning state

- Choosing the ideal location for studying

- Understanding physical triggers of the learning state

- Using music to induce a learning state

- Understanding the importance of nutrition to learning

- Proper breathing for optimum learning

- Understanding the relationship of body posture to learning

- Achieving peak emotional readiness to learn

- Using learning triggers

DO YOU ALWAYS FEEL like studying? Of course not! As a human being you experience different emotional states. Some states make you feel like exercising, watching television, or going out with your friends. Other states make you feel more serious and focused on work. During this state when you are able to study most efficiently, your brain naturally absorbs text at an accelerated rate. You feel alert, alive, and interested in the materials you must learn. At other times you are tired, bored, and uninterested in learning. You are in a negative learning state. Negative learning states can waste a great deal of your energy and interfere with your studies. Using your environment effectively can help you quickly switch into a peak learning state so you can master materials more efficiently.

It's night. Your room is pitch dark, and you want to study. How are you going to accomplish any significant work? All you need to do is turn on the light. Suddenly, your room is put into a state that is suitable for learning. Just as a light turns a dark room into a suitable area for studying, the suggestions in this chapter will illuminate your mind, enabling you to release your brain's natural ability to master information. This chapter sets up a firm foundation for all the learning that you will be able to accomplish using the speed-reading techniques described. The more suggestions you employ in your daily studying, the more efficiently you can use all this book's suggestions for mastering information. So relax, and get ready for some exciting breakthroughs that will help you create your peak learning environment.

Clothing and Props

The objects in your learning environment affect your attitude toward learning. Just as wearing a business suit makes you feel more professional than wearing a bathing suit, getting down to the business of learning by making full use of the objects in your learning environment can help you quickly switch on your learning state. There are many different props you can use to full effect. Not every prop will have the same effect upon all people. Through experience you will learn which of the following props has the most influence over your learning state. Once you discover a relationship between a prop and a learning state, always try to make use of that prop to quickly propel yourself into a more positive state.

Selecting the Proper Chair

Since a great deal of study time is spent sitting in a chair, it is important to select a chair that quickly switches on a learning state. Think about the types of desks and chairs that you see in a typical high school classroom. Are they comfortable? Or do they make you slightly uncomfortable, which helps you to stay more mentally alert? For some people a plush, soft chair helps them relax and study more efficiently. Others find a comfortable chair too relaxing, which makes them feel tired, thereby reducing their learning efficiency.

Under ideal conditions, the chair you select for studying should be used for no other activity. Since life is not often ideal, you may have to sit in the same seat for different reasons. If this is the case, try moving the chair to a different location than the one you normally use. For example, if you always sit in the same chair when you eat at your kitchen table, when studying there, you should use another seat, or move your seat to a different position at the table. Why? Your body becomes conditioned to react to its environment. Sitting in the chair where you always eat will trigger feelings of hunger and the desire to eat. More blood begins moving into your stomach and digestive tract, away from your brain. This movement of blood away from your brain makes you feel tired, sluggish and uninterested in learning. Changing the chair's position when you study can anchor new associations to this same prop. Once you change chairs or move your usual one, you will be alert, interested in learning, and prepared to absorb as much information as possible in the shortest amount of time.

Choosing the Correct Desk

For many people the desk represents the most important trigger for their learning state. Whether using an actual desk or a substitute like a table, sitting at your special work area triggers associations with learning that are essential for successful study. Choosing the proper area to sit at a desk or the proper placement for a desk is important. Try to find an area that feels right to you, that is most likely to elicit feelings conducive to work. Your desk forms a relationship between these feelings. The desk's color, drawer space, and surface all influence these feelings.

Finding the Perfect Location for Studying

What type of location triggers your study state? For some people sitting in front of a large window that opens to a world filled with visual imagery is quite stimulating. Others find looking outside distracting and prefer to sit in front of a blank wall. Do you work better in a certain room in your house, or do you find changing the location of your work gives you more variety leading to more stimulation and learning?

Sometimes different subjects are easier to learn in different locations. For example, studying science may be more easy in the kitchen than in the den, while English or history is easier to learn in your bedroom, or perhaps outside on a patio or balcony. Determine which location(s) work best for your study needs. Sitting yourself in that location will help initiate your learning state.

Using Various Physical Triggers

A variety of physical triggers can help you switch on your learning state. Some people find that a full cup of coffee placed near their study area turns on their alertness state. The smell, heat, and taste of the coffee trigger the emotions associated with study and learning. For some, putting on a comfortable bathrobe or slippers does the same trick. Perhaps a running suit or a comfortable pair of blue jeans or shorts makes you feel more alert. Whatever prop stimulates your desire to study and awakens your emotional urges to study should be carefully utilized at the beginning of any important study session.

Lighting

The Relationship of Lighting to Alertness

Good lighting is essential for successful studying. Research indicates that proper lighting induces a more positive emotional state. In fact in many regions of extreme latitude where long dark winters are common, many people are prone to a form of depression linked to a lack of lighting. The cure is often prolonged exposure to intense lighting. It is a good idea to link your studies to a well-lighted area. Howard's study area has several large cone shaped bulbs in the ceiling and he often uses a halogen light to increase the brightness level when he has to read for a prolonged period. This helps induce a more positive emotional state and leads to more successful learning.

Importance of Lighting in High-Speed Reading

The higher the intensity of a room's light, the easier it is for your eyes to discriminate the letters on the printed page. This is especially true if you are near-sighted. At higher reading speeds, good lighting can make the difference between seeing the words on the page, and seeing a blur of images that are hard to comprehend.

Avoiding Eyestrain

Eyestrain can also detract from successful reading. Make certain that your lighting source is behind or overhead. Placing lights overhead helps eliminate shadows that can cause eyestrain. Never place lamps directly in front of you. Bright light shining directly into your eyes can cause severe eyestrain and, in extreme cases cause, damage to your retina, the light-sensitive area of the eye. Prolonged exposure to intense light can decrease your visual sensitivity making it difficult to read text at high speeds.

Music

The Brain's Natural Rhythm

Scientific studies indicate that certain musical beats facilitate learning. Specifically, music with one beat per second produces an enhanced learning state. Many believe playing this type of music softly in the background while studying improves concentration and retention while reducing stress. (See page 86.)

Just the opposite effect occurs when playing loud rock or heavy metal music. The beat of this music disrupts memory and concentration. This increases the likelihood of forgetting important information.

Although Howard is a big fan of this type of music at social functions and parties, he never plays it when reading or studying. Nor should you if you desire to get peak learning results from your study time.

Accelerated Learning: Music That Can Trigger Brain-Wave Activity

Tapes or CDs of special music with computerized beats that alter the brain's wave patterns are available in many stores. While writing this book, we often listened to music that puts the brain into a Theta state. Theta waves are associated with creativity, alertness, and enhanced mental capacity.

There are also special music tapes that can be played softly in the background to facilitate learning. They are excellent for stimulating creativity while reading and writing. Like many other people, you may find music helps put you quickly into a readiness state for learning.

Temperature

When you think of an ideal studying environment do you picture a hot, sticky, muggy summer's day? Of course not! Your body is adapted to work ideally in a cool, dry climate. Whenever possible, try to establish a comfortable temperature in your studying area. If necessary, find a library or other public area that maintains the proper lighting and climate for studying. Extremes of cold or hot will disrupt your ability to efficiently learn and retain information.

Achieving Peak Physical Readiness to Learn

Nutrition

Did you ever feel sleepy and unfocused after lunch? By eating the right foods in the right sequence, you can boost your learning speed and stay alert. Recent studies of accelerated learning techniques show that proper nutrition is essential for peak learning performance. Let's take a moment to examine the positive and negative effects of certain foods on your studying.

Importance of Protein

Ingesting protein shortly before important studying has a positive effect on your alertness, memory, and ability to recall essential information. Proteins can be found in meat and in certain vegetables. We find that some health food stores have high-grade protein powder than can easily be mixed with milk. We usually take a teaspoonful in a glass of milk prior to an important studying session. It provides excellent energy without causing the sluggishness that often accompanies foods that are high in sugar. Too much protein places a strain on the kidneys so use small quantities of protein. Since some people are more sensitive to certain foods than others, it is wise to check with a physician to make certain that your health will not be adversely affected by ingesting small quantities of protein powder.

Dangers of Carbohydrates

Many students begin a study session by eating candy, ice cream, soda, or other foods high in sugar, or some other form of carbohydrates. This is a major mistake. Ingesting sugar will quickly raise your energy level, but within a short time most people experience an energy drop. Exhaustion, poor concentration, and memory loss commonly accompany the ingestion of sugar or carbohydrates such as chips, pasta, potatoes, bread, foods containing MSG, or artificial sweeteners. These chemicals have been shown to significantly reduce memory in laboratory animals.

Recent studies reveal why the ingestion of carbohydrates often precludes successful studying. Shortly after ingesting even a small quantity of carbohydrates your brain starts to secrete quantities of serotonin. Serotonin is an important chemical naturally produced in the brain. Increased levels of serotonin induce a lazy, sleepy stupor that is counter-productive for studying. On the other hand, the ingestion of protein lowers the serotonin levels and helps you get more from your study time.

Fruit can provide necessary carbohydrates without the side effects. Your brain needs glucose to fuel its peak performance. Fruit requires a minimum of digestion while delivering fuel fast. It also contains a high quantity of water. Water is also essential for peak learning states to be reached.

The Importance of Eating Food in Sequence

Did you know that the order in which you eat your food actually produces different effects on your brain's chemistry? It's true! A recent study indicates that you should always eat the protein portion of your meal first, because whatever food enters your bloodstream first determines the serotonin levels of your brain. Eating protein first reduces your serotonin level, while eating carbohydrates first raises it.

Frequent Small Meals

When studying intensely for a prolonged period of time, there is a distinct advantage to "nibbling." Taking short breaks for protein, fruit, or juice will enhance your concentration and retention of materials. Fruit is particularly helpful. The sugar found in fruit does not have the adverse effect on your brain's chemistry that many other carbohydrates are known to have. Instead it provides quick energy without the drowsiness associated with other carbohydrates. Fruit is also high in water and roughage that helps keep your body healthy and more alert.

Determining Which Message to Send to Your Brain

Remember this simple rule of thumb when deciding what to eat first: protein perks, and carbohydrates calm. You can send the appropriate message to your brain by eating the right foods first. For example when you want to relax at the end of the day, carbohydrates such as pasta and potatoes are perfect. Later they may help you sleep better, which is another key to effective learning. Determine if your brain needs stimulation or calming before starting your meal, and you'll be off to a good start at establishing a positive learning state.

Ideal Meals for Learning

1. Eat breakfast: eggs, wheat germ, fruit

2. Lunch: chicken (or other protein) and salad

3. Evening Meal: potatoes, pasta, or other carbohydrate sources

4. Snack: Use fruit to sustain peak energy levels

Water

Your body is mostly water. Drinking eight full glasses of water each day is essential for good health. Water helps your body eliminate toxins that build up throughout the day. Toxins can disrupt your focus, memory, and recall of important information. You brain also needs the water to conduct the electricity of its 20-watt electrical capacity. Studies also indicate that drinking water reduces stress. Make a habit of drinking a full glass of water every two hours, and your body will become more alert.

Breathing

More blood flows to your brain than to any other organ. Blood contains food, removes toxins, and also brings vital oxygen to your brain. Proper breathing can help put you into a relaxed, focused, and alert state with no effort. Most people breathe from the top of their chest, taking in only a small part of the air their lungs are equipped to handle. Make a habit of taking in deep breaths. Breathe from the bottom of your diaphragm and draw in complete lungfuls of air. This increases the oxygen flow to your brain, and will enable you to sustain an alert, focused state for a longer period of time.

Posture

1. Body position has a huge impact on your learning state. To discover this for yourself do the following experiment:

   • Sit in your chair and look down at the ground, breathing shallowly and then frown. How do you feel on a scale from 1 to 10?

   • Sit in your chair and look up at the ceiling. Put a big grin on your face and breathe deeply. How do you feel on a scale from 1 to 10?

   Incidentally, by performing the above exercise you have released your brain's endorphins, a potent chemical substance that produces a positive state of mind.

2. To maintain your optimum learning state, sit up straight with both feet flat on the ground. This assures maximum balance and an excellent blood flow to the brain. Always avoid crossing your legs. This restricts circulation while increasing tension in your body.

Achieving Peak Emotional Readiness to Learn

Switching On Your Brain

To help your brain work with maximum efficiency you need to get both sides working simultaneously. Your brain's left side focuses more on linear-specific information such as words, sequences, and numbers. In contrast, the right side focuses more on spatial information, such as color, patterns, feelings, and more abstract concepts. Your brain naturally switches the domination of each side every 90 minutes.

Your brain's left hemisphere operates the right side of your body while the right controls the left side of your body. Performing crossover exercises boosts your brain's performance by activating the energy of both hemispheres simultaneously. These types of exercises, which we call neurobics, sharpen reactions.

Establishing Peak Learning Triggers

Until now you have been learning how to establish environmental conditions that will trigger peak learning states. Thanks to a new science called NLP, neuro-linguistic programming, created by Dr. Richard Bandler and John Grinder, it is now possible to instantly put yourself into a peak mental state for learning by using psychological triggers.

What is NLP?

Just as modern computers use a language like DOS or Windows to run their programs, we use language to understand our world. NLP studies the relationship between our world of language and uses it to help us establish positive mental states. Often NLP uses classical conditioning to establish these positive states.

Classical conditioning was discovered by the Russian psychologist Ivan Pavlov. In his famous experiment using a hungry dog, Pavlov was able to demonstrate that an organism could be conditioned to respond to a familiar trigger. In his experiment, Pavlov rang a bell just before feeding his dog. Pavlov knew that a dog salivates when eating, and he tried to get the dog to salivate when hearing the bell. Sure enough, after pairing the ringing bell with food enough times, the sound of the bell alone triggered the dog's salivation.

Just as Pavlov was able to get a dog to salivate when it heard a bell, you can learn how to put yourself into a deep state of relaxation in order to perform at your peak learning level. You will learn how to anchor this positive emotional learning state with a trigger just as the dog's salivation was triggered by a bell. You will also learn how to establish a peak energy state to continue your studies long past your prior exhaustion point. These simple exercises will enable you to use higher reading speeds and learning techniques even when you are in a noisy environment, or taking an important examination under very tense conditions.

Entering the Alert Relaxed State

Learning to anchor a relaxed learning state is easy. First you need to establish a deep relaxed state, and then link that state to a bodily movement that would not normally be experienced. A simple anchor consists of pressing your thumb and pointer fingers together tightly while raising your hands and quickly expelling your air.

Here are the simple steps to follow:

- Press the thumb and pointer finger of both hands tightly together.

- Raise both hands and your arms upward toward the ceiling.

- Expel the air in your lungs forcefully and quickly while performing this motion.

This simple motion will become the anchor for your deep relaxed state. As soon as you experience a deep state of relaxation, perform your anchor. By continually linking your relaxed state to the anchor movements, you will soon be able to trigger your relaxed state by simply going through the motions of your anchor. Just as the bell stimulated a salivation response in Pavlov's dog, through classical conditioning, you can link your anchor to a deep state of relaxation and thereby establish your peak learning state instantaneously.

Here's a simple method for creating a deeply relaxed state. It is a technique developed at Harvard Medical School called the relaxation response.

The steps for performing the relaxation response are simple:

- Sit up straight in a chair with your feet flat on the floor.

- Close your eyes while placing your hands gently in your lap.

- Begin breathing slowly and deeply while repeating in your mind the number one.

- Say: one, one, one, one . . .

- Continue repeating until your mind wanders.

- As soon as you become aware your mind is wandering, begin repeating the next number, two.

- Continue repeating two until your mind wanders again.

- Then begin softly repeating the number three in your mind.

Each time your mind wanders simply begin repeating the next number in your series. Linking this exercise to slow, deep breathing will quickly establish a deep state of relaxation. When you are aware of a deep sense of peace, perform your anchor and picture yourself in a deep state of peace. Repeat these steps a few dozen times until you can instantly elicit your relaxed state by performing your anchor.

Several times a week link your relaxation exercise to your anchor. This will keep your response strong and ready to use whenever necessary. When you start to panic when studying for an important exam, use your trigger to quickly relax. When beginning an important examination and panic, trigger your anchor and instantly enter a state of deep, relaxed concentration. Using this anchor will multiply the power of your speed-reading many times over. It's simple, fun, and easy to use.

Entering the Peak Energy State

Sometimes a long study session requires more energy, rather than a state of relaxation. You can also establish an anchor that will energize you and enable you to perform at peak levels.

It is important that each anchor be uniquely different. Here is a simple anchor that can be linked to increasing your energy level:

- Quickly thrust both hands in front of you as if you are throwing a punch with both arms simultaneously.

- Exhale vigorously while thrusting your arms.

- Imagine your energy levels rising while performing this motion.

Raising your energy level can be accomplished by performing Exercises 1 through 4 in sequence. Be sure to perform all exercises during the same session. At the conclusion of all four exercises perform your anchor. Repeat these four exercises followed by your anchor several times until the anchor can elicit the state of mental alertness caused by these exercises. You have conditioned yourself to respond with a high energy level to your anchor. Use it whenever you feel tired, but still have a great deal of demanding mental work to accomplish. Incidentally, after stimulating yourself to a high energy level and completing your work, you may find it hard to relax. Use your relaxation trigger to put yourself into a quiet, relaxed state when you want to tone down your energy. Using these triggers will enable you to make peak use of your brain's unlimited learning power quickly and easily.

Now that you can control your learning state, you are ready to learn speed-reading.

EXERCISE 1

While standing, cross your left hand over your right shoulder and pat your back. Then place your right hand over your left shoulder and pat your back. Continue this exercise for ten repetitions.

EXERCISE 2

While standing, lift your left knee, and tap it with your right hand. Next tap your left hand on your right knee. Alternate these steps ten times.

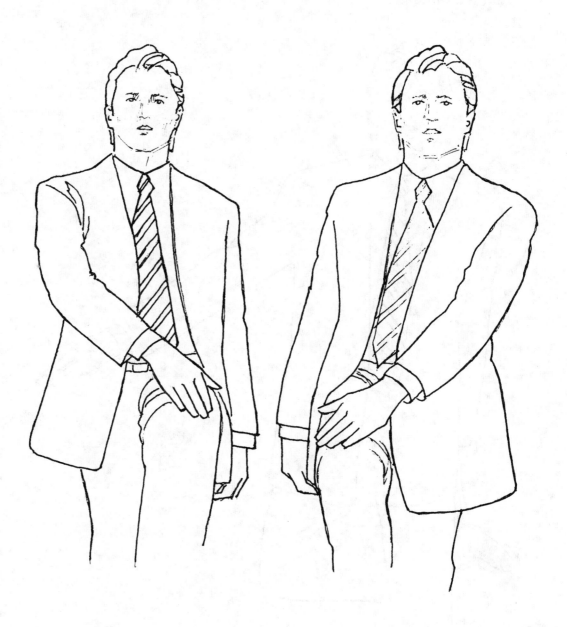

EXERCISE 3

While standing, raise your left foot behind your right knee; tap your right hand on your left heel. Then alternate and tap your left hand on your right heel. Repeat ten times.

EXERCISE 4

Finish the above sequence of exercises by rubbing your hands together until they become warm. Then press them tightly together. You should feel an instant surge of mental energy upon conclusion of these exercises.

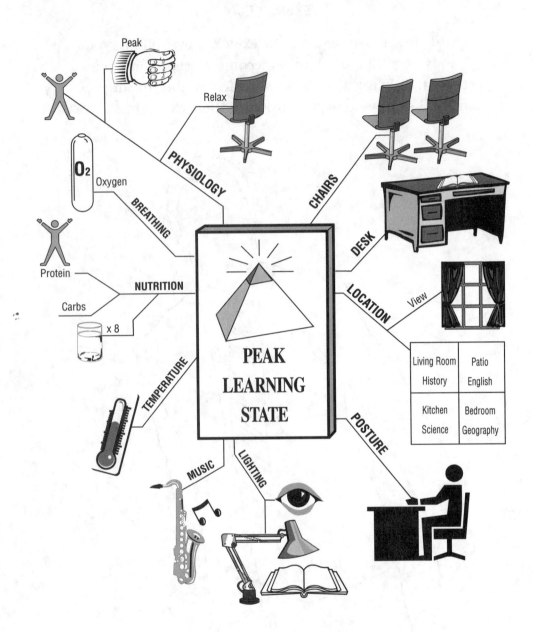

CHAPTER ONE SELF-TEST

1. List four things that you can do to make your work environment more productive.

2. Describe the relationship of lighting to alertness.

3. How can music improve learning efficiency?

4. What is the importance of protein to memory?

5. Describe the dangers of carbohydrates to memorization of details.

6. Describe an ideal meal for your brain.

7. What is a learning trigger?

8. How can you enter into a relaxed learning state?

9. How can you enter into a peak energy state?

Unit 2

The Mechanics of Speed-Reading

Chapter 2
Sharpening Your Reading Skills

Chapter Preview

- Determining your reading speed
- Proper use of the hands for speed-reading
- Page turning techniques
- Eye-hand coordination
- Expanding the visual field
- Increasing your reading speed

How to Rocket Through Text

UNDERSTANDING SPEED-READING IS easier once you know why reading is the only visual activity that is done so slowly. For example, you look at a television or movie and see the entire screen. Yet, when you look at a book, you don't see the entire page. Why are the same brain and eyes working so slowly in a book, when they work so swiftly doing everything else that is visual? During reading, your eyes turn the visual passages into an internal dialogue. As a result, while reading you tend to hear the information being seen. More simply, during reading you use your eyes to hear information on a page, instead of seeing information on a page. Think about this statement. It is very important.

Contrary to what happens when we perform other visual activities, when reading words we hear a voice in our heads. You hear this voice read the words of the text one at a time, just as you would hear the words of a conversation. Your need to hear information on a page instead of seeing it is the bottleneck that causes slow reading. Quite simply reading resembles hearing instead of seeing.

Picture yourself standing in a large group of people. Everyone around you is speaking at the same time. It is impossible to understand what they are saying. Yet, you can see all of these people at one time, just as you can hear only one word at a time while seeing all of them on the page. If you could learn to comprehend more text at a time, you would get a dramatic increase in your reading speed. Fortunately, this is an easy goal to obtain.

The largest section of the human brain is devoted to seeing. It only takes a few hours of practice to learn to see and understand large chunks of text. More importantly, your comprehension will actually get better at the higher speed.

Many speed-reading programs expect the student to conform to a specific technique. *Speed-Reading the Easy Way* is a flexible program that adjusts to your needs. In this section, we will experiment to find the speed-reading tools that are best suited to how your brain processes information. This flexibility will assure you of the highest speed possible with a minimum of effort. Some of you will read each line of text more quickly, while others will find it easy to read several lines of text quickly. Each of us is different and our brains have a slightly different way of processing information. Through experimentation you will find the technique that is best suited to your particular learning style.

Increasing your reading speed requires you to change the way your brain views text. This section of *Speed-Reading the Easy Way* will teach you how to increase your reading speed in several steps:

1. You will learn the mechanical techniques for becoming a more visual reader.

2. You will learn how to draw upon your brain's natural ability to decode text into meaningful information.

Determining Your Current Reading Speed

Less than 1% of North Americans read over 400 words per minute. Yet, according to a study by Xerox™ Corporation, you must read at least 1,000,000 words per week just to stay current in a single subject. Imagine that. Over 1,000,000 words per week! The average individual reads between 150 and 400 words per minute. Marcus reads close to 10,000 words per minute, and Howard holds the world record of 25,000 words per minute. How fast do you read? Knowing your initial reading speed will help you determine how much faster you are reading later.

You can determine your current reading speed by reading the following passage. Set an alarm clock for one minute and then read the following passage until the alarm rings:

1   A *paragraph* is a group of sentences about one topic.
2 Traditionally, the first line of each new paragraph is indented
3 about an inch, to let the reader know that a new topic is about
4 to be discussed. Block style, with no indentation, is common
5 in business writing; however, a double space between the
6 paragraphs indicates a break between ideas or topics.
7   What is the importance of this information to you as a
8 writer? The answer is clear: in every paragraph you write,
9 develop one idea fully, and don't wander from that topic to
10 another one. It is unfair to your readers, for instance, to start
11 a paragraph with *fossils* as your topic and finish with *volcanic*
12 *eruptions* as the central thought.
13   As you read the following paragraph, think about the
14 one idea that the writer develops. What is that idea?

15   Research shows that habits and life-style in the 1990s are
16   a greater risk to our health than any other factor. Where
17   pneumonia and diphtheria took their toll in the nine-
18   teenth century, smoking, poor diet, and drinking exact
19   their toll in the twentieth. These poor habits greatly
20   increase our chances of developing cancer and heart dis-
21   ease or of dying in an auto accident.

22 Explanation: The writer states the topic in the first sentence:
23 our habits and life-style, not other factors, put our health at
24 risk. The rest of the paragraph supports that statement. The
25 paragraph explains what some of the risks used to be
26 (pneumonia and diphtheria) and what they are now (smok-
27 ing, poor diet, drinking). The last sentence tells what life-
28 threatening results our habits can lead to.
29   Each paragraph must focus on one idea. Sometimes this
30 idea can be expressed in one sentence: "Thank you for con-
31 sidering this request." Usually a paragraph contains at least
32 three sentences. In business communications, however,
33 more than five or six sentences create paragraphs that invite
34 skimming. In any case, if you want your writing read, keep
35 your paragraphs to a manageable length.

36 **Purpose: First, Last, and Always**
37   Just when you thought you'd never hear it again, here's
38 another reminder: purpose is everything—or nearly everything.
39 As we said in Chapter 1, when you know *why* you're writing
40 something—to inform, to persuade, to motivate to action—
41 you're more likely to organize your thoughts effectively.
42 When you're editing your work, ask yourself, "How does this
43 paragraph fit in with the purpose of my report, letter, or
44 memo?" Furthermore, every paragraph should have the
45 characteristics of a report as a whole: a purpose, a topic, and
46 supporting ideas that develop the topic.
47   Below is a paragraph from a health report whose main
48 purpose is to inform the reader about the dangerous effects
49 of the sun's ultraviolet rays. Keep three questions in mind as
50 you read the paragraph. 1. Is the purpose of the paragraph to
51 persuade, inform, or motivate? 2. Do you think this paragraph
52 advances the purpose of the report? Explain. 3. Which sentence
53 states the topic?

54   Ultraviolet radiation from the sun can reach you and
55   burn your skin even if you're not directly in the sunlight.
56   If you love to sunbathe, you should know that 80 per-
57   cent of ultraviolet radiation can get through a layer of
58   clouds. A beach umbrella will only partially protect you
59   because ultraviolet rays reflect off the sand. Even light

60 beach clothing allows 25 percent of the ultraviolet rays
61 to reach your skin. Don't count on a swim to shield you
62 either, since 50 percent of the sun's ultraviolet radiation
63 will reach those parts of your body that are under water.

64 Let's answer the three questions stated above. The purpose
65 of the paragraph is to inform. The paragraph ties directly into
66 the overall purpose of the report because readers need to
67 know how ultraviolet radiation reaches them in order to
68 avoid the dangerous rays. The paragraph gives information
69 that dispels myths about protection from the sun. Finally,
70 the writer gets right to the point by stating the topic in the
71 first sentence.

What's Your Plan?

72 **What's Your Plan?**
73 Paragraphs don't just happen. Writing each paragraph
74 calls for some careful preparation on your part. The first step
75 is to identify your topic and then state it in a topic sentence.
76 The next step is to select details to support, or back up, the
77 topic so that your paragraph will be adequately developed
78 and unified. A *well-developed paragraph* provides enough
information to explain the topic in a meaningful way: it
79 doesn't leave the reader hanging in midair, unsure of the
80 point the writer is making. In a *unified paragraph,* every idea
81 presented is directly related to the topic sentence.
82 As you draft your topic sentence, keep in mind the *plan
83 of development* that you will be using when you write the
84 paragraph. The way you word your topic sentence and the
85 type of details you include in the paragraph will depend on
86 the plan you have chosen. Sticking to this plan will make it
87 easier for you to develop your ideas and will help keep the
88 paragraph unified.
89 There are a number of different plans that writers use:
90 • Give examples that explain or support the topic sentence.
91 • Defend the opinion stated in the topic sentence.
92 • Compare and contrast two items or ideas stated in the
93 topic sentence.
94 • Describe chronologically, or in time order, what the topic
95 sentence states.

96   • Define a word or explain a process stated in the topic
97   sentence.
98   • Link the topic sentence to an earlier topic or one to come.

Determining your initial reading speed is easy. Look at the number in the left-hand margin of the line you were reading when your alarm rang and multiply that number by 10. The result will equal the total number of words read in a minute.

For example, if you read 15 lines in one minute than you reading speed would equal 15 × 10 or 150 words per minute. If you read 35 lines, multiplying by 10 would give you a reading speed of 350 words per minute.

Write Your Answer on the Following Blank Line: _____

After completing the accelerated reading section of this book, we will prompt you to repeat this reading exercise to determine your new reading speed. You should mark down this new reading speed on the following blank line: _____.

A Word of Caution About the Following Mechanical Skills

Before you begin to learn the mechanics of speed-reading, it is important to understand some of the changes that will occur in your perception and understanding of text. As you begin to increase your reading speed and expand the chunk-size of text being read, your comprehension will briefly disappear. This occurs as your brain is learning to process printed material in a totally different fashion. It is very similar to what occurs when someone learns to swim for the first time.

Years ago, Howard was a swimming teacher. During the first lesson he taught students how to blow bubbles. As they began to blow bubbles they would look around and see expert swimmers racing across the pool, and performing intricate flip turns. Dismayed the students would turn to him and ask how blowing bubbles had anything to do with swimming. He told these students to watch how these more seasoned swimmers were blowing bubbles as they darted across the pool. With each new skill—like floating, kicking, moving the arms, and breathing—the students began to see how each one would result in them being able to swim. When you begin your speed-reading exercises, you will be blowing bubbles. It may not seem like speed-reading, but as you add additional skills it soon will lead to a mastery of high-speed learning.

The mechanical drills you are about to begin will change how your brain perceives and interprets text. Although ordinary reading causes the blood to flow to the auditory regions of the brain, when these drills are properly followed you will quickly begin to process reading material in your visual rather than in your auditory brain region. The confusion in comprehension that occurs during the early phase of this process is because your brain must switch the region used to process printed material. During the switching phase you are unable to use either your old or new technique, so confusion occurs. This phase lasts only a few short hours and will result in your reading much faster for the rest of your life. Let's begin your mastery of high-speed reading by learning how to coordinate your hands and eyes to become a more efficient reader.

Preparing for Speed-Reading

Positioning the Book

The ideal position for a book during speed-reading is flat on a table. Good lighting can also be important, especially as your eyes grow weaker with age. If you must read while standing, hold the book in one hand and use your other hand to coordinate your speed-reading.

Hand Motions

Speed-readers use their hands to control their eye movements. Research at the University of Minnesota shows that 90% of reading time is spent pausing between words for approximately one-quarter second per word. This reduces reading speed to some 240 words per minute. Using the hand to control eye movements results in a more consistent high-speed reading of larger chunks of text than are perceived during ordinary reading. Before you learn how to do this, it is important that you determine which hand to use for speed-reading.

Choosing a Hand to Use for Speed-Reading

Speed-reading requires careful coordination between the hand and the eye. Even turning pages quickly can make the difference between reaching top speed or experiencing only a modest increase. Therefore it is essential that you select the hand that is most efficient to help you master speed-reading.

Many people erroneously assume that the best hand to use is the same one they use when writing. Notice that books written in English turn from right to left. For most people turning pages with the right hand is easier. That leaves the left hand free for guiding the eye across the page. The majority of speed-readers choose the left hand to guide the eye, and the right hand to turn pages. However, you are not most people. Many right-handed people find using their left hand to guide their eye uncomfortable. It may also trigger more of a right-brain, big-picture reading experience. The best way to determine which hand you should use is by experimenting. A few years ago, Howard was a guest on the "America's Talking Cable Network." They asked Howard to read over eighteen 900-page books in ninety minutes. After reading for an hour, Howard got tired and switched hands. No one cared! Guess what? No one will care if you switch hands either. By following the instructions in this chapter, you will have the opportunity to test which method works best for you. In fact, you may decide to use a different hand at different times in your reading, just as Howard did when appearing on that television show.

Turning Pages

Let's begin by learning how to turn pages faster using the right hand. Read the following instructions and then turn to the beginning of this book to perform the steps that are described:

- Take your right hand and slide it up to the top of the right-hand page.

- Gently grasp the top edge of the page and quickly flip the page over.

- Use your left hand to keep the page from flipping over again.

- Repeat, increasing the speed with which you flip the page with your right hand.

- Do not attempt to read the text while performing this exercise.

Gently grasp the top edge of the page and quickly flip the page over.

Use your left hand to keep the page from flipping over again.

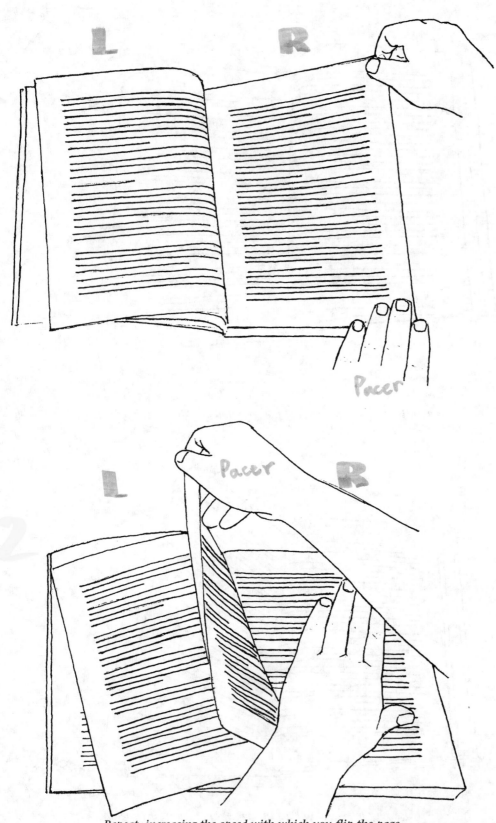

Repeat, increasing the speed with which you flip the page.

Developing Eye-Hand Coordination

You are about to learn how to use your left hand to guide your eye during speed-reading. It is this hand's function to control the eye's speed and scan of the page. Make certain that your eye follows your hand, and that your hand does not slow down to accommodate your eye. It helps to keep your left hand on a slight angle toward the center of the book. This position helps keep the pages flat when your left hand is scanning the right page. The base of the palm of your left hand will then be pressing up against the left page and keep it from snapping shut. Look at the diagram on the next page to get the proper hand position.

First Step for Using Your Hand

Place your finger on the first word on this page and slowly move your hand toward the right margin. As your finger moves from left to right, your eyes follow your finger's path and observes the text. At this point you should be moving your finger as quickly as you can and still comprehend the text. If you miss a few words that is normal. Do not go back to read a word that is missed. If you are missing many words, you are reading too quickly. It is very important that your hand go completely from the left to the right margin. Running your hand down the middle of the page places too much reliance on peripheral vision. Peripheral vision is too blurred to efficiently read words at the edges of a full-sized page. So always remember to move your hand completely from one side of the page to the other. Take a look at the diagram that follows to see how the hand motion is correctly performed. Incidentally, it is irrelevant at this point if you do not remember the material that is being read. You will learn many accelerated memory techniques later that will make it easy for you to store and retrieve information in a snap. All you need to focus on at this point is learning to speed up your visual rate of reading by using your hand. It is not important how many fingers you use to move your eye across the page. Experiment and find what is most comfortable for you. Read for a few minutes to see how comfortable you are when using the left hand to control your eye movements, and your right hand to turn the pages. If you find using your left hand makes you uncomfortable, then try using the suggestions in the next section for using only your right hand for both moving the eye and turning the pages.

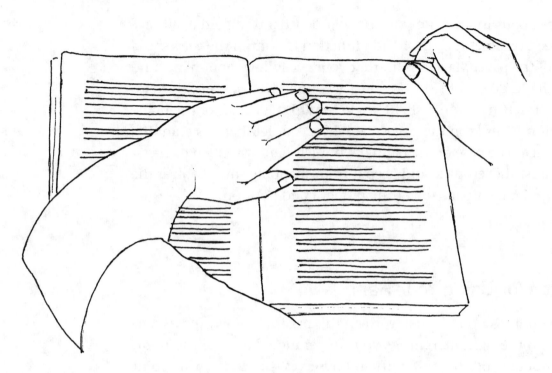

Keep your left hand on a slight angle toward the center of the book.

Move your hand completely from one side of the page to the other.

Use your left hand to control eye movements.

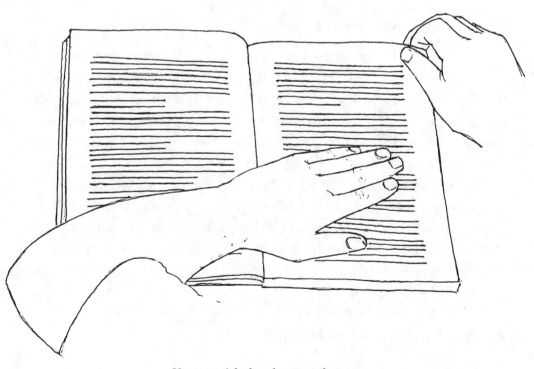

Use your right hand to turn the pages.

What If You Are Uncomfortable Using Your Left Hand?

If you found using your left hand to control your eye movements uncomfortable, then using only your right hand might be a better choice. As your right hand moves your eye from the left to the right margin, your left hand grasps the top of the left page to help keep the book open and flat. When your right hand gets to the bottom of the right side of the page you can then grasp the top edge of the page to turn it over. It will take a bit longer to turn the page using the right hand because you need to wait till you are done using that hand to move your eye. When using both hands, your right hand is already grasping the corner of the right page before your left hand gets to the bottom of the right page. This means that using both hands results in a slightly greater reading speed. However, if using both hands creates discomfort, this can dramatically reduce your ability to memorize and retain important text. It is better to read a bit slower and retain everything important than go a bit faster with a weaker retention of the material. Practice using your right hand for several minutes to determine if you are more comfortable using it to speed-read. Once you determine which hand is most comfortable, you are ready to proceed to the next set of exercises, designed to increase the number of lines that you perceive.

Expanding Your Visual Field

Your eye is designed to take in your entire surroundings in an instant. This same visual power can help you increase your reading speed by enabling your to read several lines at a time. Remember, not everyone can read several lines at a time and comprehend text. However, practice will enable you to increase your reading speed and improve your comprehension.

Begin by viewing two lines of text at a time. It is unlikely you will be able to comprehend any textual meaning during this exercise. What is important is the coordination that is developing between your hand, eye, and brain. Actually the confusion you may feel while performing these exercises is an indication that your brain is redirecting information to a different portion of your brain. After performing a few simple exercises, we will teach you how to comprehend more at your higher speed than you did at your slower reading speed.

EXERCISE 1

Turn to the first paragraph of Unit 1, chapter 1, and view two lines of text at a time while moving your hand across the page from margin to margin. Since your comprehension is quite poor, this is a splendid time for you to dramatically increase the speed with which you are moving your hand. Move your hand as quickly as possible from one side of the page to the other. Although all you will see is a blur of information, what is actually happening is your brain is perceiving the information more visually but can't turn the pictures into the sounds that you have become accustomed to hearing during reading. This means you are becoming a faster and more visual reader by using a different part of your brain, the visual area. Ultimately this will produce a much higher reading speed with better comprehension. Begin reading two lines at a time for five minutes, and when you are done return to this section of your book.

EXERCISE 2

Now you're ready to increase the number of lines being viewed at once. During the next exercise you will look at five lines at once. Remember you will not be able to comprehend the text you are viewing. All that is necessary is that you look at a larger chunk of text. This will have a profound effect on redirecting the information in text to a more visual region of your brain. Later in this book, we will show you how to make this information meaningful. Return to the first paragraph of Unit 1, chapter 1, and spend the next five minutes viewing five lines of text as quickly as possible. When you have completed this drill, continue with your next exercise.

EXERCISE 3

Now you are ready to begin viewing an entire paragraph at once. Notice we said viewing, and not reading! Once again begin reading for five minutes the first paragraph in chapter 1. Remember to move your hand as quickly as possible to force your eye to bring information to your brain at a very fast pace.

Preparing for Supersonic Reading Speed

The exercises you just completed enabled you to quickly view, or scan, large chunks of text. Now it is time to dramatically increase the rate at which you scan text. Your next exercise requires you to read an entire page in only 10 seconds. This is an easy feat to accomplish if you view large chunks of text with each movement of your hand.

EXERCISE 1

The easiest way to time yourself is by creating an audio tape. Your tape should run for a single minute. Count off each ten-second interval on the tape and make certain that you complete an entire page during each interval. Return to the first page of Unit 1, chapter 1, and begin reading the entire page in ten seconds. When you complete this exercise continue with the next one.

EXERCISE 2

Now you are going to double your already increased reading speed. Create another tape that counts off five-second intervals of one minute. Make certain that you complete an entire page before the five seconds end.

Scanning large chunks of text will make this an easy task for you to complete. Remember you will not be able to comprehend text at this speed. This drill is designed to make your brain process text more visually even without any comprehension taking place. Comprehension is very important, but it will be covered later.

EXERCISE 3

Now you are ready to double your reading speed again. Return to Unit 1, chapter 1 and read each page in two seconds. Very large chunk sizes will be needed to complete this exercise on time. Create one more audio tape of the two-second intervals of one minute. Make certain that you complete each page in no longer than two seconds. When you complete this exercise, continue with the next set of drills.

Hypersonic Reading Speed

Congratulations! You can easily scan text at a very high speed. It is time to use this ability to reach even higher reading speeds by using a simple three-minute exercise. During the first minute you will read text at your peak comprehension rate. Double that rate during the second minute without regard to your ability to comprehend. During the third minute, double your reading rate once again, still ignoring your comprehension of text. After you complete your third minute, begin your exercise anew. The first minute read for comprehension, in the second minute, double your speed, and in the third minute triple your speed. Continue reading new pages each time you read. For example, if you begin on page one, and after three minutes are on page five, begin your next three-minute exercise on page six. This exercise should be continued for twelve minutes and performed every day to help you reach peak reading speed.

What you will experience during this exercise is quite interesting. During the first minute you will comprehend the text. During the second and third minute you will not be able to comprehend, but will enter into a heightened visual awareness of text. When you slow down to read for comprehension at the start of the next exercise you will find that your new comprehension speed has increased dramatically. This will repeat each time you perform this exercise.

Speed-Reading on a Computer Screen Using a Mouse

Marcus discovered how to speed-read material on the Internet by applying these hand motions to a computer screen. It's simple. Instead of using your hand to move your eye across the page, use your computer's mouse. Set the computer screen up so that it scrolls, and quickly move your mouse from side to side. The motion of your cursor will control your eye movements very similarly to the motion of your hand in a book. This will enable you to read information on a computer screen very rapidly. For peak reading speed, we recommend printing out the copy on the screen and reading it like text.

CHAPTER BOOKMAP™

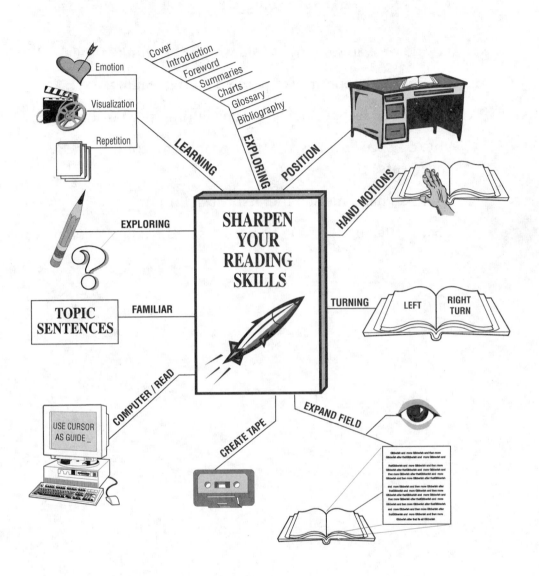

CHAPTER TWO SELF-TEST

1. Why do we read so slowly when we see and think so quickly?

2. Describe the importance of purpose during reading.

3. What is the ideal position of a book during speed-reading?

4. Why do speed-readers use their hands to control their eye movements?

5. Describe a hand motion useful for speed-reading text.

6. What is a technique you can use for speed-reading a computer screen?

Chapter 3

Integrating Reading Mechanics and Psychology

Chapter Preview

- Using topic sentences

- The advantages of reading in a familiar subject

- Getting the most from an unfamiliar subject

- Exploring text

- Asking key questions

- Relating information to life

- Importance of visualization

- The role of emotion in learning

- The role of repetition in learning

- Marking off important information

- Exploring a book's features

NOW THAT YOU UNDERSTAND the psychology of reading, and the art of scanning text faster, it is time to integrate both skills to get higher reading speed and better comprehension. Two possibilities occur as you are reading a text. You read about a familiar subject or about an unfamiliar subject. As an adult reader most of your reading will be in a familiar subject. Adults tend to read texts that are important to their work or special interests. However, as a student you frequently read texts in subjects that are required, but not necessarily of special interest to you. Different strategies are necessary for both types of reading. This chapter covers these strategies in detail.

Using Topic Sentences

A topic sentence reveals a paragraph's purpose. Most often the topic sentence is the first sentence in a paragraph. If you slow down your reading speed to read the topic sentence, and then quickly pick up your reading speed throughout the rest of the paragraph, you will attain excellent insight into the paragraph's content.

The topic sentence teaches you what important information to filter while reading. Once aware of what is important, you can look for verbs and nouns in a sentence to pick up additional details. While speed-reading, simply slow down to read the first sentence (which is usually the topic sentence) and then speed up. This will help you reach top speed in everything that you read.

Familiar Subject

Reading problems frequently occur because authors assume that information is familiar to you when it is not. Fortunately, most of the time quite the opposite occurs. Authors assume you know absolutely nothing about a subject, when actually you already know quite a bit. This occurs because writers do not actually know what a reader understands about their text's subject content. An author understands exactly what information a totally uninformed individual requires in order to learn new information from their text. So authors provide that information. However, since you are an individual who might have some experience with a text's subject content, then much of the material is already familiar to you. This simple fact can help you reach top reading speed in a familiar subject.

When encountering familiar textual information, immediately switch to your quadruple reading speed. Carefully filter the verbs describing action, and nouns that describe the people, places, and things involved in these actions. Ask the key questions of who, what, where, when, why, and how, and then look for the answers to these questions. If the information you are reading is familiar to you, then you will understand what you are reading. If you do not understand what you are reading at this high speed, then it is not sufficiently familiar. Reduce your reading speed to a more comprehensible one.

Actually, most students do just the opposite of this when reading. Let us give you an example of what we mean. Imagine you are reading a chemistry book. So far it has been technical, difficult and—dare we say it?—boring. Well, you finally find a chapter that you find interesting and easily understand. Are you in a hurry to finish this chapter and return to the rest of the difficult and challenging material, or do you want to spend extra time reviewing this interesting and easy-to-understand chapter? Many students make the mistake of lying to themselves while studying. They decide to return to the easy information they already understand. Why? The reason is simple—it requires less effort. However, it also wastes your valuable and limited study time.

Limited study time must be used to produce the best results in the least amount of time. In the future, when you encounter something you already understand, immediately switch to a much higher reading speed.

Let's do a simple exercise to practice this skill.

EXERCISE 1

The paragraph that follows contains a great deal of information that should be very familiar to you. If you encounter anything that you already know, immediately switch to your quadruple reading speed.

1 *White Blood Cells*
2 The circulatory system has the responsibility of moving the
3 blood around the body. There are two principle types of blood
4 cells: red and white. White blood cells help fight disease in
5 several different ways. Some white blood cells attack germs
6 and absorb them into themselves as an amoebae absorbs food
7 into itself. Another way that white blood cells fight germs is by

8 producing antibodies that are poisonous to these organisms.

9 These antibodies fight germs in several different ways: (1) some

10 kill the germs, (2) some prevent germs from reproducing,

11 and (3) some prevent germs from moving about.

If you have any familiarity with blood cells, this passage is not diffi-cult to read at high speed even though it contains many facts and details. Your brain's familiarity with these facts and details enables you to quickly finish the familiar sections so you can spend more time learning things that you don't know.

Unfamiliar Subject

It's safe to assume that not every book you read contains familiar information. This is especially true in school, where you frequently must learn new subjects. Fortunately, you can still increase your reading speed in most of these texts. Most texts contain only about 11 to 40% information; the rest is explanation. Explanations take the form of stories or models. Or, if you read a book about physics, you might find pictures, diagrams, and examples explaining the various concepts. For example, if you were reading about the principle of action and reaction, there might be a picture of a rocket ship taking off to illustrate action, and a picture of a balloon flying around the room as the air escapes from it to illustrate reaction. These examples help you to better understand the book's concept.

In some difficult books, you will need to read many of these examples and illustrations to understand the text. However, in other cases you may find the concepts are simple to understand. Remember that writers have to make assumptions about the difficulties that anyone reading their text may encounter. They have to assume certain questions are likely to be asked by many readers—questions that need answers. If you need this information, you will be grateful that it is provided. Yet, many times you will immediately understand what you are reading and not require all of this assistance. When this happens, immediately switch to your quadruple reading speed. If, when the example ends, you encounter new and unfamiliar information, go back to your peak reading speed (which is your highest reading speed with good comprehension). By increasing your reading speed of unnecessary information, even in an unfamiliar subject, you can reach your top reading speed.

The following is a good example of information being provided to clarify a concept that you should easily understand:

1 *A good negotiation strategy*

2   When negotiating a deal with someone it is always a
3 good idea to try to develop a win-win approach. A win-win
4 approach means that both parties are interested in seeing
5 each other succeed, and so they are flexible about what they
6 ask of each other to assure mutual success. Let us give you
7 an example of this.

8   Back in colonial America, President Jefferson wanted to
9 expand the United States further west. This occurred during
10 the Napoleonic wars. France needed money to fight a very
11 expensive war in Europe, and owned the Louisiana Territory
12 in North America that President Jefferson was very interested
13 in obtaining. Jefferson offered a large sum of money to
14 France in exchange for obtaining the Louisiana Territory.
15 This was a win-win deal. The United States obtained the
16 Louisiana territory that enabled it to expand further west,
17 and France obtained the money which it desperately needed
18 to continue fighting a costly war.

Notice how the entire example in this short reading sample added nothing to your understanding of the principle of win-win. The first paragraph provided all the information that you needed to understand the concept, while the second paragraph simply had a lot of unnecessary information that demonstrated a concept that you already understood. This will occur very frequently in many of your texts. Remember when you encounter this situation, immediately go to your quadruple reading speed until encountering new and useful information.

EXERCISE 2

Return to the speed-reading test you took earlier in this book. Since you already read the excerpt, some of its content is probably still familiar to you. If you encounter familiar information, quadruple your reading speed. If you encounter any concepts that you understand and that are followed by lengthy and unnecessary explanations, quadruple your reading. Let's see how quickly you can read by combining your understanding of the significance of the text with your ability to scan text very quickly. When you complete this exercise, continue with the next chapter in this book.

EXPLORING

The Purpose of Exploring Text

While exploring a book's chapters, you mark off information that you need to memorize or concepts that require more focus time to understand. When reviewing material, you return to these marks. Before deciding that something is difficult to learn, read the entire chapter. You may find clues or other information that make confusing information easier to understand. If you stop and struggle to understand the text, you might waste time. When you reach the end of your chapter, you will know if you still are confused with an idea. The review step is also where you use your accelerated memory skills to permanently learn important information. These skills will be covered in Chapter 4.

Asking Questions

During your review, you must select important information by asking the essential filtering questions of who, what, where, when, why, and how. Thinking about these questions and actively searching the text for answers will increase your understanding of the material. If you have difficulty answering any of these questions, it is an indication that you are looking at the text's words, without understanding their significance.

Inferential Questions

While the core filtering questions will help you master information on a literal level, inferential questions enable you to apply information on a broader scope. For example, by asking yourself, "What is my purpose, and how can I use this information?" your mental tours (or mental explorations into the deeper meaning of the text) will enable you to remember and recall information more efficiently.

Another inferential question that needs to be answered is, "Is it easy for me to understand this information?" Determining how easy or how difficult something is to learn will help you judge the amount of time it may take to master the subject. It will also help you judge your aptitude for learning the information.

Applications to Life

Picturing the use of what you are learning to practical applications is very important. For example, after graduating, many people soon lose their knowledge of mathematics, even though they spend many years studying it. Because so much mathematical information was never associated with real life applications, it is soon forgotten. Your brain is designed to remember things that are significant and interesting to you.

Questions That Need Further Information

In addition to these obvious questions, it also pays to ask yourself questions about what you don't understand. Are there additional questions raised about what you are learning that need to be answered? This type of deeper thinking not only leads to a better understanding of a subject, but also aids memory and retention by making it more significant.

Visualization

Because the brain is primarily a visual computer, converting textual information into images is a wonderful way to increase both your reading speed and comprehension. This doesn't mean that you shouldn't be able to hear anything in your mind while reading. It helps to hear the topic sentence, the verbs and nouns, the things that answer your primary questions of who, what, where, when, why, and how. But it is completely unnecessary to hear all the textual words to understand your text. The more a book is viewed like a movie instead of hearing it like a conversation, the higher your reading speed will become and the less effort it will take for you to improve your reading comprehension at faster reading speeds. In time you will find that you are seeing more and more of a movie while reading.

For example, if you were studying how bacteria infect the body, you would actually see the germs entering the body, and witness them duplicating themselves and attacking healthy cells. You see the body's defenses spring into action, and watch them devour these dangerous bacteria as they restore health. These images are very graphic. When you need to recall information about how bacteria infect the body and how your body defends itself, you now have powerful visual images that are easily recalled.

The Role of Emotion in Learning

Your brain is designed to remember things that are emotionally significant. For example, try to remember all the places you've ever driven in an automobile in your life. Impossible, right? Now have you ever been in a car accident, seen a accident, gotten lost, or gotten a speeding ticket? Can you remember anything about these events? Certainly! What's the difference? The difference is that these things had emotional significance and became quickly encoded into your permanent memory.

Your can *create* highly emotional images that will be easier for you to remember. In the last section we talked about seeing bacteria invade the body. What if you also imagined the pain, and fear associated with having a dangerous disease? Wouldn't this make the information far more important and significant to you? Absolutely. This would improve your memory of the information.

The Role of Repetition in Learning

Another key factor in memory is the repetition of information. Your brain is designed to remember things that frequently occur. When you are trying to memorize information, it helps to repeat the ideas and concepts over and over again in your imagination. In the next chapter on memory, we will give your further tips that will enable you to store and retrieve copious amounts of information with very little effort.

Two More Steps for Boosting Your Reading Speed

Until now, we have focused on techniques for increasing your reading speed with limited comprehension. Now it's time to develop procedures that will develop excellent comprehension. True speed-reading requires two steps:

- Exploring

- Examining

Until now, we have emphasized the reading phase. This is because this step takes the most time to learn, and requires the most practice. This unit of your book will teach you how to perform exploring and examining, the other two essential steps for successful speed-reading.

The Purpose of Exploring Text

Exploring text gives you the opportunity to explore the major features a text contains. At your double or quadruple reading speed you can preview an entire text in only a few minutes. In fact, previewing should *never take more* than ten to fifteen minutes.

Exploring gives you an awareness of where your text is going before you begin to study its details. For example, have you ever reached the end of a long and complicated textbook and discovered that it contained some very valuable appendices at the end? Appendices that you could have used to easily learn and understand the book's contents? Sure. Yet, you don't see these appendices **until after you have completed** your text. By then, you are done reading and can't use the valuable information contained within these appendices. Wouldn't it be helpful to know at the beginning of your reading that this information is available for you to use? Of course, and that's exactly what exploring a book does. It makes you aware of the book's useful features. At any point in your reading, you should not only be aware of where you are in the text, but also where you've been and where you are going. These insights help you to become an inferential reader with a clearer understanding of the book's contents.

Although exploring speeds are always quite fast, as you filter out information, you are learning, too—even at this lightning-fast speed. Let's examine the things you should watch for when exploring a book.

Marking Off Important Information in a Text

While exploring, and also during your examining stage, it is important to mark off information that looks important. For example, the specific information that you must memorize or learn is something you should mark off. (Later in this book we will explain in detail how to determine what information is important and what is not.) Make a habit of also marking off sections of text that you have read, but experienced difficulty understanding. For example, when reading a physics book you might read all the words but have difficulty understanding their meaning or significance.

Do not use a highlighter to mark off important information. Many students make the mistake of using a highlighter to mark off important information, but a faster and more efficient way is to use a pencil. Hold the pencil in your hand like a finger when speed-reading. If you see something important just put a simple mark in the left margin. This mark reminds you to return to that information again. Drawing a circle in the margin can distinguish something you want to memorize. By using two different marks you can differentiate between information you need to read again for understanding and the facts needing memorization.

Exploring Parts of a Book

Cover

Ignore the old saying, "You can't judge a book by its cover." It simply isn't true. You can tell a great deal about a book from its cover. The cover of a book contains information about the major features and contents, information that is worth a few seconds of your time scanning. Often, you will find that scanning a book's cover reveals whether or not a book is truly focused on your specific purpose and needs. If not, you can easily switch to another more suitable book without losing any of your valuable time.

Introduction

The introduction of a book is usually not read by students. Many students say they feel badly enough about reading the parts of a book that are assigned. Why would they want to read something that is not included in their homework? Because the introduction and the foreword of a book are almost never assigned, most people skip these sections. But there is an excellent reason for reading them. The introduction contains information about how the author handles the book's subject. It frequently contains personal information about the writer, information that may reveal a bias in favor of or against the book's subject matter. This is important information for you to know, and worth a few moments of your time to preview. You only take a few seconds on each page when exploring the introduction by reading the topic sentences and quickly viewing the verbs and nouns in the other sentences. If nothing significant is found, then you can complete your skim and begin reading the text. However, if you see something significant in the foreword or introduction, you can mark it off and return to this important textual section to read at a slower pace for more details.

Foreword

Much of what we said about the introduction applies to the foreword. Usually the foreword is a more personal statement by the writer about himself and his motives for writing the book. The bulk of a text focuses on a subject. It is the foreword and introduction that focuses on the human being writing the information. The insights you gain into his character and motives can help you filter the information in a book more objectively.

There is another important piece of information that can be contained in a book's foreword or introduction. You may find the author making references to people who influenced her or to other books that helped shape their opinions. In some cases you may have some familiarity with these other books and the people who wrote them. As a result you not only read what the author has to say about a subject, but understand where the information these opinions are based comes from. Now you can challenge or even agree with things being said by the author by using your prior experience of the materials that influenced the text.

Contents

A book's table of contents is the outline used by the author when writing the text. What a valuable piece of information! Much like a road map, the contents shows you where the book is going to take you. Previewing the contents gives you an immediate overview of the text's scope.

Don't just preview the literal meaning of a contents page. While reading the contents, analyze facts on the inferential level as well by asking yourself some of the following questions:

- Is this information relevant to my purpose?

- Have I ever learned anything like this before?

- Is this information interesting to me?

- What challenges to my understanding might this book contain?

- Are there any parts of this book that seem very easy for me to learn?

- How might I use this information?

- How much time might it take me to learn this information?

- Does this information require me to learn a subject area or use skills that I have difficulty with?

- Any other questions that may seem relevant to you.

The contents page also displays the book's structure. Many people, when first learning to speed-read, are concerned about missing important information. Reading the contents page shows you where the book is going before you get there. You can then anticipate information that you will be learning, before you actually have to master the details associated with that information. This results in greater confidence while reading at high speed.

Each Individual Chapter

Quickly skim each chapter in a book, before actually reading the text. You will find out if the chapters contain charts, diagrams, summaries, questions, or other features that may help you to better understand the contents. For example, imagine you are reading about the brain in your book. A reference is made to the cortex, and you don't know what this means. Yet, having skimmed the chapter you are aware that a picture of the brain's anatomy can be found just a few pages forward in the text. Immediately turning to this diagram you can see the brain's cortex and get a clearer understanding of information that the book described earlier.

Many students flounder when encountering unfamiliar information. Time will not be unnecessarily wasted if you take the time to use each chapter's special features. Here is where skimming really begins to pay huge dividends in time saved.

Using Questions at the End of Chapters

Often you do not know much about a text's contents. But in many texts, each chapter has study questions or chapter quizzes at the end. These questions reveal specific information that the writer feels is most important. Unfortunately, you don't find these questions until after you complete a chapter. At that point you have to go back and reread the chapter to find the answers to these important questions.

Speed-readers handle these questions more efficiently. Before reading the chapter they skim it, looking to see if there are any questions at the chapter's end. If so, these questions get read first. Mental pictures are formed around these questions, and when the textual information appears to answer a question, that textual section is marked off with a pencil and later reviewed. Questions help you filter the important information contained within a book. This strategy is especially useful in subjects that are unfamiliar to you.

Summaries

Just as many chapters end with questions, they often contain summaries of the information the writer considers essential. Using ordinary reading skills you don't find this information until after the chapter is completed. By then there is a good chance that you missed it.

Once again exploring a chapter eliminates this problem. Before reading the chapter, you see a summary describing the key information that the writer believes you should be learning from that chapter. Armed with this information, you begin to filter for the relevant details contained within the text. This is especially helpful when reading an unfamiliar subject. In that case, you must rely more heavily on the judgment of the writer to determine what is significant when you lack experience with a subject.

Visual Aids

Since the brain is primarily visual, many texts provide visual aids to make learning easier. Skimming through a book's chapters helps you locate these important visual aids, which you may use at any point during your reading to understand the textual information. For example, you may realize that an important map, chart, or diagram is located later in a book. The information it contains is helpful in understanding the material presented earlier.

Charts

Charts conveniently arrange visual information into patterns that are easier to learn than the traditional sentence form. At high speeds you can determine what kind of information is contained within a chart, and determine the significance of this information. If your purpose requires you to memorize this information, mark the margin, and return to it later.

If information contained within a chart is already familiar to you, then seeing it—even at a very high reading speed—will evoke the details that are already committed to memory. The difference here is that you are not attempting to place the information into your permanent memory; instead, you are using your already established data base to decode the information.

Using Flow Charts

Many books, especially technical and scientific books contain flow charts that clearly outline the major steps in a complex series of events. Your memory can more easily assimilate detailed information if it retains this outline. This process is called chunking down. Chunking down means that first you learn the big picture by getting a good overview of your subject. You brain will always remember things easier when it is linking new information to patterns that it is already familiar with.

Although scientific and technical books may provide flow charts, this is less common in other books. It is a good idea to create your own flow chart diagrams of complicated material. This helps your brain visualize the primary steps involved with the information. Additional details can easily be linked to this familiar information.

Diagrams

The old saying that a picture is worth a thousand words is well worth taking to heart. When a text provides visual diagrams, it is a good idea to first familiarize yourself with the pictorial information before attempting to learn textual details. These pictures will help you better comprehend technical data because your brain will have images to associate with concepts.

Pictures and diagrams sometimes occur at inconvenient portions of a chapter. That is, you may find yourself confused at the beginning of a chapter about a technical point, but there is a diagram later in the chapter that could easily help you understand it better. Skimming the chapter before reading it will make you aware of the existence of this diagram. You can turn to it immediately upon finding confusing information. Thus you may be using information out of sequence in the chapter, but in a pattern that is better suited to your learning needs. Remember the book is your tool and its information can be used in the sequence best suited to produce peak learning for you.

Index

Most students use the index of a book to look up information about a subject. While this is a good use of the index, there is another use that is equally important, but almost always overlooked. The index is also a thorough summary of all the textual details, and a very high-speed scan of an index can determine whether you are familiar with this information.

Often students misjudge a text's complexity. Most textbooks begin by reviewing information that should have already been learned. For example, a calculus book begins by reviewing algebra and trigonometry, which you should have already learned before studying calculus. For a while, a book may seem easy because it is reviewing familiar information. However after a few weeks, you reach new information and suddenly realize this is a very difficult text requiring more of your time than you anticipated.

When skimming an index at quadruple speed (or faster) all you can comprehend are details you already know. Skimming is a technique for determining how much unfamiliar and difficult information is contained within a book. If you find it difficult to skim an index, there is probably a great deal of new and unfamiliar information that will probably require extra time.

As soon as you discover that a text is going to be difficult, you can schedule your study time more efficiently at the start of a school term. The work load is usually light at the beginning of a semester, and we recommend going far ahead in your readings early on to take advantage of this light work load. Read your October and November reading assignments at the beginning of September before you have tests, papers, and exams to prepare for. You will then have an abundance of time to get your work done.

Glossary

A glossary is a complete summary of important new textual vocabulary. A high-speed skim of the glossary reveals if you are familiar with the text's language.

The glossary is also a very useful source for anticipating vocabulary questions that are frequently seen on tests, particularly when the questions are multiple choice, fill-in-the-blank, and matching.

Appendices

Appendices often contain and summarize important information in an easy-to-locate and compact format. The information contained within appendices is often invaluable, and can help you understand difficult portions of text with far less effort. Unfortunately appendices are usually found at the end of a book. For most students this means they don't see them until after they have completed the text and no longer have any use for the information. Skimming eliminates this problem.

A high-speed skim of the entire book will make you aware of the existence of any appendices before you begin reading. Now when you encounter a portion of text that could be more easily learned by using the information contained within one of the appendices, you can quickly turn to it and use that information.

Bibliography

The bibliography of a book summarizes the sources used by the author. If a subject is familiar to you, it pays to quickly skim the bibliography. You may find some of the books used as sources for your text are already familiar to you. This enables you to read the text on an inferential level. You may also find leads for additional books that can prove helpful when doing research on a subject.

CHAPTER BOOKMAP™

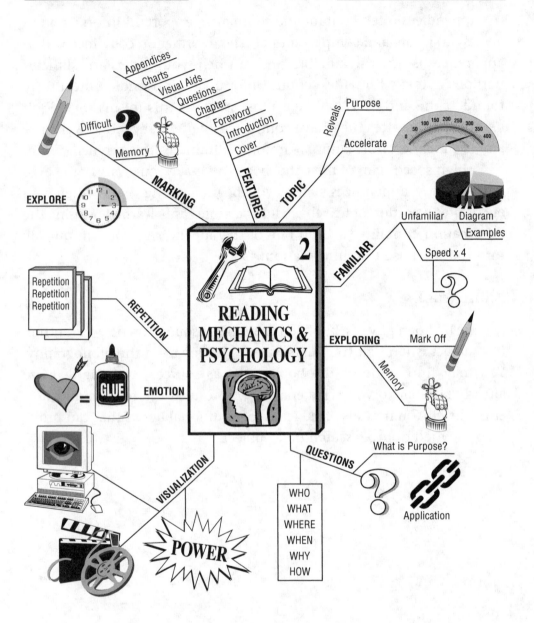

CHAPTER THREE SELF-TEST

1. How can using a topic sentence be useful during speed-reading?

2. What is a strategy you can apply to increase your reading speed in a familiar subject?

3. What is a strategy you can apply to increase your reading speed in an unfamiliar subject?

4. What is the purpose of exploring text?

5. What is inferential learning?

6. How does visualization aid high-speed learning?

7. What is the role of emotion in learning?

8. How does repetition help memory?

9. Describe the purpose of exploring text.

10. Why do you mark off important information in text?

11. What important information can be learned from a book's cover?

12. Why is it important to read a book's introduction?

13. What are the questions you should ask yourself while reading a text's contents?

14. While skimming each individual chapter, what information should you be finding?

15. How can you use the questions at the end of each chapter to enhance your learning of a subject?

16. When should you read a chapter's summary? Why?

17. How do charts simplify visual learning of text?

18. What is a flow chart, and how can it be used to master printed information?

Chapter 4

Accelerating Your Memory Power

Chapter Preview

- Introduction to memory

- The distinction between memory and recall

- The importance of putting a concept in context

- Understanding your brain's different memory storage areas

- Pegging: The secrets of modern memory masters revealed

- Mnemonics: Using the techniques of the ancient greeks

- Music: Remember hundreds of new words and definitions by using special memory music

- Flash cards: Turning on more of your brain's memory power than you ever thought possible

- Bookmapping™

- How to create a successful bookmap™

- Book Pegging™

- Physiology of memory

- Chapter summary

Introduction to Memory

How often does this happen to you? You study for a test, practice answering questions, and confidently remember the important information. Yet, when you go to the examination, suddenly your mind goes blank. What happened? Where did all that information go? Or perhaps you suddenly remember those important answers five minutes after the test's completion. These scenarios occur far too often to students. But, after mastering the powerful accelerated memory tools we share with you in this chapter, these problems will *never* again occur to you.

Memory is the ability to store and recall information. Since information varies in its level of complexity, different memory tools are necessary for mastering these various challenges. It is senseless to use the same memory tool for memorizing a math formula as you would use when reading a novel for pleasure. This chapter is chock full of useful memory tools suitable for every learning situation you will encounter when reading a text.

The Distinction Between Memory and Recall

Human memory is a complex brain activity. You possess several different types of memory storage areas, and each has a different function. In this chapter you will learn how to engage different memory activities for higher grades in half the time. The more memory regions of the brain used for storage of information, the easier it will be for you to recall the information when it is needed. For example, if you try to pick up a heavy object using just your index fingers it is difficult; if you use both hands, your grip is much stronger.

Having difficulty recalling information is different than failing to remember it. For example, when taking a biology test, you are asked to name the blood vessel carrying blood away from the heart. Last night you clearly remembered that the "artery" performs this function, but during the exam you are unable to recall it. At four in the morning you suddenly wake up and remember that the answer is "artery"! Did you really forget the answer? Of course not. If you had forgotten the answer you would not be able to remember it even after the test was over. Instead, you experienced a delay in recalling it.

Why do recall problems occur? Usually because you store answers in your memory without paying attention to where you are placing it. Let's clarify this by looking at an example from life. Suppose you work in an office with over a thousand file cabinets. Each time you receive a letter, you place it randomly in a filing cabinet. Suddenly, you need to quickly locate a very important letter. You know it can be found in one of the file cabinets—but which one? How quickly do you think you will find that important letter? Isn't this very similar to how you store information in your brain? Your brain contains countless storage areas, and you constantly store information without paying attention to where that information is being placed. Suddenly, you need information for an examination and cannot recall when you placed it. For hours, sometimes days, your brain searches for the location of this information. When found, you suddenly remember the answer to your question—often far too late to use in your examination. Fortunately there is an easy solution to this common problem.

Office filing cabinets usually use an alphabetical or chronological system to organize the information they contain. Your brain uses a very different primary system to store information. It uses your most powerful sense—vision. More area is devoted to the sense of vision than any other sense. In fact, humans have one of the most powerful visual brain regions in the animal kingdom. Using this powerful sense will enable you to quickly store and later recall important information. Arranging visual folders or impressions when reading is an efficient way to use your brain's visual power. Let's see how this visual filing system works.

Here are the visual folders created when reading a novel for pleasure:

- Location

- Theme

- Plot

- Atmosphere

- Character One

- Character Two (etc.)

When reading, imagine these folders as questions you must answer. As you read, vividly picture the answers to these questions in your imagination. For example, if you are reading the James Bond novel *Goldfinger*, picture Bond's appearance. The more specifically you can imagine his appearance, the easier it will be to recall information related to the Bond character. For example, any action James Bond undertakes in the novel appears in my imagination as a specific movie. Whenever we want to remember anything he does in the story, all we need to do is remember what he looks like. Immediately we have located the region of the brain where we have stored all of Bond's actions. Visualizing his appearance, we next scan the memory of his actions and can quickly recall anything Bond does in the novel. This same technique will work in any novel. You will never forget information because your visual movies will always be in specific memory areas linked to an easy-to-picture clue.

PRACTICE

Read a chapter in a familiar novel. While reading, focus on location, theme, plot, atmosphere, and character development. Create a visual movie for these key details, and try to recall specific information by replaying these movies in your imagination.

This visual technique is useful for remembering information when reading nonfiction books and magazines for pleasure. However, different visual folders more applicable to nonfiction are used:

- Who

- What

- Where

- When

- Why

- How

These are the same questions commonly asked and answered by a journalist or nonfiction writer. These questions organize nonfiction information during the writing process, and you can easily use them to memorize information as well. In fact, when you read the daily newspaper, you probably are already doing this unconsciously. For example, you are reading an article about former President Bush. As you read, think about how he looks or even sounds. Next associate what he is doing in the article with these familiar clues or with other familiar information about him. Whenever you need to remember anything in the article concerning President Bush, all you need to do is remember his appearance or voice and immediately you are looking in the correct region of your brain to find these details.

PRACTICE

Read an article in today's paper about a familiar individual. Run a movie in your imagination related to the questions who, what, where, when, why, and how. Link these questions to the familiar appearance of this individual. After completing the article, replay your movie by focusing on these familiar characteristics to trigger your memories. Be certain to choose someone whose characteristics are very easy for you to picture. After practicing with several highly familiar individuals, begin using less familiar individuals and focus on their described characteristics.

The Importance of Putting a Concept in Context

What did you eat for dinner ten days ago? How about twenty days ago? It's a safe guess that you don't remember. What if we asked you what you ate for dinner at the last big family gathering? Perhaps Christmas, Easter, or Thanksgiving? Now there is a greater probability that you would not only remember what you ate, but also remember many other details of the occasion. This raises an important point. It is easier to remember something when it has special importance to you.

The same is true when memorizing information. Putting information into a context that has significance helps you effortlessly remember and recall.

Too often school fails to put information into a context. No wonder students often forget what they learn as quickly as it is taught. For example, years ago Howard taught in an inner-city high school in New York City. At the end of a lesson on disease, he asked the class to name one of the five causes of disease. A student said, "bacteria." Howard acknowledged this was an excellent answer. However, when he asked this student "What is bacteria?" all the student could say was, "One of the five causes of disease." The student did not understand the meaning of the word bacteria. All he knew was that it was the correct answer to a question. Unfortunately many students learn information in school without understanding its meaning or significance. Putting information into a context eliminates this problem.

To put information into a context when reading, frequently stop and ask yourself questions that help you probe the deeper significance of what you are learning. For example, if you are reading about bacteria, you might ask some of the following pivotal questions:

- How do bacteria infect humans?

- What are bacteria?

- Where do bacteria exist?

- When are bacteria dangerous, or safe?

- Why are bacteria important?

- How can we protect ourselves or use bacteria?

Any who, what, where, when, why, and how questions will help put information into a context. Simply memorizing words without putting them into context is a waste of time and results in forgetting important facts. Simply put, how can you expect to remember something you do not understand? Make a habit of frequently asking these simple questions when reading, and you will soon dramatically improve your recall and retention of important information.

PRACTICE

Read chapter two of this book again, and frequently stop to ask yourself questions related to who, what, where, when, why, and how. Whenever possible visualize and run an imaginary movie in your mind about your questions and answers. These images and questions will put the important information into a context that is easy for you to recall and apply in the future. Throughout the rest of this book continue to frequently stop and ask these important questions. Begin doing this when reading anything that requires a high level of memory and recall. Watch the amazing memory power of your mind grow with practice!

Understanding Your Brain's Different Storage Areas

Psychologists have discovered that your brain possesses three different types of memory:

- Short-term
- Intermediate
- Long-term

Let's take a moment to examine the functions of these three memory types.

Short-Term Memory

If you survived a painful car crash would you want to remember all the details? Do you want to remember every step you take during a day in great detail? Of course not! Your brain's short-term memory lasts for a few brief seconds before extinguishing unpleasant or unnecessary information. Otherwise your mind would be crammed with useless and unwanted details.

Intermediate Memory

Intermediate memory stores information for four to eight hours before erasing it. Information that is important for a short time in your life is safely retained in this fashion. For example, you trip over a step while entering a house that you will visit only once in your lifetime. Several hours later when leaving this house you remember to be careful when reaching that step. Yet, a few hours later you will forget all memory of that step. It is a memory that no longer serves any useful purpose.

Long-Term Memory

Retaining important information in long-term memory is the goal of studying. An understanding of how long-term memory functions will help you accomplish this. Research indicates that long-term memory is a combination of several different events occurring in the brain. Important information that is repeatedly learned creates new neural pathways in your brain. This means that reviewing important information at frequent intervals will help you permanently retain and remember it.

The storage of proteins by your brain has also been linked to long-term memory. In fact, research is currently being conducted into the possibility of injecting these memory-stimulating proteins to create memory without studying. Perhaps one day you will be able to get a shot of history, biology, or math. At this point, however, science is not close to being able to accomplish this. In fact, it is quite possible it never will. However, this important research explains a very important memory occurrence that plagues most students.

To efficiently store information into long-term memory, your brain needs at least a 10-minute rest each hour. Other research indicates you may need a 10-minute rest after only 30 minutes of study. Yet, many students cram for hours when they study without taking these necessary breaks, resulting in a major memory loss of important information. Consequently students remember important information while studying, but fail to store it into their long-term memory. Without the necessary breaks, the brain stores information into intermediate memory, which lasts throughout a study session, and gives the false impression that key facts have been memorized. The next day during an exam, however, all that students remember is that yesterday they knew the answer to questions that are unanswerable today. The solution to this common problem? Take at least a 10-minute break each hour or half hour, and retention and recall will soar to new heights.

PRACTICE

Start taking 10-minute breaks every hour or half hour when studying. You will be amazed at how much more information you can recall during important examinations.

Pegging: The Secrets of Modern Memory Masters Revealed

Flipping through your television channels you have probably seen a memory master, someone who could instantly memorize and recall a random list of objects with almost magical power. Believe it or not you already possess this apparently awesome power. All you need is to learn how to release it.

Modern memory mastery actually has its roots in ancient Greece. The Greeks discovered that new information could be easily learned by linking, or pegging, it to something already familiar. The mental glue that sticks this new information onto the familiar is a vivid mental picture that has a tremendous emotional significance for you. Both pleasurable and painful emotions work, but they must be extremely intense to permanently glue new information into your long-term memory. Let's practice using this technique together.

PRACTICE

Quickly try to memorize the following list:

1. Screw

2. Bat

3. Rock

4. Soup

5. Motor oil

6. Spear

7. Tarantula

8. Lasso

9. Scissors

10. Molasses

Most likely you cannot recall these ten objects without some help. Below we list ten memory images that will help sink these objects into your permanent memory. We have linked the ten objects to ten familiar body parts using images that evoke powerful emotional responses. Both painful and pleasant emotions can anchor information into your memory. However, what one person considers pleasurable might not be considered pleasant by another. Yet, everyone can agree upon something that is painful. Since everyone will react powerfully to the same painful image, we have used these images in this memory drill. Please remember that when you construct your anchors things that are pleasurable will also work.

As you go through the following list, make a vivid mental image of what is described while experiencing the emotions evoked. The objects on our list will be linked to your body parts starting from the feet and ending at the top of your head. These body parts are used in an easy-to-remember sequence to facilitate recall of the list. In just a few minutes you will completely remember the entire list:

1. **Screw:** Imagine stepping onto a sharp screw that goes completely through your **foot**. Whenever you think about your **foot**, these powerful images cause you to remember the screw.

2. **Bat:** While playing baseball, a bat strikes and breaks your **shin**. Thinking about your **shin** immediately makes you remember a bat.

3. **Rock:** A cyclops has picked up a gigantic rock and flings it against your **knees**, instantly crushing them and causing unbelievable pain. When you think of your **knees** what do you picture? A rock.

4. **Soup:** Watch out! A bowl of boiling soup spills onto your **lap**. Ouch! It really hurts. When you think about your **lap**, you remember soup.

5. **Motor oil:** Imagine drinking a can of motor oil and feeling it settle in your **stomach**. What a horrible tasting fluid. When you think about your **stomach** you instantly remember motor oil.

6. **Spear:** A long, sharp spear is thrust into your **heart**. Feel it. React to it. When you think about your **heart**, immediately you remember the spear.

7. **Tarantula:** Imagine a big, hairy tarantula spider crawling on your **shoulder**. Oh no, it's biting you with its painful fangs. Whenever you think about your **shoulder**, instantly you remember tarantula.

8. **Lasso:** Is that a cowboy throwing a lasso around your **neck**? Watch out. He's riding away with it still wrapped around you. Besides getting a stiff **neck**, when you focus on your **neck** you will remember the lasso.

9. **Scissors:** While trimming the hair on your **face**, the scissors accidentally slip and cut a deep scar into your flesh. Thinking about your **face** immediately brings the scissors into your memory.

10. **Molasses:** Sticky molasses is in your **hair**, and roaches are crawling through it. A disgusting image, but one that is easy to recall!

Remember, powerful emotions create powerful memories. Positive emotions work just as well. Negative emotions were used in this example because everyone has a strong reaction to them.

Emotions are not the only way to peg a list into your permanent memory. Sometimes we can use other images that are as easy to remember as counting to ten. Try memorizing the following items and then read on for another set of memory-enhancing images.

1. Pen

2. Socks

3. Wheelbarrow

4. Cow

5. Starfish

6. Soda

7. July

8. Octopus

9. Cat

10. Fingers

Here are our ten images to help recall.

1. **Pen:** A pen looks like the number 1. When you think of the number one, remember pen.

2. **Socks:** How many socks do you wear? Two. When you think of the number two, remember socks.

3. **Wheelbarrow:** How many wheels are on a wheelbarrow? Three. Thinking of the number three reminds you of the wheelbarrow.

4. **Cow:** How many legs does a cow have? Four. Remember, four is linked to a cow.

5. **Starfish:** How many arms on a starfish? Five. Five reminds you of a starfish.

6. **Soda:** How many cans of soda are in a six-pack? Remembering six reminds you of soda.

7. **July:** What is the seventh month? July. Recalling seven reminds you of July.

8. **Octopus:** How many arms does an octopus have? Eight. Eight reminds you of an octopus.

9. **Cat:** A cat has how many lives? Nine. Nine is associated with cat.

10. **Fingers:** Count how many fingers you have. Ten. The number ten is associated with fingers.

Simply counting from one to ten will help you instantly recall the above list. Moreover, you can use this list to help remember numbers as well. Suppose you want to remember which section in a football stadium your seat is in. Imagine stroking a cat. What section is this? Nine. You remember breaking your fingers. What section are we in? Ten. Similarly you can remember any other number between one and ten by using these images. It's easy and fun to do.

Mnemonics: Another Technique of the Ancient Greeks

Mnemonics are another wonderful memory tool dating back to the time of ancient Greece. The Greeks discovered that a list could be recalled by associating the first letter from each item in the list with another word or phrase that triggered your recall of the original list. For example, many students remember the names of the Great Lakes by using the mnemonic *HOMES*. Here is how this mnemonic triggers the Great Lake's names:

- **H** stands for Huron

- **O** stands for Ontario

- **M** stands for Michigan

- **E** stands for Erie

- **S** stands for Superior

See how much easier it is to remember the simple mnemonic *HOMES* instead of the names of the five Great Lakes?

Mnemonics can also help you retain long lists of numbers. Take 30 seconds and try to remember the following: **ISOAR30SU**. Ready begin.

Not so easy to remember is it? Try using the following mnemonic: I Sat On A Rock 30 Stories Up. Now try to remember this number. See how much easier it is with a mnemonic?

PRACTICE

Make up a mnemonic to memorize the names of the five blood vessels in the circulatory system: artery, vein, capillary, venules, arteriole.

Music: Remember Hundreds of New Words and Definitions by Using Special Memory Music

Isn't it amazing how many song lyrics you can instantly remember—even though you never read the words? Driving in a car, you suddenly hear the first notes of The Beatles tune *Michelle*. Instantly you begin singing the words to the song. Someone asks you to sing *Twinkle Twinkle Little Star* and immediately you sing the first chorus. You can even remember the commercial jingle that goes, "you've got the right one baby uh-huh," a jingle that means absolutely nothing. Perhaps thousands of song lyrics and commercials are instantly remembered; yet, often you forget the name of a book and its author just a day after reading it. Why is it so easy to remember song lyrics to which you barely paid attention, but so difficult to remember information you diligently studied? The music makes the difference. In this section you will learn an amazing way to speed-memorize using music.

Scientists discovered that your brain has a beat, one that occurs once every second, or sixty times a minute. When music with this beat is paired with new information, your brain effortlessly encodes that information into permanent memory. Let's see how this works.

First you need the proper type of music. Here is a list of some of the acceptable music that will enable you to speed-memorize:

- Bach: Largo from Harpsichord Concerto in F Minor.

- Corelli: Largo from Concerto Number 7 in D Minor, Opus 5

- Vivaldi: Largo from Concerto in D Major for Guitar and Strings

Using the music is simple. First play the music from a stereo system at a level that can easily be taped on a hand-held recorder. Make sure the music is loud enough to hear, but not capable of drowning out your voice, which you will also be taping. Next work in eight-second increments: for four seconds, at the rate of one beat per second, say aloud the information you want to remember. Next keep silent for four seconds. Keep alternating between speaking for four seconds and keeping still for four seconds. Tape the music with your voice, and then the music alone. This new tape will enable you to speed-memorize detailed information.

For example, suppose you want to learn French. For four seconds you say, *"the word bonjour means hello."* Then for four seconds, keep silent. Each new vocabulary word is taped with its meaning in a four-second increment followed by four seconds of silence. When done, you will have a tape with as many as 400 definitions that can be mastered by repeatedly playing the tape.

Using a music memory tape has another advantage. It permits you to study during periods of the day that formerly were unavailable for learning. Anytime you can play a cassette recorder you can be learning. Suddenly some of the following times become useful for studying:

- waiting in lines

- performing errands

- driving in a car or other vehicle

- cooking, cleaning, or performing household chores

- exercising

- walking

Incidentally, a special memory music tape can be ordered by using the form at the end of this book. This tape contains over 30 minutes of music designed to help you speed-memorize.

PRACTICE

Make a list of 20 definitions you wish to memorize. Tape these meanings while playing the appropriate music in the background. Remember to work in eight-second intervals, speaking for four seconds into the tape recorder, and then just taping the music playing in the background for four seconds. Play your tape repeatedly for several hours, and then quiz yourself on the definitions. Amazingly, you will remember them without any effort!

Flash Cards: Turning On More of Your Brain's Memory Power Than You Ever Thought Possible

Wouldn't it be wonderful if you could use more of your brain's power when memorizing information? Well, the technique described below will help you use more of your senses as you're learning, which immediately makes more use of your brain's total learning capacity. Let's relate this to a common occurrence in most people's lives.

Have you ever tried to spell a word out loud and found you couldn't remember how to spell it? Yet, when you took a paper and pen you could easily write down and spell the same word. If you do not know how a word is spelled, then how can you correctly spell it by writing it down? Simple. You are using a different part of your brain when writing. Think about this. You don't spell when you speak, but you do spell when you write. What you remember are the movements made by your pen. Since you write words one letter at a time these movements are firmly embedded in the kinesthetic (movement) brain area. The same area enables blind people to read braille. As you will see in the next paragraph, this simple observation will enable you to use more of your brain when memorizing important information.

Using more of your brain to memorize is simple. First, write down on a 3 × 5 or 4 × 6 index card the information you need to remember. On one side of the card place the definition and on the other place the trigger. For example, write "bonjour" on one side of your card, and "hello" on the other. Shuffle your cards. You want a unique arrangement of the cards each time you use them. Choose your first card. If you get it right, continue with the next card. However, when you get it wrong, put that card in a separate pile. Immediately write down the word and its definition 25 times while saying it aloud. For example, write down "bonjour means hello" 25 times while saying it aloud. Writing it down uses your brain's kinesthetic region, as does moving your lips, tongue, and vocal chords. Saying it aloud stimulates the acoustical (auditory) region of your brain. Seeing it stimulates your visual region. We also recommend placing the card into a context that you find emotionally stimulating. For example, seeing someone very attractive saying bonjour to you might trigger emotional associations along with the perceptual ones.

When you complete your pile, return to the cards that you incorrectly identified and set aside. Repeat these steps until every card is correctly identified. Each day add new definitions and concepts that you must learn to your card deck. It will not matter how large the pile becomes. It will still be easy to learn. For example, how long does it take you to know that the word "bonjour" means hello? That's how long it should take you to go through every card. Only the ones that you have trouble remembering will take longer. That's O.K. You'll go through the extra steps that use more of your brain's memory power for these cards, and will soon be able to remember them.

PRACTICE

Take a dictionary and write down 20 words on one side of an index card. On the other side, write their meaning. Shuffle your deck and look at the first card. Identify its meaning. If you get it correct continue with the next card. If you make an error, write down the definition 25 times while saying it aloud. Place this card to the side. Repeat these steps for each card, until every card is correctly identified. You will be amazed at how quickly you can remember details using this technique.

Bookmapping™

Imagine yourself sitting at a desk. You are about to take a vital examination. After reading the test questions, you look up at the Bookmap to your left. (See, for example, the Bookmaps at the end of each chapter in this book.) Suddenly all the key information floods effortlessly into your mind. You smile confidently as you begin the paper, knowing that you will pass with flying colors. When you master the art of Bookmapping, the ultimate memory tool, you will consistently be able to recall key information exactly when you need it. Not only will you remember the data for tests, but you can also put information into your long-term memory so that you will remember key books you've read for the rest of your life. This will put you way ahead of 99% of the population who forget most of what they read. Once again, the Bookmapping technology is designed with your brain in mind.

This is what makes it so effective. First, your brain likes to think in pictures. For example, if we say to you, "Don't think about a yellow monkey," what do you see? If we say, "Don't think about a yellow monkey jumping on a red bicycle. Riding out to the airport on a green plane, landing in Hawaii, sitting on a beach with Marilyn Monroe, drinking a blue drink," what do you see? That's right you instantly see all of the information we told you not to think about. You did not see a string of words. The first reason Bookmapping works so well is that it accesses the brain's vast visual potential: 80% of your brain is engaged in visual processing!

The second key to retaining information is location. For example, if we ask you, "What did you have for lunch yesterday?" what's the first thing you would have to remember? That's right, where you were. Location is a very powerful system for remembering data. Bookmapping takes full advantage of this by locating the key data (information that you determine must be learned) on different parts of a page.

The third factor that helps your brain store information in long-term memory is color. The human brain is brilliantly designed to notice, enjoy, and store color in your long-term memory. In fact, to your brain, black-on-white is a monochrome that is as boring to see as a monotone voice is to hear. Bookmapping incorporates the use of at least five different colors.

Another benefit of Bookmapping is that all the information you need is contained on one sheet. So you can literally take a mental photograph of it. When Marcus does his live seminars, he asks people to raise their hands if they take notes during seminars. Every hand goes up. He then asks, "How many of you actually referred to those notes?" Ninety percent of the people stated that they do not refer to their notes after having taken them. Why? First, they are too boring. Second, they are contained in a vast number of pages. One good Bookmap is worth dozens of pages.

Another benefit of a Bookmap is that, once it is created, it can be loaded effortlessly into your long-term memory. Marcus puts his Bookmaps onto the refrigerator after completing them, thus effortlessly loading them into his long-term memory. Further benefits can be enjoyed by creating a whole wall of Bookmaps that contain information on all the key books that you need for your whole year of study. Imagine every day, effortlessly loading this information into your long-term memory. So when you do sit down to take a test, all the information is there.

How to Create a Successful Bookmap™

1. Create a strong central image. Begin by drawing a picture of the book you are Bookmapping right in the center of the page. Your eyes will naturally fall to this spot, and this picture will create the icon which will trigger all the long-term memory of the data contained in the book you've mapped.

2. Have each key, or main, branch lead to one of the most important aspects of the book that you want to remember. For example, in a book that Marcus read, called *The Seven Habits of Highly Effective People,* Marcus had one key branch for each habit. Smaller branches flow off from each main branch and contain more detailed information.

3. Use at least five different colors. This makes the Bookmap more interesting, and gives each key point a distinct appearance.

4. Use one word on each line. This allows the brain to focus on one meaning in a multitude of meanings. This again makes it simpler to recall information.

5. Include small pictures or diagrams. As we said earlier, a picture is worth a thousand words. For example, to signify the importance of listening, you might include a small picture of an ear. The brain likes recalling information that is stored in colorful pictures.

6. Realize that the more fun you have creating it, the stronger the Bookmap gets encoded into your memory. There is no need for it to look perfect. The act of creating the Bookmap does 50% of the memory work. The review creates the other 50%.

Having created your Bookmap, the most powerful way to encode it in your long-term memory is to put it in a place where you will constantly see it. For example on your mirror, refrigerator, or the area over your desk. Research shows that the longer you are exposed to any picture, the stronger the encoding in your memory. For example, Marcus was doing a seminar on Male-Female communication, and one of the students asked him a question about brain development. Marcus simply looked up and to his left and saw in his mind's eye a Bookmap of a title he had recently read. He followed the key branch down to the area that was discussing education and remembered that little girls develop their left brain first, which allows them to be great at reading, writing, and sitting still, whereas little boys develop their right brain first, which makes them far more interested in visual, and bodily kinesthetic activities. By conjuring up his Bookmap so easily, Marcus answered the question effortlessly.

Once you've created your Bookmap and reviewed it, after a short time, you can simply review it in your mind's eye whenever you are standing in a line. It is estimated that we spend five years of our lives standing in lines. This time can be learning time if you simply picture your Bookmap in your mind's eye.

You can even create a virtual library of Bookmaps. We have such a virtual library with 30 or 40 books on any key subject. Whenever you begin to study for your test, you simply review your Bookmaps, which takes about 5% of the time, and could be 1,000% more effective than traditional study techniques.

You will notice that throughout the book we have included a Bookmap at the end of each chapter that gives you the big picture, and is basically a road map to the data included within the chapter. Your brain works best when it is exposed to information visually. Almost like seeing the picture of a completed jigsaw puzzle before you begin to examine the individual pieces and start to put them together.

In the next few pages, you will see some sample Bookmaps. Also, in the workshop section of the book, you will see a Bookmap from each of the key areas that we have discussed.

Book Pegging™

Imagine being at a party where the conversation moves to what books you've read. Suddenly, someone asks if you've read *The Seven Habits of Highly Effective People* by Stephen Covey. And you say, of course, I enjoyed the book. Then you ask a different question. What is habit four, and how have you used it today? When you master the simple skill of Book Pegging, you will instantly be able to recall any key information from any book that you have read. Marcus was giving a seminar to one of the world's leading police forces. He asked the question, "Who has read *The Seven Habits of Highly Effective People?*" Twenty-five hands went up. He then said, "Name the seven habits." Not one hand went up. How often do people read books, enjoy them, but forget the information? If you forget the information, what are the chances of applying it? Book Pegging is a very simple technique, and once you master it you will instantly recall any information from any book that you have read.

Probably one of the most successful books of our time is *The Seven Habits of Highly Effective People.* If you read this book, can you tell us how effective habit number three has been in your life? Even if you've read the book, you probably don't recall the specifics of habit number three. This raises an interesting question: if you don't remember the valuable information that you read, then why bother reading it in the first place? Book Pegging is an excellent tool for storing the main features of a text. Once these main features are placed into your permanent memory, it is easy for the other details to be linked to them later.

Book Pegging applies the principles of memory pegs to specific information in a book. Let's learn to peg *The Seven Habits of Highly Effective People* to see how this concept works. As you know from studying Pegging in this book, we need to link a familiar list to the items we seek to remember in a book. A vivid and highly emotional image will help glue the new information into our permanent memory. Again we will use our body parts as the familiar items on a list. The body parts we will use for Bookmapping are:

1. head

2. shoulders

3. heart

4. belly

5. hips

6. butt

7. thighs

Let's begin with habit number one, which is **be proactive**. We'll link this habit to your head. Picture a bee stinging you on the head. How does it feel? That's right, very painful. Now whenever you think about your head, immediately you see the word bee. The word bee is associated with the phrase **be proactive**. Anytime we say head, you will say **be proactive**. You've just learned your first book peg. See how easy it is!

The second body part we will use to anchor information is your shoulders. The second habit is **begin with the end in mind**. Picture a sign on your right shoulder that says "begin." Now picture a sign on your left shoulder that says "end." Now when you picture your two shoulders you see the two signs: begin and end. Seeing these two signs reminds you to **begin with the end in mind.** Another simple book peg. By the way if we asked you to recall what you pegged to your head; immediately, you recall **be proactive.**

The third habit is **first things first**, and we must peg this to your heart area. Imagine an Olympic gold medal hanging over your heart. The medal says first place. When you picture the words first place on your heart, it helps you remember habit number three, which is **first things first.**

Let's do a quick review of the first three pegs. Remember that repetition is an important part of learning. Head makes you think? **Be proactive.** Shoulder make you recall **begin with the end in mind.** Picture your heart and you think, **first things first.** Already you have mastered three of the important book pegs.

Habit number four is **think win-win.** We will link this fourth habit to your belly. Picture the Indianapolis 500 race. The winner is being flagged as they pass over the finish line. That flag symbolizes their winning the race. Now place this same checkered flag on your belly. See the image of you winning an important race. Whenever you picture the checkered flag on your belly it reminds you to **think win-win.**

The fifth habit is **seek first to understand, and then to be understood,** and we must link this to our hips. Remember Inspector Gadget? He was a cartoon character with amazing devices popping out of different areas of his body. Well, imagine you have a magnifying glass popping out of your left hip. Out it comes and it helps you to **seek first to understand.** Next picture your right hip with two bees landing on it. Use the power of rhythm and say aloud **then be understood.** Repeat the two statements several times to place them in memory. Anytime you think about your right and left hips, immediately you remember to **seek first to understand, then to be understood.** Take a moment and recall the other four pegs you've already put into your permanent memory.

The sixth habit is **synergize,** and it must be linked to your butt. Picture the pink Energizer™ Bunny banging on his drum. He is energized! Energize and synergize sound very similar and you can use them as a hook. Imagine you are banging your buttocks like a bunny banging a drum. Instead of energize, you keep saying **synergize**. Now whenever you picture your butt you see the drum beating to the word **synergize**, and you've just completed your sixth Book Peg.

The seventh habit is **sharpen your saw**. This must be linked to your thighs. Did you ever feel like someone had cut you off at the legs? Perhaps they were using a saw. Picture a saw cutting through your thighs and immediately you will remember **sharpen your saw**.

See how easy that was!

Now let's go over our seven pegs:

1. head   **be proactive**

2. shoulders   **begin with the end in mind**

3. heart   **first things first**

4. stomach   **think win-win**

5. hip   **seek first to understand, then to be understood**

6. butt   **synergize**

7. thigh   **sharpen your saw**

You will notice at the end of each chapter, we have a Book Pegging list. This is to insure that you literally take the information contained within this book to heart. By retaining this data, you will become one of the world's fastest readers—way ahead of 99% of the population.

Physiology of Memory

Ninety percent of the what we have learned about the brain has been learned in the last five years. One of the most exciting breakthroughs is the understanding of the physiology of memory. Have you ever reviewed for a test and been confident that you knew the information, only to enter the examination room and notice that your mind goes completely blank? What happens a few minutes later when you leave the examination room? That's right, the information comes flying back. Why is this?

Your brilliant brain is designed to operate perfectly and consistently as long as you know the code. A code for running the brain is your eye movements. For example, right now just relax and count in your mind's eye the number of windows that you have in your house. Now write this number in the margin of this page. Did you notice where your eyes went? For most people, the eyes would go up and to their left. This is where visual memory is stored.

Suppose we say to you, "What does the American national anthem sound like?" Notice where your eyes go. For most people the eyes go directly across and to their left. If we were to say, "Why did you buy this book?," many people would look down and to the left as they talk to themselves: "Now why did I buy this book?" Observing others you will often see them looking like this when speaking on the telephone. When we ask, "What would Bugs Bunny look like while wearing a blue hat?," your eyes would go up and to the right. This is where you store imagination. If we were to ask you, "What would you sound like while giving a powerful presentation on speed-reading to your class?," you would look directly across and to your right. When we ask, "How does it feel to walk on a beautiful sandy beach, feeling the sand beneath your toes?," notice that your eyes go down and to the right.

Now what do you think happens during a test? Where have you been trained to look? That's right, you've been trained to look down at your paper, and you may experience a sense of memory loss. When you look down and to your left, you say to yourself, "I don't even remember studying this." When you look down and to your right, you just feel badly. So literally your eyes are bouncing from "self-talk" (or talking to yourself) to feeling badly. Now what happens when you walk out of the examination room? That's right, you look up and then all the memory comes back. But what happens if you look up during your test? The teacher is likely to say, "Look down at your own paper." How do you avoid this? Simple. First of all, lower your head all the way down during an examination, and then look to the upper left of your paper. By doing this you will still be able to switch on your powerful visual memory without looking like you are cheating.

You look up to the right to tap into your imagination and look up to the left to retrieve visual memory.

Most people look across to their right when trying to think of what to say about something.
When trying to remember a song, however, they look to the left.

When recalling what something physically feels like, people tend to look down to their right.

Most people look down to the left when trying to remember where a certain place is located.

Second, show this book to your teacher or administrator. We are training many teachers in these skills across the country. In fact, we are encouraging teachers in classrooms to build a giant mind map on the left side of the room that links the whole year's studies. This way students can effortlessly encode it into long-term memory. When this happens and students take a test, they simply look up and left, and even though the giant mind map is no longer there, their memory is still full of the information.

Another factor about memory is that to recall data, we need to be in the same state we were in as when we stored it. For example, when studying for a postgraduate examination, Marcus didn't have much confidence that he would pass statistics and math. He therefore studied in a very stressed state. Other people living in his building were very confident about statistics. And they studied in a relaxed state. On the day of the test, Marcus who had learned in a stressed state was also in a very stressed state while taking the test, and actually did better than his colleagues who had studied in a relaxed state, but were in a stressed state while taking the examination.

So what do you do to use this vital information to your advantage? When Marcus trains counterterrorist teams, it is important that these individuals are able to remember vital information during highly stressful situations. So he teaches them how to see the big picture in a relaxed, fun way. First he puts them under extreme stress so that when faced with a terrorist situation, the information automatically floats into their brain.

How can you use this vital information to make your learning more productive and effective? Simple. If you naturally get stressed when taking tests, you can turn this to your advantage. How? First, learn everything in the relaxed fun ways that we explained throughout this book. Then put yourself under stress to load that knowledge into your stressed state. How do you get yourself into a stressed state? By doing mock examinations in your home. Stress can be easily induced by getting a friend or relative to give you stern instructions: "You've got thirty minutes to do this test paper." This induces almost as much stress as you would usually have during the examination. When you do this, you will effortlessly be able to take your test.

Another solution is to learn in a relaxed state, and then use the relaxation techniques shown earlier to allow you to return to a relaxed state during the test. Then you can access information effortlessly. To achieve the optimal level of recall potential is to learn the data in a variety of states so you can have it when you need it, regardless of the state you're in.

CHAPTER BOOKMAP™

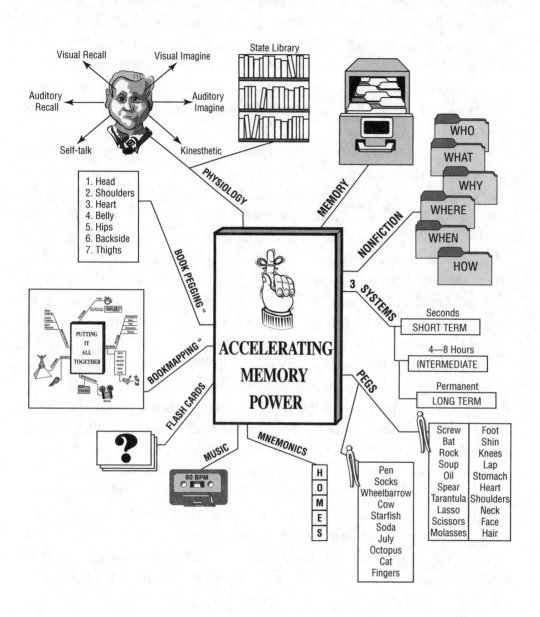

CHAPTER FOUR SELF-TEST

1. What is the difference between memory and recall?

2. What are the visual folders you can use when reading a novel for pleasure and how can you use them?

3. What are the visual folders you can use when reading nonfiction for pleasure and how can you use them?

4. Why must you put a concept into context?

5. Describe the brain's three different types of memory.

6. How can you use memory pegging for storing and retrieving information?

7. How can mnemonics be used for improving memory?

8. Why does music help improve memorization?

9. How can you use music to improve your memory?

10. Describe how flashcards can help you use more of your brain when memorizing complex information.

11. What is Bookmapping, and how can you use it to improve your recall of complex information?

12. What is Book Pegging, and how can you use it to improve your recall of complex information?

13. How can you use eye movements to increase recall of visual and auditory information?

Chapter 5

How to Study

Chapter Preview

- Understanding information challenge levels

- Using old tests to anticipate new questions

- Analysis of lecture materials

- Test-taking strategies

ISN'T IT FRUSTRATING when none of the questions you study appear on an examination? Fortunately there is an easy-to-use system that will consistently help you determine which information in a textbook is most likely to appear on your next examination. Using this system you will be able to accurately filter the most important information, and then use your speed-memory tools to permanently retain it. At the same time, you will also recognize irrelevant information that can easily be ignored. Combining these tools with your ability to read much faster will help you get higher grades in half the time!

Information Challenge Levels

Determining which information to prioritize when studying a book for a test is a snap, when you realize that the text's information is not equally challenging. The fact is there are four levels of information that you will find in any type of text. These four levels are:

- principal concept

- divisions of a concept

- main examples in each division

- specific details

It takes more effort to learn the details that occur in each level. In addition, as you go from one level to the other it takes more effort to learn the details. It's a lot like learning to play a piano. You can learn to play on the first lesson. Learning the divisions of a concept are like learning to play a few songs on the piano decently. This can take a few weeks to a few months.

Learning the main examples in each division is like learning to play a piano well. But even when you can play many types of music well, you cannot play like a professional yet.

Learning the specific details level is like learning to play a piano like a professional. This not only takes a great deal of time and practice, but also requires aptitude and skill.

Every subject is learned by going through a similiar process. First you get the main point. This doesn't take very long. Next you learn the main areas within a subject. This can take several hours, and doesn't give you much detail. Next you learn the main details. And finally you master all the nuances of a subject. Each new level of learning requires much more time and effort. That is why it is so important before studying a text to know which of these levels to strive for during your studies. The best way to determine what to focus on is by analyzing old examinations.

Analyzing Old Tests

It is common in most colleges to keep tests on file. If this isn't the case at your college, or if you are in public school, there is no reason why you can't ask your teacher for a copy of an old examination so you can better prepare for an upcoming examination. If a public school instructor refuses to cooperate you may want to consider speaking with a guidance counselor or having a parent make an appointment with a supervisor to discuss their unwillingness to help you improve your academic performance. If you're in college and your instructor is unwilling to give you an old test, we recommend taking the course with another instructor who shows a greater interest in the academic success of their students. However, there are several other options available to you if all else fails:

- Get an examination from a friend who already took the course.

- Get an examination from another instructor teaching the same course.

- Use the first examination offered in a semester as the model for future examinations.

This last choice is least desirable, because you don't know what to study until after the first test is over. At this point you may have to catch up on future tests to get a better grade. It is far better to know what you are looking for in a book even before taking the first examination. But, if this is the only way to get an examination from an instructor because all else has failed, at least you have something to fall back upon.

When looking at an old examination, you are not simply hoping that the same questions are going to appear on the next test. Instead you are trying to ascertain how many questions fall into the four different levels of difficulty described earlier. The percentages of questions asked on these levels tends to remain constant from examination to examination. Let's see how these tests can be analyzed to give us the necessary insights.

Let's use a biology test as an example. The first level of question might be about an organ system like the circulatory system. "What is the circulatory system?" is a level one question. A level two question might ask you to identify the main organs in the circulatory system. The answer would include the heart, lungs, arteries, veins, capillaries, venules, spleen, and kidneys. A level three question might ask you something about the heart. A level four question might describe the right auricle's function in the heart.

Notice that each question became more detailed, requiring more knowledge of technical information. Once you determine the pattern of the questions, you know exactly what information in the text is most appropriate to focus on. You look and say, "This seems too easy," or "This seems too hard. Past examinations rarely use this type of information." On the other hand, some of the text's information will appear to be exactly on the same level as the questions asked on previous tests. For example, this year's test might ask, "What is the function of the left auricle in the heart?" Notice how closely matched in complexity it is to the level four question. Yet they are completely different questions. The question level tends to be consistent on every examination. Once you are aware of that level, studying becomes a snap.

Analysis of Lecture Information

Even if you analyze an examination, you still will find some technical information needs to be learned. How are you supposed to ignore all the technical details in the text when you know that questions testing this level of information will appear on the exam? Simple! The technical information is supposed to be covered during class lectures. If a teacher doesn't teach you a highly technical part of a subject, and then asks a technical question about it and everyone gets it wrong, the teacher isn't doing her job. The real challenge in education is teaching things that are difficult in class so that everyone understands them. Then if a very technical question gets asked everyone gets it right. That's an accomplishment! A true educator will strive to provide clues in class to subjects that are difficult and hard to learn on your own. When technical information is covered in class, it should no longer be considered technical. At that point, you are expected to understand it, or ask your instructor questions so that you can understand it. Using this strategy, you will quickly recognize that most technical questions on tests are answered by information covered during class time or lecture.

PRACTICE

Examine the following questions from two biology examinations.

Questions: Last Year's Biology Test on Circulation

1. Name the large blood vessel that pumps oxygenated blood away from the heart.

2. The upper right portion of the heart is called the _____.

3. Describe what happens to deoxygenated blood in the lungs.

CHAPTER FIVE SELF-TEST

1. Describe the four levels of information challenge.

2. How can analysis of old exams help you select the information to study for upcoming examinations?

3. How can you get information about old examinations?

4. How can information contained within a lecture help you target what materials to study in a text?

5. How can you improve grades on essay questions?

6. Describe how you can improve your scores on standardized examinations.

This Year's Biology Test on Circulation

1. Name the large blood vessel that pumps deoxygenated blood toward the heart.

2. The lower left portion of the heart is called the _____.

3. Describe what happens to blood when it passes through the kidneys.

Notice the similarities between questions asked last year and this year? The questions are different, but they follow a pattern that is easy to identify and easy to use during studying.

More Test-Taking Strategies

How to Choose Which Questions to Answer First

Upon beginning an examination, make certain that you skim all the questions at your top reading speed. Reading at that speed you can only recognize things that are already familiar to you. If a question seems familiar, it is because a visual clue seen at high speed made it easy for you to understand it. That should be an easy question for you to answer correctly. Take a pencil and mark off all the questions that are familiar to you and don't spend more than two minutes skimming the entire exam. Using any more time than this is taking away valuable time from answering the questions on the examination.

How to Improve Your Grades on Essays

Essays are usually the toughest questions to answer on a typical examination. That is because answering an essay question requires direct recall of a subject, while most other questions simply require you to recognize an answer from among many others. You may not remember the answer to a multiple-choice question, but you may easily recognize it as one of the choices offered.

Another problem with essay questions is that they appear at the end of an examination. By the time you reach them, there usually isn't a lot of time left to finish the test. There is a simple solution to this situation. During your high speed skim of the entire examination, take some time to look at the essay questions. Make a movie picture of these questions in your imagination. Then during the rest of the test, look for any clues or information that might help you answer these questions more efficiently. It is very difficult to construct a test on a subject, and not provide any clues to information sought in an essay question. In the past by the time you reached the essays, it was too late to start looking for these clues. Now you know to read the essay questions first. You will be looking for clues to answer them while taking the rest of the examination. You will be using the information found throughout the examination to score higher grades on your essay tests.

Improving Standardized Test Scores

Few things have a greater impact on a student's academic success than her performance on standardized tests like the SAT. This single score can determine what college you attend. Some standardized tests even determine if you will be able to graduate! Here are some tips for improving your standardized test scores on future tests.

Skim the Entire Test

As with any other examination, you should skim the entire test before answering any questions. You might find some of the questions are easier for you to answer, and should begin by answering those questions first. This will guarantee that the easiest questions get completed when there is a limited time available for taking the test.

Reading Comprehension Test Question Strategies

When encountering the reading comprehension portion of a standardized test, always read the questions before reading the passage. If you don't now what the questions are, you don't know what to look for in the reading passages. While speed-reading the passages, you will know what to filter for and find it effortlessly. The amount of time it takes to complete the test will also go down as your scores go up. You will stop wasting time reading about things that are irrelevant to the questions being asked and use your test time more efficiently as well.

CHAPTER BOOKMAP™

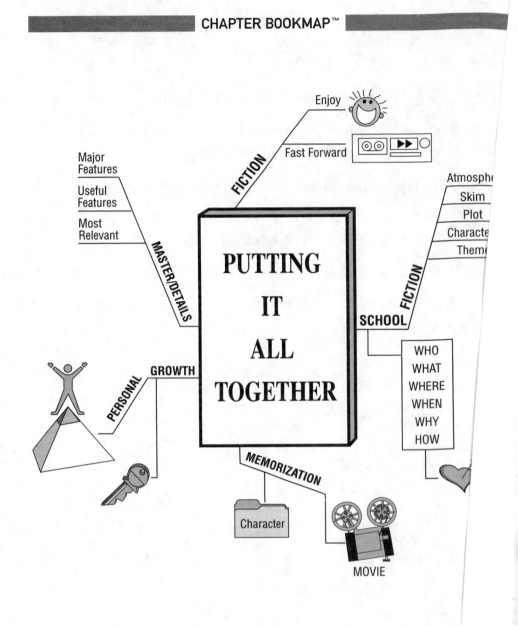

Chapter 6

Putting It All Together

Chapter Preview

- Reading fiction

- Memorization of pleasure-reading materials

- Reading for personal growth

- Mastering detailed information

NOW YOU ARE READY to put all your speed-reading techniques together into an efficient learning tool. Each tool is specifically designed for your specific reading needs.

Fiction

Although it may seem hard to believe when you are still a student, but the day may actually come when you might actually spend your money on a book for pleasure! Reading fiction for pleasure is different from reading fiction for school assignments. (Reading fiction for school assignments is covered later in this chapter.)

There are some major differences between pleasure reading and other types of reading. First, you should never explore text when reading for pleasure. Knowing the ending to an exciting novel is certain to ruin your enjoyment of the text.

Second, when reading for pleasure, you will find that very high reading speeds can reduce your enjoyment of the material. Fortunately, there is an easy way to a balance between reading your text quickly and enjoying it. It is very similar to the balance you might achieve if you were viewing a television show that you taped earlier on your VCR. What might you do when a boring advertisement interrupts your movie? That's right, you would hit fast forward and quickly return to watching the movie.

You can use this same strategy to gain maximum enjoyment during speed-reading. When your novel suddenly becomes boring, slow, or tedious, speed through this unpleasant passage. Go between two to five times as fast as your normal reading speed. Watch the topic sentences, and pay attention to the who, what, where, when, why, and how information contained within the text. As soon as your novel becomes more interesting slow down your reading speed to begin enjoying it.

For example, you might be reading a Tom Clancy novel and suddenly there are 80 pages describing how to make an atomic bomb out of a milk container. You might find this very boring information to read. Instead, you go to your top skimming speed and get through this uninteresting information. You are still completely aware of what is taking place, but reading too quickly to feel bored. Then when the information appears more interesting, you slow down to a more enjoyable reading speed.

Many students have told us that they didn't finish many novels they started reading for pleasure because they became too boring. Using this strategy described above, you will not only be able to complete every novel read for pleasure, but you will also finish them quickly. Since a large portion of text is often boring, your average speed in each book will still be quite high, and you will maintain an outstanding reading speed.

Reading Fiction for School

Reading fiction for school is completely different than reading it for pleasure. In school, you need an understanding and must be able to analyze a book, which takes more effort than pleasure reading. You definitely must skim when studying fiction. While skimming you will discover how the different plot lines develop, and other major events occurring in the major characters' lives. As a result, when you begin reading you will already know how the characters and plot are moving forward in your text. Now you are aware of where you are in the text, where you've been, and also where the text is going. This ability to peer into the future of a novel enables you to read more inferentially, and better appreciate the finer textual points essential for getting higher grades on reports and exams.

What exactly should you be looking for during your fiction reading? The filters that are essential for your understanding and enjoyment of the novel are:

- plot

- atmosphere

- theme

- character development

Throughout your reading, focus on anything in your novel corresponding to these key filters. When you see something associated to one of these filters, view it as a movie instead of reading it like a text. For example, if you are reading a James Bond novel, envision him performing the activities as if you were watching him in a movie. Your brain is highly visual, and turning text into a series of visual images will enable you to improve retention and understanding—even at high speeds.

Reading Nonfiction for Pleasure

It is probable that you will also read some nonfiction materials for pleasure. These materials can include newspapers and magazines. When reading newspapers and magazines you want to learn the key points that are mentioned in articles, but not necessarily memorize the minute details. These details can be learned when you study, and will soon be covered in this chapter.

As in reading fiction for pleasure, reading nonfiction for pleasure requires that you focus on the main details and that you use the following set of filters:

- who

- what

- where

- when

- why

- how

Any information connected to these filters should be visualized. It also helps to think about a context in which this information could be applied or used in your life or in someone else's life. Seeing information in a context makes it easier for you to retain and recall it later. Let's do a simple experiment that proves this point.

If we asked you to remember where you were 23 nights ago, you would have to think about it, and probably not remember the answer. If we asked you where you were the last time you attended an exciting party with your friends, or had an important family gathering, it would be very easy for you to recall most of the these details. The difference in this case are the context clues associated with this event, and the emotions you've linked to the clues. Whenever reading *anything*, always try to link context clues and emotional significance to what you are seeing in the text. Again, whenever possible view your text like a movie!

Memorization of Pleasurable Materials

There are many practical tools in *Speed-Reading the Easy Way* for improving comprehension and retention of all types of printed material. We would like to discuss a simple way to retain the general information learned during pleasure reading.

Your brain needs a filing system to store and retrieve information. Your brain doesn't alphabetize information, nor does it place it in chronological order. Your brain stores information primarily as visual images. Learning to use your brain's natural ability to store and retrieve these images, you are able to quickly learn pertinent information during pleasure reading. Just how do you go about doing this?

Memorizing information during pleasure-reading is simple if you use your filters efficiently. Picture all the information associated with each filter during your reading. Remember to picture this information as if you are seeing a movie instead of reading text. For example, if you are reading about Washington crossing the Delaware River during the American Revolution, visualize him standing up in a boat and crossing a frozen river. Feel the cold water spraying his face. Taste the spray. Shiver in the freezing cold weather. Experience what transpired as if it is actually happening to you. These emotions and sensory experiences help your brain store, and later retrieve, the information related to them.

A simple technique for remembering the details about fictional characters is easy to learn. First, you picture what a character looks like based upon their description in the novel. Studies show that your brain can store new information more efficiently when linking it to information that is already stored in your permanent memory. By storing images of your characters into your permanent memory you are creating hooks on which you can later hang the details about these characters' lives.

Once you have established a visual memory of how a character appears, you can then associate any activities that character performs within the text with their appearance. Visualize them acting out each event with as much specific emphasis upon their appearance as possible. Now whenever you need to recall a detail about an activity that a character was involved with, all you need to do is recall that character's appearance. Now you are searching in the specific part of your brain where you stored the images of that character's actions, and you can find this information's location in your visual folders much more efficiently.

This system is wonderful for storing information when pleasure-reading fiction. With a few adjustments, the system works splendidly for nonfiction as well. In fact, you are probably already doing this on an unconscious level when reading about a famous individual in a magazine or newspaper. For example, if you were reading an article about President Clinton, first you would recall his appearance in detail. Then you would see him actually doing what is described in the story. Now whenever you need to remember any details about what you read in the text you begin by remembering what he looks like. Now you are in the area of your brain where you stored information about his actions. Next you search for the who, what, where, when, why, and how information that you linked to the "movie" in this region of your brain. And presto! Suddenly all this information quickly appears in your conscious mind because you searched in the correct storage area.

Reading for Personal Growth

Reading materials for personal growth and to improve your personal skills and abilities is quite common. Here you are selecting a text that you believe will provide you with information for self-improvment. Unlike studying for school, this is information you seek for your own personal development and goals. The key difference is that when you study for school an instructor will be asking the questions and deciding what information is important for you to learn. When you are learning something for yourself, you get to decide what is most important and what you should be focused on.

When reading for self-growth, the first step is to skim through all the material. Unlike skimming a novel, which might ruin your enjoyment, skimming nonfiction prepares you to learn and master a subject more efficiently. During skimming, you are examining charts, diagrams, and other major features to determine their relevance or difficulty, and to see if any features are available to make it easier for you to master the text.

Once you have completed exploring the material, you are ready to begin examining its details. Explore those sections of the text most relevant to what you want to learn.

Next comes the memorization and learning of the text. This is a step that we can probably help you perform more efficiently. Many people tend to overlearn material, resulting in too much time spent trying to learn tiny, unnecessary details. At first, all you need to focus on is the key points. Get an idea of what you could do if you actually learn the subject. Next study what is necessary for getting started. Learn the details only when they become necessary. Avoid cluttering up your mind with endless details that you will probably never use. Even most computer software program users find they use about four to ten percent of the features of their software. They wind up cluttering their minds learning the other 90% and as a result even forget the four to ten percent they actually needed in the first place. Prioritize what you learn. Master details only when they become necessary. You will find yourself flying through self-development materials in a fraction of the time with far better results.

Mastering Detailed Material

Mastering detailed information is always a three-step procedure. First you explore the material for two distinct purposes. Your first purpose is to discover the major features contained within the text as well as special features that might be missing. For instance, some texts may not include a bibliography or an index. This is important information for you to know. During your initial exploration you want to determine your familiarity with the information, its appropriateness to your needs, and to discover any visual aids that might make your learning easier. Once you've finished exploring the entire book, you are ready to begin reading the first chapter. The first step in reading a technical book's chapter is to explore it once again, this time with a different purpose. You are exploring to become aware of the information contained within its useful features and to become highly conscious of these things, just as you did with the entire book's structure earlier. There is another very important purpose for this chapter exploration. You are interested in determining how large a chunk of information you can examine before it becomes too difficult to remember.

A problem many students experience when speed-reading technical information is that their minds become overwhelmed by all the new information: new ideas, new definitions, numerous complex facts. The solution is simple. Don't slow down your reading speed. Explore smaller chunks of information, determining the chunk size by what you can completely understand without difficulty. This exploration of your chapter determines just how familiar or difficult the material contained within that chapter might be for you. You must repeat this with every chapter, since even in the same book, a different chapter may present material that is familiar or unfamiliar to you, or that could be especially difficult for you to learn. Remember, your reading speed doesn't slow down. Just take smaller chunks of information at very high speed. This helps you to maximize your speed and comprehension of even the most complex text.

Once completing the second exploration of the chapter, you are ready to begin reading and examining it in earnest. During your examination, scan for information that is relevant to what you must learn using the techniques described earlier in this book. Using these techniques, you can even determine what your teachers expect you to learn for important tests. Mark off this important information in the margin by making a tick mark in the margin. This is faster and more efficient than using a highlighter. While reading, visualize and place context clues, especially emotionally significant ones, into what you are reading. Seeing text as a visual movie rather than a series of words, and putting the information into a context that is meaningful and relevant will help you understand and retain it. It is important to frequently stop and ask yourself relevant questions about what you are reading. Who, what, where, when, how, and why questions are excellent. More important, ask yourself how this information might be relevant to your life. Developing an appreciation of the relevancy of information will help you retain and comprehend it much better. Finally, use the accelerated memory skills described in this book to store and retrieve even the smallest details with confidence and ease.

CHAPTER SIX SELF-TEST

1. What common reading activity do you omit when speed-reading for pleasure? Why?

2. What should you look for when speed-reading fictional text for school?

3. What filters should you use when speed-reading nonfiction for pleasure?

4. How can you memorize information while speed-reading for pleasure?

5. Why do you skim when speed-reading for personal growth?

6. What are the three steps performed when mastering detailed reading material?

7. How can you simplify learning complicated material?

8. Instead of using a highlighter, what does the text recommend you do to mark off important details?

Unit 3

Practicing Your Speed-Reading the Easy Way Skills in Different Types of Materials

Chapter 7

Using Your Skills

In this section we will use a powerful tool to make sure you can consistently remember how to use your *Speed-Reading the Easy Way* skills. We are using an age-old technique known as an acrostic. An acrostic is a simple mechanism whereby the first letters of a key word trigger all the relevant data you need to perform a task. For us, this acrostic is SPEED:

S is for state

P is for purpose

E is for explore

E is for examine

D is for draw a Bookmap.

By simply remembering the acrostic SPEED, all the key components for accelerated reading will automatically open up in your mind. So, to review. In order for you to read at speeds well ahead of 99% of the population, you simply have to remember these five simple steps:

1. **State.** It is vital that you get your body's system into a state for maximum absorption, comprehension, and retention. You can achieve this by simply using the exercises detailed within the book. For example, practice correct nutrition because protein perks and carbohydrates calm. Ensure a good blood supply to the brain by doing neurobics. Ensure that you sit at a desk in a chair that is appropriate for you, or that you wear the right clothing with the right music in the background. You can fully enter the appropriate state by simply using your thumb trigger.

2. **Purpose:** When you clearly notify your brain the purpose of your reading, your mind becomes a magnet, automatically attracting the key data that you need to recall into your long-term memory. Clearly by stating your purpose you prepare your mind to read at lightning speed while retaining the key data that you are likely to need.

3. **Explore the book.** Once again we highlight the fact that only 11% to 40% of the book contains the key data that you need. So by reading the front cover, the back cover, the introduction, the contents page, the first paragraph, the last paragraph, the last chapter of the book, reviewing the diagrams, using the index, the glossary, and the appendices, you can explore the book in a few minutes and then decide whether or not to read it. Half of the art of speed-reading is not reading. That is, you use your techniques to decide what books not to read. Once again this links back to your purpose. When you have a crystal clear purpose your brain will accelerate you through the irrelevant and direct you to that which will be most beneficial to you.

4. **Examine the book.** At this stage you simply take a pencil and accelerate through the book marking anything that requires further comprehension or that you want to lock into your long-term memory. By using this technique you free your mind from thinking, "What if I miss something? What if I don't understand something?" Anything that you don't understand or remember you simply mark with a pencil mark. This will allow you to rocket through the book at lightning-fast speed. You will even begin to get a little angry with the publisher if you are not getting any useful information from the text. Remember the purpose is to add new data to your memory bank.

5. **Drawing the Bookmap.** At this stage you take all of the key areas that you marked in the book and convert it into a one-page visual memory system—the Bookmap. Remember the keys to Bookmapping are to have a central image, to have the key information coming off the major branches, to use five different colors, and to use pictures that are worth a thousand words. You can then display the Bookmap on your refrigerator, mirror, wall, closet, or anywhere you are likely to see it on a regular basis and

then load it into a long-term library. With this technique alone you will be able to read far ahead of your classmates and retain the information permanently.

So by remembering this simple code you will always be able to speed-read and get through work at lightning speed.

In the pages that follow you will have the opportunity to apply your *Speed-Reading the Easy Way* skills to various types of reading materials. Let's look at what you can do to maximize your learning efficiency in each chapter.

Perform two explorations of each reading selection. During your first exploration look for the general features that can prove useful to your understanding:

- Use music and other devices to put yourself into a learning state.

- Look for the flow pattern of the materials.

- Pay close attention to any subheadings.

- Are there any charts, diagrams, pictures, or other visual aids you can be using?

- Look out for any questions asked throughout the chapter—look for the answers to these questions.

- Is there any new vocabulary that is unfamiliar to you? Learn this vocabulary.

- Are new words and concepts marked off from the rest of the text by bold-faced type, italics, or anything else that is easy to spot at high speeds?

- Mark off important information in your text with a tick mark.

- Frequently ask yourself literal, implied, and inferential questions to see if you are understanding the material's true meanings.

- Filter all information by seeking information in the text that falls under the categories of who, what, where, when, why and how.

- Look for new and important concepts that are unfamiliar to you, and ask yourself questions about the applications of these concepts.

- Determine how relevant the information is to your purpose. Should you even be reading this material?

- Put new information into a context that is easy to picture and recall.

- Explore the end of the chapter by looking for summaries, questions, or any important features that will help you determine what to prioritize during your reading.

During the second exploration of your chapter perform the following:

- Determine how large a section of text you can read before you have difficulty understanding, storing, and retrieving the information.

- Determine your level of familiarity with the material.

- Mark off important information in your text with a tick mark.

- See if any sections are easy for you to understand and if they contain a lot of familiar material. If so, prepare to read these sections at a higher reading rate.

Now examine your text. Using the insights gained from your exploration be prepared to:

- use music and other devices to put yourself into a learning state

- find the answers to important questions

- look for information contained within any summaries

- form literal, implied, and inferential questions about important, new material

- create context clues around important, new, and unfamiliar material

- mark off important information in your text with a tick mark

- create a Bookmap of the key points contained within each chapter

- use your memory techniques to store and retrieve important information

Let's begin to put your skills into practice. In each practice exercise, we will help you focus on making the correct decisions for peak learning, and will highlight our suggestions so you can work with us to improve your learning skills. In effect, we will enable you to see the information you are learning through our eyes, thus empowering you to understand how an experienced speed-reader views information in text. Our spontaneous remarks will help you develop the same ability to spontaneously think your way through even the most complex text. Remember that all the suggestions we made at the beginning of this unit should be applied to every exercise, and that our additional suggestions scattered throughout your practice exercises are there to help you focus on certain aspects of these suggestions at one time, and do not negate the importance of performing all of the suggestions made earlier.

Putting Your Knowledge to Work

PRACTICE READING 1: BIOLOGY

1 # CHARACTERISTICS AND
2 # RELATIONSHIPS OF LIFE

3 *What do we know about:*

4 • *how to decide whether an object is alive?*

5 • *the chance that life can currently arise from*
6   *nonlife?*

7 • *the age of the earth, and of continuous life on*
8   *earth?*

9 • *the possibility that ancient life was based on*
10   *RNA, not DNA?*

11 • *the possibility of our possessing genes that might*
12   *cause aging?*

13 • *how the maximum human life span might be*
14   *increased?*

15 • *defining the moment of death?*

16 • *looking for clues of relationships among*
17   *organisms?*

18 • *the five kingdoms (or are there six)?*

> Notice that this chapter has an introduction summarizing its key points. Pay careful attention to these main points, and focus carefully upon textual information related to this information.

19 ## LIVING ORGANISMS SHOW CERTAIN
20 ## CHARACTERISTICS

21   It is paradoxical that the quality known as life is at the
22 heart of biology, yet explaining it is still beyond the capacity
23 of biologists. A complete explanation will have to await the
24 time when life can be created in the laboratory by properly

25 organizing the chemical components of protoplasm (living
26 matter). Biochemists have progressed far in the analysis of the
27 constituent chemicals found in cells and of the reactions in
28 which they participate. Nevertheless, no one can claim total
29 knowledge of the organization and interactions that bind these
30 into an entity that is truly alive.

31   Regardless of the form of life, whether a bacterium, tree, or
32 an elephant, there appears to be a remarkable uniformity in its
33 chemical composition. A good generalization is that organisms
34 look more alike when examined nearer the molecular level,
35 and more diverse when examined at organizational levels
36 more complex than molecules. Another way of saying this is to
37 note that there are now approxi-
38 mately one million recognized
39 species on earth, but that all of
40 these diverse types of organisms
41 utilize identical (or very similar)
42 molecules and do very similar
43 things with them.

> Pay careful attention to information contained in lists. It is a method of emphasizing important information.

44   What are the functional and
45 structural characteristics of living organisms that make them
46 different from nonliving matter? Let us begin a list.

47   1. Certainly one of the most striking things about any organism
48   is that it is *highly organized*. Furthermore, this organization
49   is arranged in a hierarchy. A convenient way to describe
50   this is to examine the following list, arranged from simplest
51   to most complex.
52   *Levels of organization, arranged hierarchically:*
53   submolecular chemical structures
54   molecules
55   subcellular structures (organelles)
56   cells
57   tissues
58   organs
59   systems
60   whole organism
61   interactions among organisms
62   Within this hierarchy, each component or level forms the
63   next (more complex) component.

64   Each of these components will be examined in detail in
65   following chapters, but it is appropriate at this point to discuss
66   more fully one of them—the cell. One of the most funda-
67   mental statements in biology is that which is
68   usually called the *Cell Theory*. It actually con-
69   sists of two related statements. First, virtually
70   all living matter is composed of one or more
71   cells. (Viruses are a possible exception; it can
72   be argued that they are nonliving since they
73   cannot exist apart from the cells in which
74   they reproduce.) Furthermore, any cell alive
75   today has its origin in a preexisting cell. Divi-
76   sion of many organisms into small cellular
77   units should not be interpreted as a separation
78   into simple units. The cell has a complex
79   arrangement in which there is a division of
80   various processes among its components, as
81   will be demonstrated in several later chapters.
82   Cells of multicellular organisms perform
83   processes common to all cells, plus additional
84   processes for which they are specialized. For
85   instance, a muscle cell carries on many self-
86   maintaining activities that all cells must do
87   and also uses specialized structures unique to
88   itself that perform the activity of contraction.
89 2. Another characteristic of living organisms is that they
90   *capture*, *store*, and *utilize energy*. For plants and plant-like
91   microorganisms, this involves intake of pure energy in
92   the form of light and then conversion of it to the bonds of
93   foods that are then synthesized from simpler chemicals. For
94   all other organisms, the matter entails capturing (eating or
95   absorbing) food containing energy that can be ultimately
96   traced to sunlight. Usually, energy-holding molecules are
97   stored for some period of time after being made, either in
98   their original form or after being converted to more stable
99   (and usually larger) molecules such as polysaccharides or fats.
100   For all organisms, the eventual utilization of energy involves
101   a complex series of chemical reactions that break the bonds
102   of food molecules and thus release the energy for use.

> Notice how the author has put important vocabulary into italics. Look for other words in italics as well.

> Are you asking yourself how much of this new information you can read before it becomes hard for you to retain? Are you asking yourself literal, implied, and inferential questions to be certain that you are learning and not simply looking at this information?

103
104
105
106
107
108
109
110
111
112
113

3. Some of the energy that an organism captures will be used in *growth and reproduction*. Overall growth of a multicellular organism often involves reproduction on the cell level—each cell in a region splitting to become two, followed by increase in size of each daughter cell. Reproduction of an entire

> Can you picture any of these events happening? Can you see any of this information in a context of something related to real life? This will help you understand and retain your information better.

114
115
116
117

organism can be *asexual* (splitting off or budding of a portion of a mature organism), or *sexual* (cooperative combining of components from two mature organisms to form a new individual).

118
119
120
121
122
123
124
125
126
127
128
129
130

4. Another characteristic of living organisms is that they are *responsive to variables in the environment*. That is, they are capable of sensing changes in their environment, then they do the appropriate thing to ensure their continued health. Obviously, organisms vary considerably in the kind and degree of response. We are most familiar with the quick interaction of nerves and muscles in animals, but there are slower responses too. For example, sunlight and gravity influence the direction of growth in trees. Animals such as the sponges, which have no nerve cells or muscles, reproduce in response to a favorable combination of environmental conditions.

131
132
133
134
135
136
137
138
139
140
141

Appropriate responsiveness also occurs *within* an organism, since the internal environment constitutes a source of variability. The condition of being able to maintain optimum internal conditions is termed *homeostasis*. An example of a homeostatic mechanism is the constant monitoring of

> Do you need to read this example? Or did you understand the concept? Remember that only 11 to 40% of the information you read actually needs to be learned. Go to a higher reading speed when unnecessary information is provided by the author.

142 blood acidity or alkalinity (pH) in a person, with chemical
143 changes occurring to move it in the appropriate direction
144 when it deviates from a narrow (optimal) range.
145 5. The examples of response described above are all short term;
146 that is, they are rather quickly reversible changes during the
147 course of a single organism's life span. There is another sort
148 of responsiveness to the environment, which
149 involves an entire population of organisms and
150 extends over more than one generation. This
151 property of all organisms is termed *evolutionary*
152 *adaptation*. If a population includes organisms
153 that differ somewhat from each other, and if
154 these differences enable some form(s) to have a
155 greater chance of surviving and reproducing
156 than others, then the conditions are right for
157 the composition of the population to change
158 as generations go by. Since the expected
159 change makes the population (as a whole) more likely to
160 survive and thrive, this long-term responsiveness is a useful
161 *adaptation* to an environment.

> Consider placing each of these important concepts or points onto a flash card, and using the memory suggestions for flash cards to memorize and retain all these important details.

---

162 ## ONLY ORGANISMS CAN PRODUCE
163 ## ORGANISMS

164 Until it was disproved in a series of experiments
165 beginning in the late *1600s*, the *general belief was*
166 *that life can constantly arise from dead matter in a*
167 *spontaneous fashion*. Mice, insects, snails, and other
168 forms of animal life were supposed to come from
169 mud or putrefying matter. *In 1688, Francisco Redi*
170 *put pieces of meat into containers, some of which he*
171 *left open, some covered with netting fine enough to*
172 *exclude flies, and some covered with paper. The meat*
173 *decayed in all the containers, but maggots developed only in the*
174 *open ones. Flies were attracted to the meat beneath the netting but*
175 *laid their eggs on the netting when they could not get to the meat.*
176 *The eggs hatched into maggots on the netting. He concluded from*
177 *these simple observations that maggots came from insect eggs, not*
178 *from dead meat.* Among others supporting Redi's views was

> We will use a different typeface for the important information in this next section to make it easier for you to find these important details.

179 *Louis Pasteur*, who with his *sterilization experiments in the 1860s*
180 clinched the belief *that life must come from preexisting life*. He
181 proved that *bacteria had to be introduced into sterilized (nonliving)*
182 *materials before decay could occur*, but they *did not originate sponta-*
183 *neously* within them. In combination with Redi's work this
184 *ensured the downfall of the idea of spontaneous generation.*

185 # HOW DID THE FIRST LIFE
186 # APPEAR ON EARTH?

187   It is appropriate now to address the question of the *original*
188 beginnings of life on earth. There is evidence that the ancient
189 earth did not have nearly the same conditions of atmosphere
190 and temperature that we see now. Therefore, the ancient
191 appearance of living organisms from nonliving materials within
192 that different environment cannot be ruled out.

193 ### The History of Life on Earth is Very Long
194   What do we know about the age of the earth, and when
195 life first appeared? Most scientists agree that the earth formed
196 over four billion years ago. Our way of tracking the story of life
197 on earth rests mostly on fossilized remains of organisms and
198 their artifacts, usually to be found in mineral formations. Over
199 the last 50 years, several reliable methods have been developed
200 that can provide an age estimate for rock formations in which
201 fossil imprints are found, or for actual remains of organisms.
202 These methods are usually based on the physics of the decay
203 rate of radioactive atoms (see Chapter 15). With the help of these
204 techniques, two important statements have become generally
205 accepted. First, life on earth has existed for a very long time.
206 The most ancient fossils currently known have been dated as
207 being about 3.5 billion years old. Second, those oldest materials
208 were provided by very simple organisms, which nevertheless
209 had shapes similar to those of some modern organisms. More
210 specifically, the oldest known organisms were bacteria, which
211 are the simplest of the modern types of cellular organisms.
212 (However, recent findings suggest that single-celled eukaryotic
213 organisms, those that are not bacterial, have ancestry going back
214 to approximately the same time.)

215 **We Can Speculate on Primitive Conditions for First Life**
216   Of course, it is very difficult to know what the earth and its
217 atmosphere were like at a time so far removed from the present.
218 Based on knowledge of modern emissions from volcanoes, and
219 assuming no photosynthetic activity (a property of some living
220 organisms), the atmosphere of a lifeless earth would probably
221 have had carbon dioxide (CO_2), carbon monoxide (CO),
222 hydrogen sulfide (H_2S), hydrogen cyanide (HCN), gaseous water
223 (H_2O), and gaseous nitrogen (N_2), but very little free gaseous
224 oxygen (O_2). The surface temperature would be expected to be
225 very hot, but cool enough for some liquid water to collect.
226 Note that, while the hypothetical mix of materials at the
227 ancient earth's surface is different from that of the modern
228 earth, the fundamental rules of chemistry and physics by
229 which the materials would interact are not presumed to be dif-
230 ferent from those we currently see operating.
231   The question is, would such an inhospitable setting be
232 suitable for a series of spontaneous events to occur that would
233 culminate in living cells capable of reproducing and becoming
234 the ancestors of all the life we see now? We will never know for
235 sure whether such things actually happened. We can only devise
236 experiments that test whether they could have happened,
237 with certain suppositions being made. One way to do this is to
238 set up a controlled micro-environment that mimics what we
239 think the earth's surface might have been like, then observe
240 what happens. Many such experiments have been done since
241 the early 1950s. They indicate that very simple molecules can
242 combine to make many of the complex molecules (amino
243 acids, sugars, nucleotides, and polymers of these) that we know
244 must be part of living organisms. Furthermore, these large
245 molecules can sometimes be found in organized structures not
246 unlike those found in cells.
247   Perhaps the most important class of molecules that would
248 have to be formed in order to ensure a successful emergence of
249 life is a polynucleotide used to store and release information.
250 Although most modern forms of life use DNA for this purpose,
251 there is much support for the idea that most primitive life
252 would have relied upon the closely related RNA. The major

253 evidence for RNA is that it can
254 catalyze chemical reactions much
255 as protein-based enzymes do.
256 Thus, in a primitive situation
257 where only a minimum of mole-
258 cule types would be present, RNA
259 could do double duty by holding
260 information for reproduction of
261 cells and also catalyzing impor-
262 tant reactions.

263   In summary, there are in-
264 triguing clues in modern settings
265 that are not inconsistent with
266 the idea that living cells could
267 have been formed from natural
268 processes on the surface of a
269 primitive earth. However, it must be said that other existing
270 hypotheses cannot be ruled out unless physical evidence is
271 found to do so. Among these is the long-held belief in many
272 societies that at least some steps
273 in the beginning of life were
274 supernatural events directed by a
275 Supreme Being. Another idea is
276 that life on earth arrived from
277 elsewhere, perhaps by way of
278 comets or meteorites. A related,
279 less encompassing hypothesis is
280 that life formed on earth, but
281 was nudged toward the critical
282 moment by the arrival of com-
283 plex organic molecules via comets
284 or meteorites. In either case, one
285 is still left with the question of how life or its preceding mole-
286 cules might have formed on some other celestial body. It is
287 obvious that we are far from resolving the fundamental question
288 of the origin of life.

> Notice how the author stressed the most important class of molecules. Pay attention to these clues. Have you been chunking down the size of information you need to learn in this section? Remember, the more unfamiliar and complicated the information, the smaller the chunk of text you should be reading.

> Have you been paying attention to the key topics mentioned at the beginning of this unit? Have you seen any of these important points covered in the text and made a special effort to form context clues around them?

289 ORGANISMS UNDERGO THE PROCESSES
290 OF EMBRYONIC DEVELOPMENT,
291 MATURING, AND AGING

292   When uninterrupted by accidents, individual life spans
293 pass through distinct, distinguishable phases. For multicellular
294 organisms, the first phase is that of the embryo, which is prob-
295 ably the period of greatest change. During embryonic life, the
296 organism undergoes rapid cell division (going from one cell to
297 as many as trillions), growth in overall volume, movement of
298 cells to form tissues and organs of proper shape and position,
299 and specialization of cells to begin their useful functions for the
300 body. For some organisms, such as the mammals, this period
301 ends at birth, when the young animal becomes
302 physically separated from its mother. For many
303 other organisms, however, the entire embryonic
304 development has occurred away from the mother,
305 and the next phase is signaled by some other sig-
306 nificant event such as hatching (some fishes,
307 many invertebrate animals), or rapid growth of
308 already specialized parts (many land plants, with
309 growth of stems and roots). In all cases, embryon-
310 ic life is followed by a period of maturation that
311 culminates in the organism's becoming capable of reproduc-
312 ing. Finally, in many (but, intriguingly, not all) species there is
313 an aging process that ends in death.

> Do you feel any special emotional significance to death? Use this powerful emotion to help you picture, peg, and retain the details described in this section.

314   Any discussion of aging should begin with the reminder
315 that most individual organisms in their natural habitat are killed
316 long before they have the opportunity to age. For instance, it
317 has been observed that 99 percent of wild field mice die before
318 they are one year old (from disease, starvation, or the action of
319 predators), even though they would be likely to live up to four
320 years in the protected environment of a laboratory or pet
321 store. Even though field mice can demonstrate aging, virtually
322 none actually do so in a natural setting. Some people have
323 speculated that aging (leading inevitably to death) is an inherited
324 mechanism whose function is to weed out organisms that have
325 already passed their genes to the next generation and are taking
326 up valuable space and resources. However, the observation

327 that aging almost never has the chance to occur in nature
328 would seem to reduce the force of this argument, and make it
329 less likely that there are aging genes or death genes.

330 **Some Organisms Seem to Avoid Aging**
331   Some organisms never seem to age, even if given the chance.
332 Many trees continue growth and reproduction for their entire
333 lives, with only the ravages of physical and biological attack
334 causing death. Bristlecone pines are estimated to live longer
335 than 4,000 years, with no apparent natural limit. As an example
336 in the animal realm, some fish species appear to have no innate
337 age limit. Single-celled organisms, such as bacteria and proto-
338 zoans, do not age if given the chance to reproduce. The only
339 reason that a population of bacteria does not increase forever
340 is that its members eventually run out of nutrients and space
341 to occupy.

342 **Many Animals Have Characteristic Life Spans**
343   On the other hand, vertebrate
344 animals demonstrate maximum
345 life spans that are characteristic
346 of their species, when given the
347 chance to avoid rigors of the
348 wild. Among long-lived vertebrate
349 animals are tortoises, known to
350 live over 200 years; carp, 150
351 years; falcons, 160 years; eagles,
352 over 110 years; parrots, 100 years;
353 and crows, 70 years. Among
354 domesticated animals, dogs may
355 live more than 20 years (average
356 10); cats, more than 30 years
357 (average 14); cows, 30 years; and
358 horses, 50 years. The typical
359 length of human life in devel-
360 oped countries has increased
361 dramatically the last 100 years, a
362 tribute to our increasing knowl-
363 edge of nutrition, disease control,
364 and surgery.

Do you need to know the life spans of all these animals, or is it enough to recognize that significant differences exist? What might explain some of these differences in life span? Can you apply any of this information to increase your own life span? Is this interesting to you? Notice how some very detailed information can suddenly become very important if you link it to important context clues related to your life.

365   In 1900, it was estimated that 63 percent of Caucasian
366 American males who could have reached the age of 40 had actu-
367 ally done so. In 1940, 85 percent had succeeded in living to that
368 age. However, there is no indication that the *maximum* human
369 life span has increased. Almost no survivors exist past the age of
370 100 years, and the very small fraction doing so is gone before
371 many more years have passed. (Currently, no one has been
372 proven to have lived over the age of 121 years). Over the past cen-
373 tury (when reliable records were first widely available), this max-
374 imum has remained steady. It would appear, therefore, that many
375 organisms have a natural aging process and a resulting maximum
376 life span that are heritable along with all of their other species-
377 characteristic shapes and functions. What is not known at this
378 time is the exact cause of this inevitable loss of ability.

379 **There Are Multiple Hypotheses on the Cause of Aging**
380   Within an organism some cells types continue to undergo
381 reproduction throughout life; and in some ways, retain a
382 youthfulness that nonreproducing cells gradually lose. For
383 instance, within a tree the growing stem and root tips and
384 cambium (the growing layer that increases the diameter of
385 stems and roots) remain perpetually capable of reproducing.
386 In the human, actively dividing unspecialized cells like those
387 in the lower layer of epidermis and blood-forming tissue do
388 not show the usual signs of aging that eventually appear in
389 nondividing cells.
390   When normally nondividing cells are transferred to the arti-
391 ficial environment of a culture vessel, and given unlimited nutri-
392 tional supplies and room to grow, they often revert to a relatively
393 undifferentiated condition and go into rapid reproduction just
394 like their embryonic ancestor cells. However, even here there is
395 often a change that eventually occurs—many cultured cell pop-
396 ulations stop reproducing when about 50 cycles of mitosis have
397 occurred, after which the cells begin to show signs of aging.
398   Some feel that aging is intimately tied to metabolic rates—
399 the rates at which the multitude of chemical reactions are
400 occurring within cells. During the summer, when honeybees
401 are most active, the workers live from three to six weeks; yet
402 they survive much longer periods during the winter when

403 they are relatively inactive. In temperature-regulating animals,
404 including the birds and mammals, there seems to be some
405 correlation between speed of living, size, and length of life.
406 During the day the tiny hummingbird reaches a peak of meta-
407 bolic activity among the highest known for any animal. So
408 much energy is expended that it feeds almost continuously to
409 keep from starving. The bird would die of starvation at night
410 were it not to go into a state of hibernation during which its
411 metabolic rate is strikingly reduced. Hummingbirds live only a
412 few years. On the other hand, the long-lived elephant has a
413 relatively low metabolic rate.

414   Perhaps related to the metabolism hypothesis is the observa-
415 tion that rats with significantly reduced access to food tend to
416 live as much as 30 percent longer than those given unlimited
417 amounts. The most prominent physiological effect of semi-
418 starvation in this species is the prolongation of the juvenile
419 period of life (retardation of sexual maturity); it is this extension
420 that leads to a longer total life span. Thus, this study may be a
421 stronger link between aging and reproduction than between
422 aging and metabolic processes.

423   Another possible critical factor in cellular aging is the accu-
424 mulation of toxic materials that inevitably occurs in a very
425 active cell. Such molecules could act directly on vital cell
426 processes, or indirectly by increasing the rate of mutations in
427 vital genes. This is an attractive idea, but no specific occurrence
428 of such accumulation has been documented.

429   Currently, the most popular model for cellular aging is
430 based on accumulation of errors in genes. Rather than postu-
431 lating the existence of genes whose function is to cause aging,
432 this is an assertion that all genes necessary for normal life
433 gradually become defective because they undergo attack during
434 the course of life. Errors accumulate and genes become less
435 efficient in directing cell activities. It is well known that a vari-
436 ety of physical and chemical insults occur at the gene level,
437 and that they can come from outside the organism (e.g., X
438 rays, asbestos), or from within (free radicals produced in every
439 cell). If errors in genes can occur at any time, and if they are
440 sometimes kept as long as the genes are present, then it is log-

441 ical that more and more would accumulate as the cell grows
442 older. It is probable that a number of defects have to be pre-
443 sent simultaneously before a cell or a whole organism shows
444 the classical signs of aging and then dies.

445   Can cells detect gene errors and correct them?
446 There are several mechanisms in a normal cell for
447 this important activity. It is possible that these
448 maintenance and repair mechanisms gradually
449 lose effectiveness, and that errors eventually accu-
450 mulate. This idea can be linked to the concept of
451 natural selection. It would be in the best interest
452 of a species to attempt to repair errors up to the
453 time of reproduction, but there would be no use-
454 fulness for a repair mechanism to continue vigor-
455 ous activity after genes have been passed along to
456 new individuals, since the continuity of the
457 species has already been ensured by successful
458 reproduction. Thus, according to this hypothesis, natural
459 selection would favor an error-correcting mechanism only up
460 to the point of successful reproduction. Then there would be
461 no selection operating for organisms to continue protecting
462 their genes after that point. If such a view is correct, a strategy
463 to elongate the normal human life span would involve finding
464 ways to decrease the damage to genes, or to increase the effi-
465 ciency of repair mechanisms, or to prolong the length of time
466 that repair mechanisms continue to work well, or a combina-
467 tion of all of these. Of course, the sociological, psychological,
468 and demographic consequences of significantly increasing the
469 life span of humans would be matters of much debate, should
470 such biological methods come into existence.

What might be some of the debatable questions suggested by the author. Learn to go beyond what is mentioned in text. Infer meanings. Think. Question. Analyze. Apply the full power of your mind for learning by applying these principles.

---

471 DEATH IS A DIFFICULT EVENT
472 TO MONITOR

473   Drawing a sharp line between life and death is
474 a problem. The glib response when asked to define
475 death is that it is the cessation of those activities
476 that occur in a living organism: gaining and using

Interesting thought questions that you should be looking to answer.

477 energy, reproducing, responding to environmental changes,
478 and the like. However, there are many exceptions. Would a
479 sterile person be considered dead, just because of an inability
480 to reproduce? Would a portion of a body be considered dead
481 just because it could no longer respond to nerve messages?
482   On the level of the individual cell, the moment of death is
483 difficult to document, because a cascade of several events is
484 likely to occur. If, for instance, a specific poison enters the cell
485 and causes cessation of vital energy-releasing reactions, it may
486 take some time for consequences to appear. Minutes or hours
487 later there will be important changes, such as lack of move-
488 ment and breakdown of intracellular structures. Eventually it
489 becomes quite apparent that the cell has died, but death came
490 by a series of events over a period of time.
491   A multicellular organism's death may be even more difficult
492 to document. Large portions of a tree may be dead when
493 examined on the level of individual cells, but enough of it
494 might be operating to allow energy conversion, growth, and
495 reproduction to continue indefinitely in certain portions.
496 Progressive loss of function might continue for decades before
497 the entire plant is truly dead.
498   Of course, the definition of human death is very important
499 to us. For many centuries, the critical signs to be looked for were
501 cessation of heartbeat and breathing. We now know that a per-
502 son can survive several minutes in the absence of these activities,
503 and there are documented cases in which a drowned person
504 revived after more than twenty
505 minutes without breathing
506 (helped by lowered oxygen need
507 in extremely cold water). It is
508 now apparent that various por-
509 tions of the body do not die
510 simultaneously under the same
511 conditions. At normal body tem-
512 perature cells of the brain (requir-
513 ing much more oxygen than
514 most other cells) begin to die within a minute after being
515 deprived, while muscles (including heart muscle) can survive for
516 much longer periods. Because the human brain controls so

> Ask yourself why the moment of death might be difficult to determine? Is this the same for all organisms? If not, what are some of the differences?

517 much of the rest of the body's functions, its irreversible death has
518 come to be considered the end point of a person's functional life,
519 even if other organs can be artificially maintained alive.

520 SYSTEMATISTS STUDY HOW ORGANISMS
521 ARE RELATED TO EACH OTHER

522   Throughout this chapter there has been ample evidence that
523 all living organisms have a number of features in common. But
524 of course we also see many strikingly different characteristics, by
525 which we distinguish them and apply names for identification.
526 The scientific process of placing organism types into appropriate
527 categories, and using that information to understand relation-
528 ships and ancestries, is carried out within the discipline called
529 *systematics*. Many other fields of biology depend greatly upon
530 the work of systematists, who provide a grand scheme of the
531 diversity of life within which various specialized studies must
532 find their place.

533   Even at first glance it appears that systematizing the great
534 number of organisms living on this earth is an impossible task.
535 Indeed, we now believe that there are many more kinds of
536 organisms out there than we ever believed before, and that it
537 may not be feasible to catalog all modern species. Nevertheless,
538 the rewards, both theoretical and practical, of gaining as much
539 knowledge as possible about biodiversity make the attempt
540 worthwhile.

541 Structural and Functional Similarities Are Clues
542 in Deciding Relationships

543   The best way to proceed is to
544 see which organisms share charac-
545 teristics that might reveal some
546 degree of kinship. One can quick-
547 ly see that some organisms resem-
548 ble each other more than others.
549 A horse is obviously more closely
550 related to a cow than to a snake,
551 just as a peach tree is obviously
552 more closely related to a cherry

Here again is an example. Do you need this information to understand the point? If not, go to a higher reading speed to find the next important point.

553 tree than to a daisy. These similarities make possible the lumping
554 of large numbers of organisms into relatively few categories
555 based on major characteristics that they have in common.

556   Systematists do not agree totally on all aspects of classifica-
557 tion, but as time passes they are gradually constructing a natural
558 system based on relationships.
559 They replace artificial groupings
560 based on superficial resemblances
561 by natural groupings based on
562 genuine similarities arising from
563 common origins. This branch of
564 biology takes its clues from many
565 sources, such as gross anatomy,
566 cellular and molecular structures,
567 embryological development, and
568 fossil records.

What are some of the ways systematists create their systems of organization? Can you picture them carrying out any of these techniques?

569   The easiest way to begin is to look at obvious anatomical
570 structures of adult specimens. In many cases, however, visual
571 evidence of actual kinship is obscure, so biologists are often
572 forced to turn to procedures in physiology, embryology, and
573 genetics to clarify some of the less apparent relationships. An
574 example of one that puzzled zoologists for a long time is the true
575 position of the strange-looking sea squirts that grow attached
576 to surfaces in the oceans. At one time they were classified with
577 clams and snails. Finally someone studied their development
578 and discovered that the larval stage has a temporary support-
579 ing rod identical to the notochord in the chordate animals.
580 Then they were correctly placed with humans, fishes, and
581 other chordates.

582   A pitfall to avoid is drawing conclusions from superficial
583 appearances. The whale may appear similar to a fish, or the bat
584 may appear similar to a bird, but
585 both whales and bats are mam-
586 mals. Their body forms are adap-
587 tations to the environment in
588 which they live. The Spanish
589 moss of the southern United
590 States may be mistaken for a true
591 moss until a closer examination
592 reveals it to be a flowering plant

What are some easy mistakes that an inexperienced systematist might make? How can you prevent this from happening?

593 belonging to the pineapple family. There are numerous cases
594 in which animals are mimics, such as the insect that looks like
595 a rose thorn and a type of fly that looks like a stinging bee.

596   When studying seed plants, one may find temporary use
597 for artificially grouping them into such categories as trees,
598 shrubs, and herbs, or annuals, biennials, and perennials, but
599 these are based on some conspicuous characteristics with no
600 regard for their natural positions. These groups are useful to
601 describe body form or duration of life but are fallacious indica-
602 tors of any common ancestry. Sometimes, subtle features are
603 the most accurate indicators of relationships. For instance, the
604 locust or mimosa trees, by virtue of their size and general
605 appearance, would seem at first to be close relatives of oak or
606 maple trees, but they have entirely different kinds of flowers,
607 and are properly placed in the pea family with such un-treelike
608 plants as the clovers and beans.

609 ## THE FORMAL CLASSIFICATION
610 ## OF ORGANISMS IS A PRODUCT
611 ## OF SYSTEMATISTS

612   Very little was done toward finding a workable method of
613 classification until Linnaeus (1707–1778), a Swedish naturalist,
614 laid the foundation of a new system. Until his day, attempts at
615 placing organisms into categories were almost
616 entirely artificial. Even Linnaeus did not have the
617 ideas of origins and kinships as they are under-
618 stood today. Nevertheless, his system of using four
619 groups—*class, order, genus,* and *species*—provided a
620 nucleus for a really workable system. His four cat-
621 egories, plus some additional ones, are still in use.
622 A major contribution of Linnaeus was the estab-
623 lishment of a system of giving to each living organ-
624 ism a two-part Latin name, a *binomial*.

Did you notice all the new vocabulary in this section? Have you placed these important definitions on flash cards?

625   The first word in a binomial is the organism's genus, and the
626 second is its species. For instance, a common North American
627 butterfly is in the genus *Danaus*, along with many related
628 butterflies, and its species name is *plexippus*. The butterfly's
629 binomial is, therefore, *Danaus plexippus*. Its genus name indi-

630 cates relationship with other butterfly species that share many
631 characteristics, and the species name provides a unique desig-
632 nation for this member of the genus. Perhaps you know this
633 butterfly by its common English name, the Monarch. In
634 everyday usage among English-speaking North Americans that
635 name suffices, but someone outside North America may rec-
636 ognize another butterfly by that same common name. A
637 Spanish speaker in Mexico,
638 where the butterfly is common,
639 will not be familiar with the
640 English name, and a number
641 of Native American languages
642 undoubtedly have their own
643 words for this butterfly. Upon
644 reflection, it becomes obvious that
645 assigning a unique internationally
646 recognized binomial to this animal
647 greatly enhances communication,
648 at the same time that it provides
649 clues to relatedness.

> Do you need to know about the butterfly in detail, or simply understand the principles about biology systematics this example is used to explain?

650 The following outline shows the major categories (*taxa*;
651 singular, *taxon*) used in the modern system of classification.
652 The outline also includes the classification of one common
653 North American plant and one animal as illustrations.

654 CATEGORIES	WHITE OAK	HUMAN
655 Kingdom	Plantae	Animalia
656 Phylum (pl. Phyla)*	Tracheophyta	Chordata
657 Class	Angiospermae	Mammalia
658 Order	Fagales	Primates
659 Family	Fagaceae	Hominidae
660 Genus (pl. Genera)	*Quercus*	*Homo*
661 Species (pl. Species)	*alba*	*sapiens*

662 *The term *division* is used for plants.

663 The largest numbers of individuals are included in the
664 upper categories because they need to have fewer characteris-
665 tics in common. Those characteristics are considered of major
666 importance and apply to all individuals in lower categories. For

667 example, the fundamental characteristics of a king-
668 dom are found in all groups within that kingdom.
669 Or to express the relationship differently, all the
670 lower groups are included as a part of a higher
671 group because they have certain characteristics in
672 common. Many systematists consider that
673 Kingdom Animalia is composed of more than fifty
674 phyla; Kingdom Plantae is composed of ten divi-
675 sions. At the opposite end of the scale are the smallest cate-
676 gories, where individual types of members are fewer but where
677 their members have more characteristics in common.

> It would be important to learn the taxonomic names, but not the names of the specific organisms used in this example.

678   One might be wondering why not all systematists agree
679 on, say, the number of animal phyla. It should be kept in mind
680 that we do not yet know exact relationships, and that the
681 same evidence might be interpreted differently by two people.
682 One expert might consider a particular characteristic as being
683 very important and assign all organisms carrying it to a unique
684 phylum. Another person, looking at the same characteristic,
685 would consider it fundamental enough to delineate a class but
686 would not give it a separate phylum designation. Keep in
687 mind the idea that science is a dynamic area of human
688 endeavor, which is constantly being corrected as additional
689 evidence and insights accumulate.

690 **Organisms Are Either Prokaryotes or Eukaryotes**
691   An important set of characteristics has been used to divide
692 all cellular organisms into two categories, *prokaryotes* and
693 *eukaryotes*. These are not part of the formal hierar-
694 chy shown in the list above, but help to place
695 organisms into that system. The cell of a prokary-
696 ote *lacks* two important characteristics that are
697 found in any eukaryotic cell—a membrane sur-
698 rounding its genetic material (a nuclear membrane)
699 and a set of other structures that are also membra-
700 nous (mitochondria, endoplasmic reticulum, etc.).
701 These and other less easily observed differences
702 lead biologists to conclude that modern prokaryotes
703 and eukaryotes should not be considered to be
704 very closely related. Indeed, while most think that prokaryotes

> What important facts can be drawn from the differences between eukaryotes and prokaryotes? What significance does this have in the overall concept of evolution and systematics?

705 preceded eukaryotes, there is some recent evidence that the
706 eukaryotic line has just as long a history on earth, and may not
707 be derived from the prokaryotes.

708 **Kingdoms Are the Largest Classification Categories**

709 The highest ranking formal category of classification is the
710 kingdom, which encompasses many organisms sharing very
711 significant characteristics. Even at this level it is difficult to
712 decide how to place organisms in a way that accurately depicts
713 their degree of similarity and their lineage. Historically, the
714 first way to do this was to use just two kingdoms, Plantae and
715 Animalia. Eventually, systematists realized that more kingdoms
716 would have to be designated in order to accommodate those
717 organisms that were clearly different from either plants or
718 animals. Since 1969, a five-kingdom system has been the one
719 most used by biologists, but many now argue for the addition
720 of at least one more kingdom. These six kingdoms are intro-
721 duced below.

722 1. The smallest kingdom is *Archaea*, composed of bacteria-like
723   single-celled organisms (lumped with the true bacteria in a
724   kingdom called Monera if a five-kingdom system is used).
725   These and the true bacteria are the only known prokaryotic
726   organisms. Most members of Kingdom Archaea are found
727   living under extreme conditions—high heat, low pH, or
728   great saltiness. Molecular data published in 1994 indicate
729   that modern Archaea may be more closely related to the
730   eukaryotic kingdom than are the true bacteria.

731 2. If one prefers a six-kingdom system, the true bacteria are
732   placed in Kingdom *Bacteria*. These are the more common
733   prokaryotes, of which about 4,000 distinct species have
734   been identified (although many more are probably awaiting
735   our discovery).

736 3. Kingdom *Protista* includes the simplest modern eukaryotic
737   organisms. However, it should be pointed out that even these
738   are far more complex than the prokaryotic organisms. One
739   indicator of this is that a typical algal cell, a Protistan, con-
740   tains about ten times as much DNA as a typical bacterium
741   (although both phyla show much variation from these
742   averages). There is some controversy as to whether certain

743   organisms belong in Kingdom Protista. Certainly all single-
744   celled eukaryotic organisms are Protista. This includes many
745   kinds of algae and all of the organisms called protozoa.
746   Organisms about which there is difference of opinion include
747   the multicellular algae (often placed in Kingdom Plantae)
748   and some fungus-like organisms (sometimes placed with
749   multicellular organisms of Kingdom Fungi). Well over 60,000
750   species of Kingdom Protista have been identified.

751   4. Kingdom *Plantae* includes all of the multicellular organ-
752   isms that carry on photosynthesis to capture energy (but
753   see the controversy over multicellular algae, above). Of the
754   approximately 265,000 identified plant species, fully
755   235,000 are the familiar ones that reproduce using the
756   structure called a flower. Nonflowering plants include
757   mosses, ferns, and others.

758   5. Most of the multicellular organisms that cannot perform
759   photosynthesis, but must rely on gathering food molecules
760   from outside the body are in Kingdom *Animalia*. In addition
761   to their method of capturing energy, animals differ from
762   plants in a number of other features. This indicates to biol-
763   ogists that ancestries of animals and plants diverged a very
764   long time ago.

765   6. Kingdom *Fungi* includes a wide variety of organisms that
766   were once considered to be plants. Some of its members are
767   mushrooms, yeasts, and molds. The fungi were originally
768   lumped with plants because of their immobility and
769   plant-like external morphology. Closer examination
770   revealed an inability to perform photosynthesis and
771   many other biochemical differences that
772   demanded a unique kingdom for these
773   organisms. Still, many biologists considered
774   them to have descended from the plant king-
775   dom. In the early 1990s several independent
776   studies at the biochemical level led to a
777   rather startling conclusion: the fungi appear
778   to be more closely related to members of
779   Kingdom Animalia. According to the best
780   data now available, fungi and animals may
781   share a common Protistan ancestor, and the

> What are the six different types of kingdoms? What are their differences? What are their similarities? Are some of them larger? Are any of them more important to you? Why?

782   fungi can no longer be considered as degenerated or spe-
783   cialized offshoots from Kingdom Plantae or from photo-
784   synthetic Protista. Over 100,000 fungal species have been
785   classified.

786   **The Species Is the Most Fundamental Classification Unit**

787   The taxonomic category called *species* (singular and plural)
788   is the narrowest. To the nonscientist, it is usually equivalent to
789   what is meant when the word kind is used. It may come as a
790   surprise to learn that this most fundamental of all taxa is also
791   one of the most difficult to define, and is the subject of much
792   debate among biologists. Historically, the species has most
793   often been defined as a group of similar individuals, usually
794   differing little from one another and differing distinctly from
795   members of other species. Under this definition, species have
796   generally been named and described on the basis of clearly
797   visible external characteristics and (less often) internal anatomy.
798   However, more recently a biological (rather than anatomical)
799   criterion has become the norm. The biological definition of a
800   species is *a group of natural populations whose organisms can*
801   *successfully reproduce among themselves, and cannot successfully*
802   *reproduce with organisms of other groups.* The term *successfully*
803   *reproduce* means that reproduction occurs to bring an appro-
804   priate number of offspring into existence, *and* that those off-
805   spring themselves are able to reproduce. Some closely related but
806   distinct species can reproduce (producing a hybrid organism),
807   but this hybrid will be sterile. Some systematists hesitate to
808   place two groups into a single species if reproduction occurs but
809   produces an abnormally small number of offspring compared
810   to the number resulting from mating within a group.

811   From the foregoing paragraph, it becomes obvious that the
812   biological definition of species has potential for being more
813   clear-cut, since it provides a test that can be put to any
814   groups—the test of reproduction. However, this method may
815   be very expensive in terms of time and money. Therefore, it is
816   not surprising that the great majority of newly described
817   species is still defined by the less rigorous criteria of anatomy.

818   The species may sometimes be divided into *subspecies, variety,*
819   *form, breed, race,* or *strain.* These divisions are not always clearly

820 definable and may sometimes refer to the same
821 thing. The subspecies is used by some biologists to
822 separate variants of a species having a distinct geo-
823 graphical distribution. Variety often means the
824 same thing as subspecies, but it is also used in spe-
825 cial senses for discontinuous variants of an inter-
826 breeding population or for variants horticulturally
827 produced. Breed is used in connection with dogs
828 and other domesticated animals; strain in con-
829 nection with crops having physiological differ-
830 ences such as disease resistance; and race in
831 connection with humans. All categories below
832 that of the species are subject to much interpretation and are
833 to be avoided unless their use clearly helps in identification or
834 in showing relationships.

What is a species? Can you think of any good examples? Are some animals hard to classify as a species? Which ones? Why might they be difficult to classify? Any ideas on how to go about doing this?

835 **STUDY QUESTIONS**

836   1. What are the two general statements that com-
837   prise the Cell Theory?
838   2. List the recognized levels of organization
839   found in a living organism, beginning with
840   the smallest (submolecular structures) and
841   progressing toward the largest.
842   3. What are good examples of quick responses to
843   the environment, and slower ones? Can respon-
844   siveness of living organisms extend beyond
845   individual life spans?
846   4. According to current scientific estimates, how
847   long did the earth exist without any form of
848   life?
849   5. Why do some molecular biologists suggest that
850   this was once an RNA-based world of life?
851   6. Has the typical human life span increased dur-
852   ing the past century? Has the maximum life
853   span done so?
854   7. Describe the hypothesis relating cellular aging
855   to accumulation of genetic errors. Do cells have
856   ways of correcting such errors?

Did you read and learn these questions before reading the chapter? What pictures can you form about these questions to make them easier to recall during your reading? Can you distinguish between questions that are literal, implied, or inferential? Can you think of additional questions that may help you improve your understanding of the material?

8. How does a natural system of classification differ from an artificial one?

9. From what fields of biology has information been obtained to clarify relationships among organisms? From what branch of biology was information obtained to clarify the taxonomic position of sea squirts?

10. What naturalist was responsible for laying the foundation of the system of classification in use today?

11. For every identified organism, a binomial name is given. What are the classification categories shown by the binomial?

12. How could one distinguish a eukaryotic cell from a prokaryotic cell? Which kingdom or kingdoms include(s) prokaryotes?

13. Why is the number of kingdoms still controversial among systematists?

14. Kingdom Fungi was once part of Kingdom Plantae. Why was it necessary to split it away?

15. What is the biological definition of species? Why is this definition sometimes hard to apply to real organisms?

PRACTICE READING 2: CHEMISTRY

1 *Theme 3* MATTER

2 Matter is material that has mass and occupies space. All mat-
3 ter can be classified as being either a pure substance or a
4 mixture. Furthermore, matter can exist as either a solid, a
5 liquid, or a gas and can undergo transition among these
6 three phases. Chemistry can be considered to be the study of
7 the properties of matter.

8	**INDIVIDUAL KEYS IN THIS THEME**
9	*8* Pure substances
10	*9* Mixtures
11	*10* Chemical and physical changes

12 *Key 8* Pure substances

13 **OVERVIEW** *A pure substance has a unique set of*
14 *physical and chemical properties. These properties*
15 *characterize that pure substance.*

16 **Elements** are pure substances that cannot be
17   chemically separated or decomposed into sim-
18   pler substances. There are a total of 103 known
19   elements.

20 An **atom** is the smallest unit of an element having
21   all of the characteristics of that element.

22 **Compounds**, chemical combinations of elements, are pure
23   substances in which the component elements are present
24   in fixed proportions. They are uniquely characterized by
25   their properties, which are different from those of the com-
26   ponent elements.

Did you see what themes will be covered in this unit?
Pay attention to the overview that follows.
Overviews are summaries and should be carefully explored prior to examining the text for details.

27 A **molecule** is the smallest unit
28 of a compound.

29 As an example, carbon tetrachlo-
30 ride (CCl_4) is a compound
31 that is a dense liquid at room
32 temperature. It can be chem-
33 ically broken down into its
34 component elements, carbon
35 (C, a black solid) and chlorine
36 (Cl_2, a yellow-green gas).

37 Chlorine is an example of an
38 element that exists as a
39 diatomic molecule in its ele-
40 mental form (Cl_2). A **diatomic**
41 **molecule** is a molecule that
42 contains two atoms.

Notice how this text uses bold-faced type to delineate important new definitions. Pay careful attention to any other words that are bold-faced. Consider using the flash card technique to memorize this new vocabulary. Don't examine more information than you are capable of remembering. Remember to chunk down complicated information.

43 *Key 9* Mixtures

44 **OVERVIEW** *Mixtures have variable physical properties and*
45 *can consist of elements or compounds (or both) brought together in*
46 *any proportion. Mixtures may be formed between any combination*
47 *of gas, liquid, and solid.*

48 Mixtures are commonly divided into two kinds:
49 • **Heterogeneous** mixtures are made up of two or more
50 physically discernible parts or phases.
51 • **Homogeneous** mixtures consist of components that can-
52 not be individually detected.

53 Homogenous mixtures are usually called **solutions**.

54 In a two-component system, the major component is called
55 the **solvent** and the minor component is called the **solute**.

56 **Aqueous** solutions have water as the solvent.

57 If the components of a solution can be mixed in any
58   proportion, they are said to be **miscible**.

59 A **colloid** (or **colloidal suspension**) is a mixture in
60   which the particles of the lesser phase are
61   intermediate in size between those present in
62   homogenous mixtures and those in hetero-
63   geneous mixtures; typically, they are on the
64   order of 10 to 10,000 Å in diameter.

65 The **Tyndall effect** is the scattering of light by a
66   colloidal suspension because of the fact that
67   the size of the suspended particles is on the
68   order of magnitude of visible light.

Are you asking yourself literal, implied, and inferential questions about this material? Are you visualizing the information rather than simply hearing the words? Are you discriminating between important information, and the examples used to make it easier to understand?

69 *Key 10*   Chemical and physical changes

70 **OVERVIEW**   *Chemistry is the study of the chemical and physical*
71 *properties of matter and how chemical substances undergo change*
72 *or **reaction**. **Phase transitions** occur when a substance is trans-*
73 *formed from one state (phase) to another; they are physical changes.*

74 Changes are classified as being either physical changes or
75   chemical changes:
76   • In a **physical** change, a **physical property** (a property
77   that can be studied without changing the identify of the
78   substance) is being modified. Melting and
79   boiling are examples of physical changes and
80   the melting and boiling points of a substance
81   are physical properties of that substance.
82   • In a **chemical change**, a **chemical property**
83   (a property that can be studied only at the risk
84   of changing the identity of the substance) is
85   being modified. The fact that carbon burns
86   (reacts) with oxygen to form carbon dioxide is
87   an example of a chemical property of carbon.
88   Once the reaction takes place, one substance
89   has been converted into others.

Is any of this information familiar to you, or easy to learn? Can you increase your reading speed in the easier parts of this text? Are you remembering to use your hands to keep your eyes moving to new information?

90 Properties can be classified as being intensive or extensive:

91 • An **intensive property** does not depend on the amount of
92   material present; for example, temperature.

93 • An **extensive property** depends on the amount of material
94   present; for example, mass or volume.

95 Elements or compounds, can exist in any of the three **states of**
96   **matter**: solid, liquid, or gas. For example, the compound
97   represented by the chemical formula H_2O exists as ice
98   (solid), water (liquid), and steam (gas).

99 The **melting point** is the temperature at which a solid changes
100   to a liquid.

101 The **boiling point** is the temperature at which a liquid changes
102   to a gas.

103 The **condensation point** is the
104   temperature at which a gas
105   changes to a liquid (the same
106   temperature as the boiling
107   point).

What are the different states of matter? How are they different? What significance do you attach to these different states? How might you relate this information to the different states of water to help you remember it better?

108 The **freezing point** is the tem-
109   perature at which a liquid
110   changes to a solid (the same
111   temperature as the melting
112   point).

113 The transition from a solid directly into a gas is known as
114   **sublimation**, which occurs at the **sublimation point**.

PRACTICE READING 3: PHYSICS

1 THE NATURE OF PHYSICS

2 WHAT IS PHYSICS?

3   Physics is a branch of knowledge that
4 attempts to establish relationships among natural
5 phenomena. These phenomena are a part of our
6 sensory experiences from everyday life. As human
7 beings, we use these sensory inputs to make deci-
8 sions about the world around us, decisions that
9 are based on recognized patterns of orderly events
10 (like the rising and setting of the sun, the changes
11 in seasons, the migrations of animals, and the
12 movements of objects).

13   Occasionally, we come across situations that
14 seem to occur randomly. These discrepant events
15 challenge the routine of predictability that is the
16 foundation of the scientific method. Many of
17 these naturally occurring random events display
18 orderly tendencies on average, which means that
19 while individual events might be random, the
20 occurrence of a large number of events may
21 indeed be predictable. This *statistical* behavior of
22 natural phenomena will come in handy when we
23 consider the interactions of large numbers of interacting par-
24 ticles such as those that make up a gas.

25   In order to understand how these causal relationships are
26 established, we must first adopt a set of rules by which all
27 observers might be led to similar conclusions. There is a
28 caveat, however, that if we restrict our decisions too rigidly,
29 then we may be forced to make conclusions that are contrary

Explore this unit looking for the numerous tables and other visual aids that will make this complicated subject easier for you to learn. Remember to chunk down difficult ideas into smaller pieces that are easier for you to learn.

Notice that this book uses italics to highlight important new vocabulary. Look for other words in italics.

30 to information obtained from our senses and the real world. In
31 physics, the former happens all the time, however, the nature
32 of science demands that we always be describing real events. It
33 is to these *rules of reasoning* that we now proceed.

34 RULES OF REASONING WHEN
35 DOING PHYSICS

36   The branch of knowledge that develops these rules of reason-
37 ing about the world is called *philosophy*. Philosophy differs
38 from science in that the scientific method demands that
39 experimental evidence verify a prediction made using the
40 rules of reasoning (or logic) to be discussed here. Thus, the
41 ancient school of Greek Philosophy called φιοικοσ (*physikos*) or
42 natural philosophy developed from abstract thinking about
43 how the universe works into a systematic experimental disci-
44 pline.

45   In physics we usually employ two modes of reasoning
46 called inductive and deductive. *Inductive reasoning* begins with
47 an accumulation of specific phenomena, and then we make
48 conclusions about a general concept. This is the basis of experi-
49 mental science. In a controlled experiment, we vary one
50 quantity *independently* and then observe what happens to
51 another quantity called the *dependent* quantity.

52   The relationship is established by comparing the effects of
53 the changes. If the dependent quantity does not change at all,
54 the relationship is referred to as being *constant*. If the dependent
55 quantity increases the independent quantity increases, the
56 relationship is referred to as being *direct*. If the dependent
57 quantity decreases the independent quantity increases, the
58 relationship is referred to as being *inverse*.

59   *Deductive reasoning* begins with a general premise, and then
60 we draw conclusions about particular aspects of that concept.
61 Syllogistic reasoning is one type of deductive reasoning.
62 Consider this standard example:

63   All men are mortal.
64   Socrates is a man.
65   Therefore, Socrates is mortal.

66 If the truth of the first two statements is valid, then the con-
67 clusion is judged valid. Notice that the first statement is an all-
68 inclusive general statement: All men are mortal.

69   An example from physics might be something like this:

70   Gravity accelerates all free bodies near the earth at the same
71   rate. A sheet of paper and a pencil are both bodies near the
72   earth. Therefore, if the paper and pencil are free, they will
73   both fall with the same acceleration.

74   If you try this example, you will find that the sheet of
75 paper floats down at a constant speed because of air resistance.
76 Therefore, in light of the counterexample, we are forced to
77 either discount or modify the original premise. In science, we
78 often choose to do the latter.

79   In his treatise, *Principia*, outlining much of what we now
80 call *classical Mechanics*, Sir Isaac Newton presented, more com-
81 prehensively, these rules of reasoning which we can keep in
82 the backs of our minds as we proceed to study physics:

83 1. We are to admit no more causes of natural things than such as
84   are both true and sufficient to explain their appearances.
85 2. Therefore, to the same natural effects, we will assign the
86   same natural causes.
87 3. The qualities of bodies that do not increase or decrease in
88   amount and are found to belong to all bod-
89   ies, as far as we can determine from our
90   experimental instruments, will be called *uni-*
91   *versal qualities* of all bodies.
92 4. In experimental science we look at conclu-
93   sions inferred by general induction from
94   phenomena as being accurate and very nearly
95   true, notwithstanding any contrary hypotheses
96   we may consider, unless some new phenom-
97   ena occurs which causes us to modify these
98   conclusions.

What is the importance of reasoning to physics? What things might be studied according to physics' principles? What things probably would not be easy to study by using physics?

99 ESTABLISHING RELATIONSHIPS
100 IN PHYSICS

101   Relationships are based on quantitative comparisons using
102 the rules of reasoning just described. To begin with, we ascribe
103 to quantities of matter *fundamental characteristics* that can be
104 used to distinguish them. Among
105 these are mass, length, and electric
106 current. And since the universe
107 undergoes constant change, we
108 add time to this list.

109   Quantitative comparisons are
110 based on assigning a magnitude
111 and a scale to each of these
112 quantities. The magnitude indi-
113 cates the relative size of the
114 quantity, and the scale provides
115 the rule for measurement. Another
116 term we could use instead of *scale*
117 is *unit* or *dimension*. Specifically,
118 the units assigned to mass, length,
119 and time (and several others) are
120 called *fundamental units*. In
121 physics, we use the International System of Units (SI, for *Système*
122 *International d'Unités*) and some of the more common units are
123 presented in Tables 1 and 2.

> Is any of the information shown in this table familiar to you? Is it easy to understand or confusing? What pictures can you use in your imagination to make it easier to learn this material? Take some time and think about what you are learning. Don't just read the words. Ask important questions.

124   **TABLE 1. FUNDAMENTAL SI UNITS USED IN PHYSICS**

Quantity	Unit Name	Symbol
Length	meter	m
Mass	kilogram	kg
Time	second	s
Electric current	ampere	A
Temperature	kelvin	K
Amount of substance	mole	mol
Plane angle	radian	rad

133   The units in Table 2 are called *derived* since they can be
134 expressed in terms of the fundamental units shown in Table 1.

135

TABLE 2. SOME DERIVED SI UNITS USED IN PHYSICS

Quantity	Unit Name	Symbol	Expression in Other SI Units
136			
137 Force	newton	N	$kg\text{-}m/s^2$
138 Frequency, cyclic	hertz	Hz	cycles/s
139 Frequency, angular	—	—	$rad/s = 1/s$
140 Pressure	pascal	Pa	$N/m^2 = kg/m\text{-}s^2$
141 Energy, work and heat	joule	J	$N\text{-}m = kg\text{-}m^2/s^2$
142 Power	watt	W	$J/s = kg\text{-}m^2/s^3$
143 Electric charge	coulomb	C	As
144 Electric potential (EMF)	volt	V	$J/C = J/As = kg\text{-}m^2/As^3$
145 Capacitance	farad	F	$C/V = A^2s^4/kg\text{-}m^2$
146 Resistance	ohm	Ω	$V/A = kg\text{-}m^2/A^2s^3$
147 Magnetic flux	weber	Wb	$Vs = kg\text{-}m^2/As^2$
148 Magnetic flux density	tesla	T	$Wb/m^2 = kg/As^2$
149 Inductance	henry	H	$Wb/A = kg\text{-}m^2/A^2s^2$

150   One way to establish a relationship between
151 two physical quantities is by means of a graph. If
152 the graph indicates that for one value of the inde-
153 pendent quantity we assign one and only one
154 value for the dependent quantity, then we have a
155 *functional relationship*. This usually means that the
156 relationship can be represented by an algebraic
157 equation.

158   Certain relationships produce graphs that are
159 immediately recognizable. Usually, we plot a
160 graph using *Cartesian coordinates* (see Chapter 3)
161 and represent the independent quantity along the
162 horizontal or *x axis*. When there is no change in
163 the dependent quantity for any change in the
164 independent quantity, then we obtain a horizontal
165 line as in Figure 1.

How good is your knowledge of mathematics? Is it helping or hurting your understanding of physics? Would reviewing some of your math skills help you better understand this information? Don't be lazy. Always strive to use your best abilities to learn everything necessary.

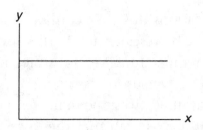

166 **FIGURE 1.** *Constant relationship.*

167 If there is a constant change in the dependent quantity
168 proportional to the independent quantity such that both
169 increase (or decrease) simultaneously, then we say the rela-
170 tionship is a *direct relationship*. When the dependent quantity
171 decreases while the independent
172 quantity increases (or vice versa),
173 we have an *inverse relationship*.
174 Now these relationships can be
175 either linear or nonlinear.
176 Examples of linear direct and
177 inverse relationships are present-
178 ed in Figures 2 and 3.

Pay careful attention to
the following visual aids.
Look at the references
to them, and think
about their significance.

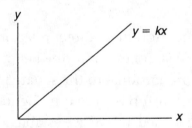

179 **FIGURE 2.** *Direct relationship.*

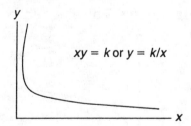

180 **FIGURE 3.** *Linear inverse relationship.*

181 The graph of a linear direct relationship is diagonal straight
182 line that starts at the origin. This is desirable since it makes the
183 form of the equation simpler. This equation can be expressed
184 as $y = kx$, where the constant k is called the *slope* of the line.

185 Direct relationships that contain *y intercepts* other than the
186 origin can be rescaled to fit this form. One example is the
187 absolute temperature (Kelvin) scale. Instead of plotting Celsius
188 temperature versus pressure for an ideal gas (and getting
189 –273°C as the lowest possible temperature), we rescale the
190 temperature axis such that the lowest possible temperature is
191 defined to be 0 K and then obtain the familiar gas law rela-
192 tionships defined for absolute temperature only.
193   There are two typical nonlinear direct relationships that
194 appear often in physics. The first is the *parabolic* or *squared rela-*
195 *tionship.* For example, in freely falling motion, the displace-
196 ment of a mass is directly proportional to the square of the
197 elapsed time. A graph of this relationship is shown in Figure 4.

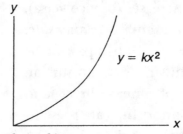

198 **FIGURE 4.**   *Parabolic relationship.*

199   The other nonlinear direct relationship is called the *square*
200 *root relationship.* For example, the period of a swinging pendulum
201 is directly proportional to the square root of its length. A graph
202 of this relationship is shown in Figure 5.
203   Having looked at how we establish relationships in physics,
204 we are then left with the question of how to identify key concepts
205 when doing physics. This is an important aspect of learning,

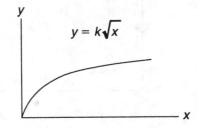

206 **FIGURE 5.**   *Square root relationship.*

207 studying, reviewing, and doing physics. The remaining chapters
208 in this book will be devoted to answering this question as well
209 as to reviewing most of the content material covered in a stan-
210 dard college physics course. Let's get started!

PRACTICE READING 4: PSYCHOLOGY

1 *Theme 1*   PSYCHOLOGY
2   THEN AND NOW

3 Modern psychology is a
4 broad discipline with many
5 subdisciplines, each of which has
6 its own rich history and each of
7 which might define psychology
8 in its own distinctive way. But,
9 setting aside differences between
10 the subdisciplines in what they
11 study and at times how they go
12 about it, there's still a lot of com-
13 mon ground. And there are many
14 milestones in the history of psy-
15 chological theory and research
16 that are commonly agreed upon.
17   Theme 1 explores where psy-
18 chology came from and where it
19 is today.

Note which themes are presented in this section. Look for key information related to these themes. Are any of these themes familiar to you? Which ones? How familiar? Are any of these themes unfamiliar or difficult for you? Decide how to invest your time in learning the material by planning more time for unfamiliar or difficult themes.

	INDIVIDUAL KEYS IN THIS THEME
20	
21	*1* Defining Psychology
22	*2* Psychology before the 20th century
23 24	*3* Psychoanalysis: The first force in modern psychology
25	*4* Behaviorism: the second force
26	*5* Humanistic psychology: The third force
27 28	*6* Other approaches and where psychology is today

---

29 *Key 1*   Defining psychology

---

30 **OVERVIEW**   *Modern psychology is defined as the*
31 *scientific study of behavior and mental processes.*

> Pay attention to overviews. They are summaries that can help you prepare for what is coming.

32 The term **psychology** has its roots in Greek terms
33 *psyche*, indicating life or self, and *logos*, indi-
34 cating reasoning and logic. Consistent with the
35 origins of its name, psychology is potentially
36 concerned with studying and understanding the behavior
37 of any living organisms that qualify as animals. But the
38 emphasis is on humans. And though psychological
39 research methods often involve groups of subjects, the
40 overall goal is to understand the individual.
41 • **A subject** is any living organism that is the focus of
42   study and research, from small and simple creatures
43   such as flatworms, all the way up to humans.
44 • **Research on groups** most often looks at processes that
45   help explain the behavior of the individual in the sense
46   of what behavior is typical and what behavior is most
47   likely and what causes that behavior in the first place.

48 **Scientific study** has many requirements, most of which relate
49   to providing knowledge that is reliable and factual. Like any
50   true science, psychology strives to be objective, empirical, and
51   systematic as it observes and collects data, and it proceeds
52   by testing hypotheses and generating theories.
53 • **Objective** means that observations are not affected by
54   any hopes or preferences or other possible biases on the
55   part of the researcher.
56 • **Empirical** is closely related to objective, meaning that
57   the same observations can readily be made by anyone
58   and therefore can be taken as fact. Note that researchers
59   at times use sophisticated laboratory equipment that not
60   just anyone could manage, but the observations are still
61   empirical.
62 • **Systematic** has to do with how observations are collected
63   and also what observations are collected. In other words,

64   researchers must have a plan and then execute the plan in
65   an orderly way if the research is to be meaningful and useful.

66   • **Hypotheses** are educated guesses and predictions about
67   what will happen under specific conditions and circum-
68   stances. Although psychological research is sometimes
69   exploratory and open-
70   ended, it is more often
71   oriented toward testing
72   specific hypotheses.

73   • **Theories** are statements
74   that organize and summa-
75   rize research and informa-
76   tion. In turn, theories often
77   generate the hypotheses
78   that are tested by research.
79   And theories are never
80   "true" or "false"; they are
81   simply accurate or inaccu-
82   rate with regard to what is
83   under consideration. In
84   other words, theories can
85   never be *proved*, though
86   they can and should be
87   *supported* by research.

> Did you notice how this chapter puts the important new definitions in bold-face type? Did you set up flash cards to memorize them? Can you think of a mnemonic that might help you organize your information easily? Are you playing memory music in the back-ground while studying? Have you used music to memorize anything you've learned thus far?

88 **Behavior** is a broad term that has different meanings in psy-
89   chology depending upon the context. In the definition of
90   psychology, behavior refers to absolutely anything the subject
91   does, whether it's overt or covert.

92   • **Overt behavior** is that which can be observed and mea-
93   sured empirically, whether it's external to the subject
94   (environmental) or internal (physiological-biological).

95   • **Covert behavior** is that which cannot be observed directly
96   and empirically—as yet. Thinking and remembering are
97   examples: Psychologists can empirically observe various
98   kinds of brain activity, but can't yet empirically observe
99   what a person is actually thinking or remembering.

100   • **Behaviorism**, in contrast, is a term often used in refer-
101   ence to the idea that *only overt behavior* can be studied

102   scientifically (Key 4). Modern psychologists do not tend
103   to take such an extreme view, as indicated in
104   the definition. And yet, modern psychology is
105   often characterized as a "behavioral" science.

106 **Mental processes**, then, are **covert** behavior, and
107   the standard definition of psychology specifies
108   mental processes mainly for emphasis on what
109   psychology is today. Also note that **cognition**
110   is a popular term for thinking, remembering,
111   perceiving, problem solving, and many other
112   mental processes that can only be studied indi-
113   rectly and *inferred* from overt behavior—so far.

> What does the term behavior mean to you? What are the different mental processes? How might these different processes be studied? What problems do these studies have in common?

114 ## *Key 2*   Psychology before the 20th century

115 **OVERVIEW** *Modern scientific psychology traces some of its*
116 *origins back to the logic and ideas of the ancient Greeks, skipping*
117 *forward from there to the philosopher-scientists near the end of the*
118 *Renaissance. The following are concepts and major thinkers often*
119 *cited.*

120 **Associationism** began with Plato and especially Aristotle, who
121   proposed that we learn and understand by forming mental
122   associations between events we observe.
123   • **The principle of temporal contiguity**, for example, is
124   that we tend to associate two events and think of them
125   as related to each other if they occur more or less at the
126   same time. Such principles are still considered impor-
127   tant in understanding learning and memory.

128 In the 17th century, Rene **Descartes** wrote extensively on the
129   issue of "mind" and "body," proposing that the two are
130   somehow separate entities that interact to determine who
131   we are and what we know. Today, psychologists still differ
132   in their views of mind and body, though many assume that
133   mental processes must somehow correspond to underlying
134   neurological functioning. Descartes was also an early advo-
135   cate of the view that came to be known as nativism.

136 • **A nativist view** emphasizes **nature** in the form of genetics
137   and heredity in accounting for who we are and what we
138   know. To say that intellectual skills, personality character-
139   istics, and morality are mostly innate and built-in is to
140   take an extreme nativist position.

141 Also in the 17th century, Thomas **Hobbes** and then John **Locke**
142   argued instead that who we are and what we know comes
143   entirely through our basic senses, with emphasis on the
144   learning of associations between the events we observe. In
145   Locke's view, each person is a "tabula rasa" at birth, to be
146   shaped and molded by experience. This became known as
147   the extreme empiricist position.
148 • **Tabula Rasa** means "blank slate," implying that nothing
149   psychological is innate or built-in. And, as it happened,
150   Locke also believed that we are amoral and inherently
151   "bad" unless society teaches us to be "good."
152 • **An empiricist view** emphasizes **nurture** in the form of
153   environment and experiences. To say intellectual skills,
154   personality characteristics, and morality are mostly
155   learned is to take an extreme empiricist position.
156 • **Empiricism** in a different sense, however, is the basis for
157   all modern science. Empirical science requires that you
158   have observations and facts to back up what you say, as
159   discussed in detail in Key 7.

160 In the 18th century, Jean Jacques **Rousseau** retaliated with an
161   extreme nativist position on morality, proposing that we
162   are inherently good unless society corrupts us into being
163   bad. Both the empiricist and the nativist views of where
164   "morality" comes from are still alive today, though modern
165   psychologists don't tend to endorse either in the extreme.

166 In the 19th century, the influence of Charles **Darwin** and the
167   theory of natural selection as an explanation for evolution
168   eventually gave rise to the functionalism proposed by
169   William **James**, a major founder of psychology.
170 • **Functionalism** stressed the idea that who we are and what
171   we know is strongly influenced by adaptation to the
172   environment, a view still popular in psychology.

173 Meanwhile, Wilhelm **Wundt** founded the first
174   experimental psychology laboratory in 1879,
175   using a research method called introspection
176   and using an overall approach that came to be
177   known as structuralism.

178   • **Introspection** means looking inside oneself
179   and trying to describe what's going on. In a
180   sense, this general approach is still used
181   throughout psychology, especially in clinical
182   psychology, with regard to insight and under-
183   standing oneself.

184   • **Structuralism**, later named by E. B. **Titchener**,
185   was the view that human conscious experi-
186   ence (and therefore much of the psychological
187   world) could best be understood by break-
188   ing it down into component parts. Thus,
189   trained observers introspected and reported
190   what they experienced, and the structuralists
191   tried to formulate general theories based on
192   their subjects' reports.

What are some of the important views on behavior cited in this section? Who are some of the important individuals associated with these ideas? What do these ideas mean? Where can these ideas be used in your life? When would you use this information for your own purposes? Why are some of these ideas more useful than others? How can these ideas be applied to learning about psychology?

---

193 ***Key 3*** Psychoanalysis: The first force in
194   modern psychology

---

195 **OVERVIEW** *Historians designate three major "forces" that*
196 *shaped modern psychology, the first of which was Freud's psycho-*
197 *analysis.*

198 **Psychoanalysis** (Key 57) grew out of the clinical work of
199   Sigmund **Freud** that began just before the beginning of the
200   20th Century, and has had many advocates and students
201   since. Freudian (classical) psychoanalytic theory assumes
202   that all motivation comes from within the person, as a
203   result of "instinctual" desires that are basically hedonistic.
204   In complex ways, personality then results from how we
205   perceive and deal with our instinctual desires—especially
206   sex—plus our interactions with parents and others during
207   infancy and early childhood. Later psychodynamic theorists
208   who diverged from Freud's "classical" psychoanalysis are
209   discussed in Keys 29 and 59.

210   • **Hedonism** here means seeking pleasure and avoiding
211   pain, with little concern about anything else—such as
212   other people's feelings.
213   • **Psychodynamic** theorists and practitioners placed much
214   more emphasis on conscious processes than on the
215   unconscious, instinctual processes Freud proposed.
216   • Carl **Jung** was an early student of Freud who broke away
217   from classic psychoanalytic theory and instead empha-
218   sized a more abstract "collective unconscious" as the
219   primary source of motivation and personality.
220   • Alfred **Adler** was another early student of Freud who
221   rebelled and stressed "striving for superiority" over self
222   and environment as primary.
223   • Erik **Erikson** was an early student of Freud who went
224   along with most of Freud's theorizing and expanded it
225   into a theory of lifelong personality development, though
226   with much more emphasis on social interactions.
227   • Karen **Horney** was a later psychodynamic theorist who
228   contributed to the increased emphasis on conscious
229   processes and who also developed a much more con-
230   temporary explanation of male-female differences in
231   personality than that proposed by Freud.

232 *Key 4*   Behaviorism: The second force

233 **OVERVIEW**   *The early behaviorists rejected what they saw as*
234 *the deep and unobservable mysteries of psychoanalysis (and also*
235 *structuralism). The impact of the behaviorists exists throughout*
236 *modern psychology, though with emphasis on conditioning and*
237 *learning as discussed in Theme 8.*

238 Psychology was dominated from the turn of the century into
239   the 1950s or so by what is often called "strict" of "S-R"
240   behaviorism. This approach emphasized scientific study
241   taken to the extreme that *only empirical data* and *overt*
242   *behavior* were acceptable. Who and what we are with regard
243   to motivation and personality, for example, was viewed in
244   terms of the consequences of our behavior—usually as a
245   result of reinforcement and punishment, though still with
246   the assumption that we are basically hedonistic.

247 • **The S-R behaviorists** formulated their research on
248 "stimulus-response" relationships, where a **stimulus** is
249 any sensory event the subject is capable of detecting
250 and a **response** is any behavior the subject is capable of
251 performing. Stimuli and responses are overt and empiri-
252 cally observable, and therefore acceptable to the S-R
253 behaviorists. In turn, the S-R behaviors argued that *all*
254 behavior could be explained and understood that way.
255 The S-R behaviorists also tended to study learning and
256 behavior using laboratory animals, within the view that
257 the basic "laws" of behavior apply equally to lower animals
258 and to humans. The behaviorist approach is discussed
259 in detail in Theme 8.
260 • E. L. **Thorndike** was an early behaviorist and educator
261 best known for the law of effect (Key 43), which is in
262 essence that living organisms tend to repeat behavior
263 that leads to reinforcement and not to repeat behavior
264 that leads to punishment.
265 • Ivan **Pavlov** was the originator of classical conditioning
266 (Key 41), in which responses are understood in terms of
267 associations between stimuli.
268 • J. B. **Watson** was a researcher and general spokesperson
269 for S-R behaviorism, perhaps best known for his arguments
270 that the human infant is a tabula rasa, in keeping with
271 Locke's view.
272 • B. F. **Skinner**, somewhat later than the rest, but with
273 perhaps the greatest influence of all, refined and
274 extended S-R behaviorism into what became known as
275 operant conditioning (Key 42), which is based entirely
276 on observable behavior and its consequences.

---

277 *Key 5* Humanistic psychology:
278 The third force

---

279 **OVERVIEW** *In the 1950s, a third force emerged and came to be*
280 *known as humanistic psychology. With emphasis on self and dis-*
281 *tinctly human motives, humanistic psychology was a reaction*
282 *against both psychoanalysis and S-R behaviorism.*

283 The founders of **humanistic psychology** (Key 60) objected to
284 the basic hedonism of psychoanalysis and behaviorism alike,
285 arguing that too much emphasis had been placed on the
286 "animal" side of human nature. The humanists proposed
287 that we have uniquely human, positive motives that include
288 sharing, belonging, helping others, and especially achieving
289 one's own unique potential, with the effect that personality
290 must be understood in such terms. Relatedly, personality is
291 best understood from a phenomenological perspective.
292 • **The phenomenological perspective** stresses trying to see
293 things from the individual's own unique point of view.
294 • Carl **Rogers** was one of the founders of humanistic psy-
295 chology, with his emphasis on the person-centered
296 approach. Rogers argued that we should understand the
297 individual as being motivated toward getting in touch
298 with self and achieving a sense of fulfillment in life, noting
299 that each individual is unique and therefore can only be
300 understood from his or her
301 own unique point of view.
302 • Abraham **Maslow** was
303 another founder, best
304 known for his hierarchy of
305 needs: biological and hedo-
306 nistic needs are at the bot-
307 tom to be satisfied first;
308 above that are characteristi-
309 cally human needs such as
310 belongingness, esteem, aes-
311 thetics, and especially self-
312 actualization. Self-actualiza-
313 tion essentially means
314 achieving one's own unique potential.

> What are three major forces that shaped psychology? How are they similar? What are some of their differences? Are any of these ideas familiar to you? How might you apply this information to your life or the life of someone else?

---

315 *Key 6*   Other approaches and where
316   psychology is today

---

317 **OVERVIEW**   *Modern psychology can be understood in part as*
318 *a result of the three dominant forces discussed previously, but other*

319 *ways of looking at things were developing at the same time and*
320 *have had major impact. Today, psychology is distinctly cognitive*
321 *and increasingly biological.*

322 **Gestalt psychology** was concerned primarily with perception,
323   problem-solving, and other cognitive processes—at a time
324   when the S-R behaviorists were in control and rejected the
325   study of cognitive processes as wholly unscientific. Gestalt
326   psychologists are discussed in Keys 21 and 46.
327   • **Gestalt** means, basically, that the whole is more than the
328   sum of the parts. Thus, Gestalt psychology was in part a
329   reaction against the structuralists and their attempts to
330   break consciousness down into separate components.

331 Perhaps ironically, **early cognitive psychology** as such also
332   traces in part to the work of the behaviorists, notably those
333   who encountered serious obstacles to the explanation of
334   behavior in strict S-R terms. For example:
335   • Clark **Hull** and colleagues dedicated themselves to S-R
336   explanations of behavior and devised extensive formulas
337   to predict behavior both under specific and general cir-
338   cumstances. However, the formulations became so elabo-
339   rate and so far removed from what was directly observable
340   that in the end—most agree—it was covert behavior
341   that was actually being studied.
342   • Much of the work of Edward **Tolman** (Key 46), during
343   the heyday of S-R behaviorism, was designed to refute it.
344   Tolman argued, for example, that animals in mazes (one
345   way of studying animal learning) use **cognitive maps** to
346   find their way around. Thus, in effect, the animals *think*
347   rather than simply perform mechanical responses to the
348   stimuli present.

349 Hence, down the line occurred what has become known as **the**
350   **cognitive revolution**—especially from the 1960s on. In large
351   part, this revolution grew out of a widespread realization
352   throughout psychology that humans (*and* other animals)
353   could not be understood adequately in strictly behavioristic
354   terms. But the development of information-processing theory

355 and computer science also helped a lot by providing a
356 starting point for the scientific study of that which can't be
357 directly observed as yet. Many thousands of research
358 efforts later—with respect to the first three forces—the
359 cognitive revolution has affected all areas of psychology,
360 from the study of learning and memory to the study of
361 abnormal behavior and treatment.

362 • **Information-processing theory** as applied to humans
363 treats behaviors such as thinking and remembering as
364 sequential, beginning with input and then proceeding
365 through various kinds of processing to output in the
366 form of memory storage or overt behavior. By studying
367 characteristics of the input and the output, the mental
368 processing that took place in between can be inferred
369 scientifically.

370 • **Computer science** has helped by providing the capabil-
371 ity of creating "models" for human mental processes,
372 through which theories can be tested in great detail.
373 That doesn't mean, or course, that computers and
374 humans "think" the same ways (Key 47).

375 Otherwise, modern psychology is also strongly influenced by
376 ongoing advances in the **biological** and **medical** sciences.
377 As more sophisticated measurement techniques and better
378 ways of understanding physiological processes develop in
379 those disciplines, psychology comes closer to understand-
380 ing relationships between mind and body.

381 • **Biopsychology**, for example, focuses on the extent to
382 which behavior can be traced directly to physiological
383 processes in the brain.

384 • **Behavioral medicine** studies and applies the methods
385 and approaches of psychology to the diagnosis and
386 treatment of physical illnesses (Key 72).

387 And nowadays, psychologists still have professional preferences
388 about how to look at things and what methods to use in
389 studying behavior and perhaps controlling and changing it.
390 But modern psychologists tend to be eclectic and therefore

391   disinclined to look at things only one way.

392   • **Eclectic** means taking the best from differ-
393   ing and sometimes conflicting theories and
394   approaches, as the situation warrants. In
395   particular, being eclectic means recognizing
396   that the global theories and explanations
397   such as those of the first three forces in psy-
398   chology may be helpful in understanding
399   the behavior of one individual but not nec-
400   essarily that of everyone, or perhaps in one
401   situation but not in another.

Did you recognize any of the psychological ideas used in this book? Can you see how you can apply abstract information toward the solution of real problems? Does seeing abstract information applied to a real-life situation help you understand and comprehend it better? How might you use this approach to learn other things more effectively in the future?

PRACTICE READING 5: ACCOUNTING

1 THE ACCOUNTING
2 EQUATION

3 Some Basics

4 *WHAT IS ACCOUNTING?*

5 Accounting is the art of organiz-
6 ing, maintaining, recording, and
7 analyzing financial activities.
8 Accounting is generally known
9 as the "language of business."
10 The accountant translates this
11 accounting information into
12 meaningful terms that are used
13 by interested parties. Every orga-
14 nization, whether organized for
15 profit, nonprofit, charitable, reli-
16 gious, or governmental purposes
17 requires accountants.

18   Accounting may be divided
19 into three areas: (1) public
20 accounting, (2) private account-
21 ing, and (3) governmental
22 accounting. The public accoun-
23 tant, usually an employee of a
24 CPA firm, is employed as an
25 independent contractor by a
26 business to perform an auditing
27 function: to review the account-
28 ing system used by the business, check the correctness of finan-
29 cial statements, and give an opinion. The public accountant
30 also prepares income tax returns and provides management
31 advisory services. The private accountant, usually employed
32 by a business, records business activities and prepares periodic

Accounting is a very visual subject. Explore this excerpt for all the visual aids and make frequent use of them when reading about technical information that uses these visual aids. Remember to chunk down difficult material to a size that is easy for you to learn. While exploring, notice this unit has numerous exercises. If you are having a problem understanding a concept make use of them, but if the ideas are easy for you to understand, increase your reading speed and move quickly through unnecessary examples.

33 financial statements. The governmental accountant
34 performs the same functions as a private accountant
35 but is employed by a federal, state, or local
36 governmental agency.

37 WHO USES ACCOUNTING
38 INFORMATION?

39 Accounting information is used by everyone. The
40 manager of an organization, who is charged with the
41 responsibility of seeing that the enterprise is prop-
42 erly directed, calls upon the accounting informa-
43 tion provided to make appropriate decisions.
44 Investors in an enterprise need information about
45 the financial status and future prospects of an orga-
46 nization. Bankers and suppliers grant loans and extend credit to
47 organizations based on their financial soundness as evidenced
48 by accounting information. Customers are concerned about a
49 company's ability to provide a product or service. Employees are
50 concerned about the ability of the employer to pay wages and
51 fringe benefit packages.

> What is accounting, and what information can it provide? Is it interesting to you? Is it easy? When might you use this information? Is this information important? Can you use the importance of this information to make this subject more interesting to you?

52 WHAT INFORMATION DOES AN
53 ACCOUNTANT GATHER?

54 The accountant keeps track of all "business transactions."
55 A business transaction is any business activity that affects
56 what a business owns or owes, as well as the ownership of that
57 business.

58 What Are Assets?

59 Those things that are owned by any business orga-
60 nization are known as ASSETS. In order for an item
61 to be considered an asset, it must meet two
62 requirements: (1) it must be owned by the organiza-
63 tion, and (2) it must have money value. OWNER-
64 SHIP is the exclusive right to possess, use, enjoy,
65 and dispose of property. MONEY VALUE exists if a
66 buyer is willing to pay money to a seller for the
67 property.

> Did you notice how this book capitalizes important vocabulary words? Are you prepared to learn these new definitions using a memory technique?

68 *EXERCISE 1*

69 From the following list of items,
70 indicate by checking the appropri-
71 ate box which items are or are not
72 assets.

Are these exercises useful or a waste of your valuable time?

73

Item	Yes	No
74 Automobile		
75 Jewelry		
76 Apartment (Rented)		
77 Clothing		
78 Money		
79 Typewriter		
80 Checks		
81 Library Book (On Loan)		
82 Shopping List		
83 IOU from a Friend		

84 *EXERCISE 2*

85 Prepare a list of ten assets that you personally own. You may
86 include the assets listed in Exercise 1, but attempt to list as
87 many other personal assets as you can.

88 *EXERCISE 3*

89 Prepare a list of ten assets that a business organization would
90 own. Attempt to list business assets that an individual might
91 not have.

92 KEEPING TRACK OF ASSETS

93 Since there apparently are so many different kinds of assets, how
94 does the accountant keep track of all the assets? The accountant
95 does not keep track of all the assets individually, but rather com-
96 bines assets of a similar nature into common groups. For exam-
97 ple, an individual or business organization may have such assets
98 as coins, bills, money orders, and checks. These assets would be
99 placed in a category or grouping known as CASH. Thus, any
100 money, regardless of its actual form, would be known and cate-
101 gorized as cash. Cash also includes money in bank accounts of
102 the individual that is available for payment of bills.

103 *EXERCISE 4*

104 Test your ability to assign specific assets to categories. Place the
105 assets listed below under the asset category headings that follow.
106   Traveler's checks, tables, truck, typewriter, adding machine,
107 lamp, pencils, chairs, stationery, wrapping paper, automobiles,
108 coins, money in bank, light bulbs, desk, pens, currency, show-
109 cases, computer, software programs, computer printer, and
110 toner cartridge.

| 111 | | | *Furniture and* | *Office* | *Delivery* |
112 *Cash*	*Office Supplies*		*Fixtures*	*Equipment*	*Equipment*

113   1. What is the difference between office supplies and office
114   equipment?
115   2. A toner cartridge is considered an office supply, even
116   though it is an integral part of the computer printer. Why?
117   3. Will we replace a typewriter as frequently as a typewriter
118   ribbon? Why or why not?
119   4. What type of asset is a supply? (Short-life or long-life?)
120   5. What type of asset is a computer? (Short-life or long-life?)

121 *TYPES OF ASSETS*

122 As the previous exercises indicated, assets may take many
123 forms. While they may be grouped together into categories as
124 in Exercise 4, they may also be considered to be tangible and
125 intangible assets as well. A tangible asset is one that can be
126 readily seen, and possibly touched, such as those previously
127 illustrated. They are physical assets. An intangible asset is with-
128 out physical qualities, but has a value based on rights or priv-
129 ileges belong to the owner.
130   The assets of an organization are usually divided into four
131 categories: (1) current assets, (2) investments, (3) property, plant,
132 and equipment, and (4) intangible assets.

133   CURRENT ASSETS are defined as cash and other assets that
134 can reasonably be expected to be converted to cash, used up,
135 or sold within one year or less. Examples of current assets
136 include cash, accounts receivable (obligations due from cus-
137 tomers), and supplies.

138   INVESTMENTS are generally of a long-term nature, are not
139 used in the normal operations of the organization and are not
140 expected to be converted to cash within the year. Examples
141 of investments are stocks and
142 bonds of other organizations.

143   PROPERTY, PLANT, AND
144 EQUIPMENT are long-term or
145 long-life assets that are used in
146 the continuing operations of the
147 organization and are expected to
148 be used by the organization for
149 more than a year. These kinds of
150 assets are also known as "Plant
151 Assets." Examples of these assets
152 are land, building, machinery,
153 and equipment.

> **What are different types of assets? Which ones might apply to your situation? Can you picture any of these assets? Do these pictures help you understand the asset definitions better?**

154   INTANGIBLE ASSETS are usually of a long-term nature and
155 have no physical substance but are of value to the owners of
156 the organization. Examples of these assets are patents, copy-
157 rights, goodwill, franchises, and trademarks.

158 ***EXERCISE 5***

159 Place the following assets in the appropriate columns of the
160 form following them: cash in bank, office equipment, First
161 National City bonds, patents, accounts receivable, office sup-
162 plies, notes receivable (due in ninety days), building, office
163 machines, furniture and fixtures, mortgage notes receivable
164 (due in six years), store equipment, petty cash, goodwill, factory
165 supplies, and merchandise.

166 | *Current Assets* | *Investments* | *Plant Assets* | *Intangible Assets* |
|---|---|---|---|
| | | | |
| | | | |
| | | | |

167 **A COMMON WAY TO EXPRESS ASSETS**

168 We have indicated that the accountant keeps track of all business
169 transactions. So far, the only business transactions we have
170 discussed are things that the organization owns, namely
171 assets. In order to keep track of these assets, there must be a
172 common way of expressing these assets. The common way of
173 expressing the value of items in a business is known as the
174 MONETARY PRINCIPLE. All business transactions are recorded
175 in terms of money. Money is the only factor that is common to
176 all assets as well as to other items we will shortly be discussing.
177 If we were to say that we have the asset "office supplies," the
178 accountant would express the ownership of this asset in terms
179 of a money value assigned to it. The money value assigned
180 would be based on what the office supplies had cost when
181 they were purchased. If we acquired office supplies that had cost
182 us $50, we would then say that the value of the asset office
183 supplies is $50. All things owned by and owed to an organiza-
184 tion, as well as the ownership of the organization, will be
185 expressed in terms of money value. Money or cash becomes the
186 common denominator in presenting accounting information.

187 *Determining Money Value of Assets*

188 In the case of the office supplies illustrated, the value assigned
189 was based on the cost of the item. This is known as the COST
190 PRINCIPLE. The cost assigned to the asset not only includes
191 the purchase price, but also transportation charges, installation
192 charges, and any other costs associated with placing the asset
193 into use by the organization.
194   While every form of organization previously mentioned
195 uses accounting information, we will assume from this point
196 on that we are dealing with a profit-making business. We will
197 further assume that the business is that of a single owner (sole
198 proprietorship). A SOLE PROPRIETORSHIP is a business that is
199 formed by one individual. This individual is considered the
200 owner of the business and receives any profits that the business
201 earns and sustains any losses that the business may incur.
202 The assets which the business owns are separate and apart
203 from the assets that the owner may personally own. This is
204 known as the BUSINESS ENTITY CONCEPT.

205 ***EXERCISE 6***

206 Mr. Jones, the owner of a limousine business, purchases an
207 automobile from the Friendly New Car Dealership. The pur-
208 chase price of the automobile is $12,760. There are make-ready
209 charges of $385, delivery charges of $125, and applicable state
210 sales taxes amounting to $893.

211   **1.** Determine the cost as which the new automobile should be
212   recorded on the books of Mr. Jones's business.
213   **2.** If, upon leaving the dealership, Mr. Jones was offered
214        $14,500 for the automobile, at what price should the new
215   automobile be recorded on his records? Why?
216   **3.** Does Mr. Jones own the asset automobile? Why or why not?

217 ***EXERCISE 7***

218 Mr. Glenn is negotiating to buy a parcel of property for his
219 business. The seller of the property is asking $170,000 for the
220 property. The assessed value of the property for property tax
221 purposes is $125,000. The property is presently insured by the
222 owner for $135,000. Mr. Glenn originally offered the seller
223 $130,000 for the property. Mr. Glenn and the seller have agreed
224 on a purchase price of $150,000. Shortly after the purchase is
225 made by Mr. Glenn, he is offered $175,000 for the same property.
226 At what price would Mr. Glenn record the property on the books
227 of his business?

228 ***Recognizing the Proprietor's Ownership***

229 The proprietor in beginning a business contributes assets to the
230 business. These assets contributed may consist of cash, supplies,
231 or equipment. Each asset is assigned a money value based on
232 the cost of the asset to the proprietor. Since the proprietor is
233 also the owner of the business, those assets contributed represent
234 the proprietor's ownership or equity in the business. A record is
235 set up by the accountant to repre-
236 sent the proprietor's ownership in
237 the business. This record is called
238 CAPITAL.

239   CAPITAL is the ownership of
240 the assets of the business by the
241 proprietor. For every asset that

> Can you distinguish the difference between capital and equity? How are they used by an accountant?

242 the proprietor contributes to the business there is a corre-
243 sponding value assigned to the record of proprietor's capital. A
244 term frequently used interchangeably with capital is EQUITY.
245 In this instance, equity represents the ownership of the assets
246 of the business by the proprietor.

247 *EXERCISE 8*

248 Ms. Taylor began a business on April 1, 199-, contributing to the
249 business the following assets: Cash, $3,000; Office Supplies,
250 $275; Office Equipment, $700; Furniture and Fixtures, $2,100.
251 Determine the value of Ms. Taylor's ownership (CAPITAL) in
252 the business.

253   1. What is the total value of the assets that Ms. Taylor con-
254   tributed to the business?

255   2. What is the value of Ms. Taylor's ownership in the business?

256 *Assets = Capital*

257 From the above relationship we can develop a simple equation
258 which relates assets to capital. This equation will be expressed
259 as: ASSETS = CAPITAL. Thus, if Ms. Taylor contributed to the
260 business assets valued at $6,075, the equation would be
261 expressed as:

262   ASSETS = CAPITAL
263                    $6,075 = $6,075

264   If at some future date the proprietor contributes additional
265 assets to the business, both the value of the total assets and the
266 value of the capital will increase by the same amount, thus the
267 equation would remain in balance. Should the proprietor
268 decide to take an asset out of the business for personal use, this
269 will cause a corresponding decrease in the value of the total
270 assets and the value of the total capital.

271 *EXERCISE 9*

272 Using the chart presented below, show the effects on the equation
273 caused by the following business transactions. After you have
274 recorded the transactions on the chart, add the individual
275 columns and verify that the equation is still in balance.
276 (Remember that assets are set up in various categories depending

277 upon the nature of the asset. If a business uses an existing asset
278 to acquire another asset, this will only cause a change in assets.
279 There will be no effect on the proprietor's capital. Transactions
280 4 and 5 should not affect capital; they represent an EXCHANGE
281 OF ASSETS.)
282   1. The proprietor invested $5,000 cash in the business.
283   2. The proprietor invested a typewriter valued at $250.
284   3. The proprietor took $200 out of the business as a perma-
285   nent reduction in investment.
286   4. The proprietor purchased supplies for the business, pay-
287   ing for the supplies with $75 in cash from the business.
288   5. The proprietor purchased an adding machine for $50,
289   paying with cash from the business.

	ASSETS			=	CAPITAL
No.	CASH +	SUPPLIES +	EQUIPMENT	=	CAPITAL
1					
2					
3					
4					
5					
TOTAL					

299 **EXERCISE 10**
300 List the following headings on a sheet of paper. Cash + Accounts
301 Receivable + Store Supplies + Office Supplies + Furniture and
302 Fixtures + Equipment = Capital.
303   Record the following business transactions in the appro-
304 priate columns. Identify each by number and after each trans-
305 action is recorded, verify that the equation is in balance by
306 FOOTING (adding) the columns. The proprietor of the business:
307   1. Invested $20,000 in the business.
308   2. Purchased furniture and fixtures for use in the business
309   paying $1,200 in cash.
310   3. Purchased store supplies paying $170 in cash.
311   4. Purchased equipment for use in the business paying
312       $1,500 in cash.
313   5. Loaned a business associate $750 in cash which he promised
314   to repay in ten days.

315   6. Contributed office supplies to the business that had a
316   value of $60.
317   7. Received a check for $300 in partial payment of the
318   amount that his associate had owed him.
319   8. Permanently reduced his investment in the business by
320   taking out a desk worth $100 and $900 in cash.
321   9. Returned equipment previously purchased and received a
322   cash refund of $175.
323 10. Bought office supplies paying $65 in cash.

324 *Expressing Borrowed Assets*

325 In the previous two exercises we practiced recording business
326 transactions that affected assets and capital of the business.
327 The owner of a sole proprietorship will use the assets he or she
328 contributed to the business to acquire other assets that the
329 business needs to function. In some circumstances there may
330 be inadequate assets available to meet the needs of the business.
331 When this situation occurs, it may be necessary for the business
332 to obtain the needed assets from other sources.

333   The most obvious way in which additional assets can be
334 obtained for the business is by borrowing. When cash or any
335 other asset is borrowed, the firm is said to have incurred a debt
336 or liability. Regardless of what is borrowed, it is customary to
337 repay the obligation in cash. When the obligation is initially
338 incurred, the business obtains the asset borrowed. At the same
339 time, a liability is incurred which has to be recognized as an
340 obligation of the business. Until the debt is paid, the creditor
341 (the person to whom the money is owed) is said to have a
342 claim upon the assets originally loaned. A LIABILITY is defined
343 as the ownership of the assets of a business by it *creditors*. Notice
344 that this definition of a liability is identical to the definition
345 of capital, except for the last word. (Capital is the ownership
346 of the assets of a business by the *proprietor*). Since a liability is,
347 by definition, not an asset or ownership as evidenced by capital,
348 it becomes necessary to establish a third classification of items,
349 namely that of liabilities. Since a liability is closely associated
350 with the ownership of the business assets, it is shown on the
351 equation on the same side as capital. The term *equity* as previ-
352 ously discussed was used synonymously with *capital*. Equity

353 signifies ownership, thus it represents both capital and liabilities
354 in this case. The final form of the equation, which is generally
355 known as the ACCOUNTING EQUATION, is:

356   ASSETS = LIABILITIES + CAPITAL

357   Liabilities may take many
358 forms. If the owner of a business
359 has to borrow money and orally
360 promises to pay back the obliga-
361 tion, this obligation would be
362 known as an ACCOUNT PAYABLE.
363 If the promise made took the
364 form of a written document,
365 such as an IOU or a promissory
366 note, then the obligation would

> What are different types of borrowed assets? Do any of these apply to you? Can you think of a model you can create about this that could be placed on a flash card?

367 be known as a NOTE PAYABLE. Regardless of the form that the
368 actual obligation takes, its placement in the accounting equation
369 would remain the same. Let's assume the following information:

370   ASSETS = LIABILITIES + CAPITAL
371          $14,000 =   –0–   + $14,000

372   The business borrows $6,000 from a local bank. What
373 would happen to the various classifications within the
374 accounting equation? Show the new totals (balances) as a
375 result of recording the transaction.

376   ASSETS = LIABILITIES + CAPITAL
377          $14,000 =   0   + $14,000
378   +$ 6,000 =   +$6,000   +   0
379          $20,000 = $6,000   + $14,000

380   If at a later date the loan is repaid, determine the effects of
381 the repayment on the total value of the assets, liabilities, and
382 capital.

383 *EXERCISE 11*

384 Calculate the value of the missing element of the accounting
385 equation in each of the numbered situations:

386   ASSETS = LIABILITIES + CAPITAL
387 1. $6,000 = $2,000 + ?
388 2. $5,500 = ? + $2,300
389 3. ? = $4,500 + $3,650
390 4. $10,550 = $485 + ?
391 5. $8,400 = ? + $8,400

392 *EXERCISE 12*

393 A. L. Brandon is the owner of the Brandon Small Appliance
394 Repair Shop. On January 1, 199-, the assets, liabilities, and pro-
395 prietor's capital in the business were: Cash $2,000; Accounts
396 Receivable $400; Supplies, $500; Equipment, $6,000; Accounts
397 Payable, $900; A. L. Brandon, Capital, $8,000. The business
398 transactions for the month of January were as follows:

399 1. Paid $300 of the outstanding accounts payable.
400 2. Received $100 on account (part payment) from customers.
401 3. Purchased $250 worth of supplies on account (on credit).
402 4. Returned a defective piece of equipment that was pur-
403   chased last month and received a cash refund of $1,200.
404 5. Borrowed $1,000 from a supplier, giving word to repay
405   the loan in thirty days.
406 6. Paid creditor $200 on account (part payment)
407 7. Purchased equipment for $800, giving $200 cash and
408   promising to pay the balance in sixty days.
409 8. Bought supplies paying $65 cash.
410 9. Received a $250 check from customer on account.

411   Set up a chart using a form similar to that in Exercise 10.
412 Record the January 1 balances immediately under the various
413 assets, liabilities, and capital item headings. Record the business
414 transactions listed above. Be certain to label each transaction
415 with the corresponding number assigned, and foot the columns
416 after each transaction has been recorded to verify the balance
417 of the equation. Notice that every business transaction has

418 a minimum of two changes.
419 Transaction 7 has three changes,
420 but notice that the dollar change
421 is equal, thus the equation in
422 this case, as with all the business
423 transactions, remains in balance.

> Are you remembering to chunk down difficult material into smaller and easier to learn chunks? Are you maintaining your learning state? Are you anchoring energy when you need it? Are you staying focused?

424 What Are Revenue,
425 Expenses, and Profit?

426 Every business exists primarily to
427 earn a profit. This profit is realized
428 through REVENUE received by an organization as a result of
429 the sale of a service or product by that business. Our primary
430 concern will be with a business that provides a service. Examples
431 of persons in service-oriented occupations are accountants,
432 lawyers, doctors, beauticians, real estate and insurance brokers,
433 and travel agents. The resulting profits of a service business
434 belong to the owner (sole proprietor) of the enterprise. The
435 revenue generated through the services provided are recognized
436 as an increase in the capital of the owner. This is justified
437 because the profits that the business earns belong to the owner
438 of the business, and the revenue received should be reflected
439 in the record of ownership.

440 *RECORDING REVENUE*

441 If revenue of $500 cash is received by the business, this revenue
442 should be recorded as an increase in cash of $500 and a resulting
443 increase in proprietor's capital of $500. Revenue may be received
444 in forms other than cash. An organization may receive payment
445 for services rendered in the form of other assets such as supplies,
446 equipment, and even someone's word to pay at a future time
447 (accounts receivable). The effects on the accounting equation
448 will still result in an increase in the specific asset received and
449 a corresponding increase in capital.

450   An increase in the proprietor's capital will result from not
451 only an investment by the owner, but also as a result of revenue
452 received for services provided.

453 ### *RECORDING EXPENSES*

454 Profit and revenue are not the same. PROFIT represents the
455 income that a business has earned after certain adjustments
456 have been made. Revenue is one component which permits
457 the recognition of profit. Every business, regardless of its
458 nature, must incur certain costs in order to operate. These
459 costs are known as EXPENSES. Expenses are generally referred
460 to as the "costs of doing business." Examples of expenses that
461 businesses incur are rent expense, insurance expense, salary
462 expense, and supplies expense. Expenses are also known as
463 "necessary evils," because they must be incurred in order to
464 obtain revenue which ultimately will be translated into profits
465 for the business. While we learned that revenue causes an
466 increase in capital, an expense will have the opposite effect
467 and result in a decrease in capital.

468   If rent expense for the month amounting to $300 is paid, this
469 will result in a decrease in the asset cash and a corresponding
470 decrease in proprietor's capital.

471   A decrease in the proprietor's capital will result from a per-
472 manent reduction in the owner's investment in the business,
473 from the proprietor taking assets out of the business, and now
474 as a result of the payment of an expense.

	Transaction	*Effect on Proprietor's Capital*
475		
476	Owner's investment	Increase
477	Owner's withdrawals	Decrease
478	Revenues	Increase
479	Expenses	Decrease

480 ### *HOW REVENUE AND EXPENSES AFFECT CAPITAL*

481 When the proprietor makes the initial investment or subse-
482 quent investments in the business, this investment is said to
483 be PERMANENT in nature. An assumption is made that the
484 assets contributed through the investment will be used in the
485 business on an ongoing basis to maintain the business and
486 contribute toward future growth. The revenue and expenses
487 which affect capital are also used to determine if the business
488 has earned a profit. Since profit is determined periodically,

489 these records (revenue and expenses) are considered to be
490 TEMPORARY in nature. Also, when the proprietor borrows assets
491 from the business, this withdrawal is considered temporary.

492   PERMANENT CAPITAL = Proprietor's Capital (Investment)
493   TEMPORARY CAPITAL = Revenue, Expenses, Withdrawals

494   In order to distinguish temporary capital from permanent
495 capital, the accountant maintains separate records for each
496 specific kind of temporary capital account. An ACCOUNT is a
497 separate record maintained for each category of asset, liability,
498 permanent, and temporary capital record. The proprietor's capital
499 account is only affected by changes which are considered to be
501 permanent in nature. Business transactions which result in the
502 receipt of revenue or the payment of expenses will be recorded
503 in separate specific accounts. These accounts will increase and
504 decrease in the same way as if the changes were made directly
505 to the proprietor's capital account.
506 Just as revenue would be consid-
507 ered as an increase in the propri-
508 etor's capital, it is expressed as an
509 increase in the specific revenue
510 account. An expense, as a cost of
511 doing business, has a decreasing
512 effect on the proprietor's capital.
513 Business transactions directly
514 affecting these expenses, while
515 increasing the value of the indi-
516 vidual expense, still have a
517 decreasing effect on the propri-
518 etor's capital.

> What do you understand about revenue and expenses? Is there anything unclear to you? Return to what is causing the problem. Analyze it. Think about it. If you understand the ideas, then quickly move to the next idea that is unfamiliar to you.

519 **_EXERCISE 13_**
520 Upon finishing law school, Carolyn Goldstein set up a law
521 practice. During the first month, she completed the following
522 business transactions:

523   **1.** Invested $3,000 cash in the business.
524   **2.** Purchased a law library for $1,200 cash.

525 3. Received $500 for services rendered.
526 4. Purchased office supplies on credit for $150.
527 5. Paid rent for the month amounting to $300.
528 6. Sent a bill for $1,100 for services rendered.
529 7. Sent a check for $50 in part payment of accounts payable.
530 8. Received $200 from customers as a result of services previ-
531   ously rendered and recognized.
532 9. Sent a check for $60 to the local utility company for costs
533   incurred in beginning service.
534 10. Borrowed $200 from the business (show the effect of this
535   loan in the Carolyn Goldstein drawing account).

536   Set up a chart using a form similar to that in Exercise 12.
537 The following account headings are to be used: Assets—Cash,
538 Accounts Receivable, Office Supplies, Law Library; Liabilities—
539 Accounts Payable; Capital—Carolyn Goldstein, Capital; Carolyn
540 Goldstein, Drawing; Income from Services; Rent Expense;
541 Utilities Expense. Record the business transactions listed
542 above making certain to verify the balance in the accounting
543 equation as a result of each business transaction. Remember,
544 revenue increases capital. Expenses decrease capital. Drawing
545 decreases capital.

546 Summing Up

547 Accounting is the art of organizing, maintaining,
548 recording, and analyzing financial activities.
549   Accounting information is used by managers
550 of all business organizations. Others who may
551 have an indirect financial interest in the organiza-
552 tion also make use of accounting information.
553   Business transactions represent economic events
554 that affect the financial condition of the business.
555 The position of the organization is represented by
556 assets, liabilities, and capital.
557   Assets represent anything that is owned and
558 has money value. Assets are organized into groups.
559 These groups are current assets; investments, prop-
560 erty, plant, and equipment; and intangible assets.

Did you remember to read this summary first? Did you use this summary to better prepare yourself for what you learned in this chapter? How can you use this summary to make certain you learned all the important information?

561   The assignment of costs to all noncurrent assets is based
562 upon the cost principle. The cost to be assigned to the asset
563 includes all costs necessary to make the asset operational for
564 the business.

565   Liabilities are the claims upon the assets of the business by
566 its creditors. Liabilities may either be short-term or long-term
567 obligations. Accounts payable expected to be paid within a
568 year are short-term obligations. Notes payable, if not payable
569 within a year, are considered long-term liabilities.

570   Capital is the ownership of the assets of the business by the
571 proprietor.

572   The accounting equation is:

573   ASSETS = LIABILITIES + CAPITAL

574   Capital may be divided into two categories: permanent
575 and temporary. Permanent capital represents the investment
576 that the owner makes in the business. Temporary capital rep-
577 resents revenue, expenses, and drawing (withdrawal).

578   All businesses are in business for the purpose of earning a
579 profit. This profit can be determined by comparing revenue
580 with expenses. The excess of revenue over expenses represents
581 profit. If expenses exceed revenue, the result is known as a loss.
582 Resulting profit or loss will cause a change in the proprietor's
583 capital.

PRACTICE READING 6:
READING COMPREHENSION IN STANDARDIZED TESTS

1 Questions 31 to 35 refer to the following passage.

2 **HOW DO CREATIVE INDIVIDUALS BEHAVE?**

3   Discoveries in science and technology are
4   thought by "untaught minds" to come in
5   blinding flashes or as the result of dramatic
6   accidents. Sir Alexander Fleming did not, as
7 (5) legend would have it, look at the mould on a
8   piece of cheese and get the idea for
9   penicillin there and then. He experimented
10   with antibacterial substances for nine years
11   before he made his discovery. Inventions and
12 (10) innovations almost always come out of
13   laborious trial and error. Innovation is like
14   hockey: Even the best players miss the net
15   and have their shots blocked much more
16   frequently than they score.
17 (15) The point is that players who score
18   most are the ones who take the most shots
19   on the net—and so it goes with innovation in
20   any field of activity. The prime difference
21   between innovators and others is one of
22 (20) approach. Everybody gets ideas, but
23   innovators work consciously on theirs, and
24   they follow them through until they prove
25   practicable or otherwise. They never reject
26   any thought that comes into their heads as
27 (25) outlandish. What ordinary people see as
28   fanciful abstractions, professional innovators
29   see as solid possibilities.
30   "Creative thinking may mean simply the
31   realization that there's no particular virtue in
32 (30) doing things the way they have always been
33   done," wrote Rudolph Flesch, the language

This section will help you practice your reading comprehension in fiction and nonfiction for standardized tests. Pay very careful attention to the questions. Read the questions first. Always pay careful attention to words that change the meanings of questions such as "not have in common."

34   guru. This accounts for our reaction to
35   deceptively simple innovations like plastic
36   garbage bags, and suitcases on wheels that
37 *(35)* make life more convenient: "How come
38   nobody thought of that before?"
39   Creativity does not demand absolute
40   originality. It often takes the form of throwing
41   an old ball with a new twist.
42 *(40)*   The creative approach begins with the
43   proposition that nothing is as it appears.
44   Innovators will not accept that there is only
45   one way to do anything. Faced with getting
46   from A to B, the average person will
47 *(45)* automatically set out on the best-known and
48   apparently simplest routing. The innovator
49   will search for alternate courses which may
50   prove easier in the long run and are bound
51   to be more interesting and challenging even
52 *(50)* if they lead to dead ends.
53   Highly creative individuals really do march
54   to a different drummer.

55 **31.** Which person would the author probably consider to
56   have an "untaught mind" (line 2)?
57   (1) a high school dropout
58   (2) a citizen of a society that restricts personal freedom
59   (3) a superstitious person
60   (4) a person ignorant of the method of laboratory
61   experimentation
62   (5) a practical businessman

63 **32.** According to the author, what separates innovators from
64   noninnovators?
65   (1) the variety of ideas they have
66   (2) the number of successes they achieve
67   (3) the way they approach problems
68   (4) the manner in which they present their findings
69   (5) the background they possess

70 33. According to the author, what is the common response
71   to a new invention?
72   (1) surprise at its simplicity
73   (1) acceptance of its utility
74   (1) questioning of its necessity
75   (1) dependence on its convenience
76   (1) resistance to its use

77 34. In lines 38 and 39, the author uses the imagery of
78   throwing the ball to explain the
79   (1) significance of form
80   (2) importance of a fresh perspective
81   (3) importance of practice
82   (4) relationship between science and athletics
83   (5) ease of creation

84 35. In keeping with the context of the passage, what would
85   the innovator probably state about going from Point A
86   to Point B?
87   (1) A straight line is the most direct and proven approach.
88   (2) The shortest route is the most advantageous.
89   (3) The most challenging route will eventually prove to
90   be the easiest.
91   (4) The advantages of several routes must be carefully
92   considered.
93   (5) The best route is the mode widely known.

94 <u>Questions 36 to 40</u> refer to the following com-
95 mentary on the plays *Romeo and Juliet* and *West*
96 *Side Story*.

97   **HOW DO *ROMEO AND JULIET* AND**
98   **_WEST SIDE STORY_ COMPARE?**

99   What glorious verse falls from the lips of
100 Shakespeare's boys and girls! True, there is a
101 rollicking jazzy vigor in such songs of *West*
102 *Side Story* as the one of Officer Krupke, but it
103 *(5)* pales alongside the pyrotechnical display of

Again read the questions first. Be careful to observe the author's opinions and not base your answers on your opinions that might be completely different! Remember to run a visual movie of what is described in the text to make it easier to understand what is being described.

104   Mercurio's Queen Mab speech. There is

105   tenderness in "Maria," but how relatively

106   tongue-tied is the twentieth-century hero

107   alongside the boy who cried, "He jests at scars

108 *(10)* that never felt a wound." "Hold my hand and

109   we're halfway there," say Maria and Tony to

110   each other, and the understatement touches

111   us. But "Gallop apace, you fiery-footed steeds"

112   and the lines that follow glow with a glory that

113 *(15)* never diminishes. The comparisons of

114   language could be multiplied, and always, of

115   course, Shakespeare is bound to win.

116   Without its great poetry *Romeo and Juliet*

117   would not be a major tragedy. Possibly it is

118 *(20)* not, in any case; for as has frequently been

119   remarked, Shakespeare's hero and heroine

120   are a little too slender to carry the full weight

121   of tragic grandeur. Their plight is more

122   pathetic than tragic. If this is true of them, it

123 *(25)* is equally true of Tony and Maria: for them,

124   too, pathos rather than tragedy. But there is

125   tragedy implicit in the environmental situation

126   of the contemporary couple, and this must

127   not be overlooked or underestimated.

128 *(30)* Essentially, however, what we see is that all

129   four young people strive to consummate the

130   happiness at the threshold on which they

131   stand and which they have tasted so briefly.

132   All four are deprived of the opportunity to do

133 *(35)* so, the Renaissance couple by the caprice of

134   fate, today's youngsters by the prejudice and

135   hatred engendered around them. All four are

136   courageous and lovable. All four arouse our

137   compassion, even though they may not

138 *(40)* shake us with Aristotelian fear.

139   Poets and playwrights will continue to

140   write of youthful lovers whom fate drives into

141   and out of each other's lives. The spectacle

142   will always trouble and move us.

143 36. The author of the selection implies that
144   (1) the songs of *West Side Story* lack strength
145   (2) the language of *West Side Story* leaves us cold
146   (3) the language of *Romeo and Juliet* lacks the vigor of
147   that of *West Side Story*
148   (4) the poetry of *Romeo and Juliet* will prevail
149   (5) the speech of *West Side Story* can compete with the
150   verse of *Romeo and Juliet*

151 37. In comparing the language of *Romeo and Juliet* with that
152   of *West Side Story* the author
153   (1) takes no position
154   (2) likes each equally
155   (3) favors that of *Romeo and Juliet*
156   (4) favors that of *West Side Story*
157   (5) downplays the differences

158 38. Both plays share a common weakness. That weakness is
159   (1) the stature of their heroes and heroines
160   (2) the absence of deep emotion
161   (3) their dramatic construction
162   (4) the lack of substance of their themes
163   (5) the lack of linguistic power

164 39. The couples in the two plays share all of the following
165   EXCEPT
166   (1) a pathetic situation
167   (2) lack of opportunity to achieve happiness
168   (3) courage
169   (4) inability to instill fear in the reader
170   (5) inability to arouse pity in the reader

171 40. The couples in the two plays differ in the nature of
172   (1) their plight
173   (2) their ultimate fate
174   (3) the cause of their tragic situation
175   (4) their attractiveness
176   (5) their love for one another

177 **ANSWERS TO QUESTIONS 32–40**

178 32. 3
179 33. 1
180 34. 2
181 35. 4
182 36. 4
183 37. 3
184 38. 1
185 39. 4
186 40. 3

PRACTICE READING 7: AMERICAN HISTORY

A NATION OF IMMIGRANTS

APPROACHES TO HISTORY

The Method of the Historian

Many people think history is a set of facts, explaining what happened in the past, that everyone should learn. They believe that by memorizing this material, they will know history. Unfortunately, this is only partly true. The truth is that history is a record of the past, and consists of information historians have gathered to explain, as best they can, what occurred before the present. You might ask, "What is the difference between these two statements?" The answer is that the latter statement avoids the word facts, and suggests the method historians use to gain an understanding of the past.

"Facts" come in all degrees of accuracy, something that can be hard for the inexperienced student of history to accept or understand. Part of the historian's method is to evaluate facts. For instance, you may be familiar with the statement "Columbus discovered America in 1492," and believe it to be a fact. Historians have considered the evidence and agree that Columbus came to the Americas in 1492—that is, 1492 according to the calendar used by most people in the United States but not 1492 according to the Jewish or Chinese calendars. Therefore, we must be clear what we mean when we state a "fact," because it may not be universally understood. More importantly,

Begin by skimming the entire chapter. Pay careful attention to the topics covered. Ask yourself, "Is this new information or familiar? Is it difficult or easy information to learn? Is it interesting or uninteresting? How much time do I need to master this material?" Also look for summary and questions at the end of the chapter to help frame what information to focus on during your actual reading of this unit. Also notice important *key point to remember* outlined on the top of page 198. How can you use this information to focus on important information?

34 | we know that there were Native Americans already in
35 | the Americas, and other Europeans had come here—they
36 | had all "discovered" America long before Columbus. So
37 | to be accurate, you need to rephrase the statement so it
38 | reads, "Columbus rediscovered America for the Europeans
39 | in 1492 AD."
40 | The historian's method begins with the collection
41 | and questioning of so-called factual information. Once
42 | historians have collected a good deal of information—
43 | often referred to as data—they study it and develop
44 | explanations of how these facts relate. These explanations
45 | are hypotheses[1], since there is no way we can be certain
46 | just how the events, the facts, of the past were understood
47 | and related to each other.
48 | The historian's method is very similar to the method
49 | used by scientists. Using the so-called scientific method,
50 | the scientist collects data, develops a hypothesis about
51 | why the observed data behaved the way it did, and then
52 | prepares experiments in the laboratory to prove the
53 | hypothesis by running the test over and over again to
54 | show the data will always perform the way the
55 | hypothesis states.
56 | Unfortunately, once historians have developed a
57 | hypothesis as to why events occurred in a particular way,
58 | they cannot run an experiment over and over again to
59 | prove the hypothesis. Historians' hypotheses cannot be
60 | tested the way scientists' are. Therefore, there is always
61 | an element of uncertainty in what historians write.
62 | Historians must rely on careful research and analysis
63 | of information. They must be aware of their own personal
64 | views and try to be objective.
65 | Information such as the statement about Columbus
66 | becomes important only when used to support a
67 | hypothesis; it is of little significance alone. As you study
68 | history, you must learn the facts (data), but a fact is
69 | meaningful only when it helps to support a hypothesis
70 | about how past events occurred. As a student of history,

[1]*hypothesis* A calculated guess; an improved theory or explanation offered
as a way to understanding.

71 | you need to understand the hypotheses the writer of
72 | history is supporting, and judge how well they are proven
73 | by the facts presented. Then you need to ask if there are
74 | additional facts that might disprove the hypothesis.
75 | In conclusion, historians do not think of history as a
76 | mere collection of facts but rather as a series of hypotheses
77 | or explanations of the past supported by factual evidence.
78 | Historians often attempt to keep their personal biases
79 | out of their interpretation but it always is present.
80 | Because there is no way to finally prove what exactly
81 | happened in the past, there are often several explanations
82 | or interpretations of the past. Historians often disagree.
83 | Have you ever experienced a situation in which you and
84 | a friend, or you and your parents, disagreed and each
85 | presented an explanation with evidence that the other
86 | person would not accept? That can happen in history.
87 | As you read on, think what the hypotheses of the author
88 | are, and ask yourself how sound the evidence is to support
89 | the position presented.

90 **Introduction**

91   We are a nation of immigrants. Some of you
92 reading this book may be immigrants yourselves;
93 most of you will know people in your communities
94 from Asia, Latin America, or Europe, who recently
95 came to America as immigrants. All of us have
96 ancestors who were immigrants—some voluntary,
97 some forced. The immigrant experience is one that all Americans
98 have shared from the earliest to arrive—the Native Americans—
99 to the most recent arrivals from Cambodia, El Salvador, or East
100 Germany.

101   We will begin this study of American History with a brief
102 look at the first immigrants, the ancestors of today's Native
103 Americans, and those who followed before the arrival of
104 Christopher Columbus. By realizing we all share in some way
105 this immigrant experience, and that it is still a current issue,
106 the past will become closer and easier to understand.

> What does the introduction reveal about the purpose and content of this chapter?

107 I. NATIVE AMERICAN IMMIGRANTS

108 The First Immigrants

109   The first immigrants who came to the North American
110 continent were the nomadic[1] ancestors of the Native Americans.
111 By the best estimates of historians,
112 sometime around 50,000 years ago, *Native Americans*
113 several related groups began crossing *arrive in North*
114 the Bering Sea over a land bridge *America over a land*
115 between Siberia and Alaska. From there *bridge. They were the*
116 they moved south and east, and their *first to "discover" the*
117 descendants populated the North and *lands of the Americas.*
118 South American continents.

119   These first groups were nomads who hunted animals and
120 gathered fruits and berries. During the last Ice Age they moved
121 south away from the cold. Later, as the ice receded, the land
122 bridge over which they had come was flooded, cutting the
123 new arrivals off from their places of origin.

124   This pattern of separation from home, from all that was
125 familiar, has been repeated over and over again in the history
126 of the Americas. Can you think what it would be like to be
127 completely cut off from all familiar places? All immigrants
128 share this experience.

129   What would such immigrants bring with them, either now
130 or 50,000 years ago? Many have brought just what they could
131 carry. Often that is not much, and in the case of the first
132 immigrants it may have been little more than furs for clothing,
133 some crude hunting tools, and perhaps baskets or fur sacks for
134 gathering food.

135   The most important thing immigrants brought with them
136 was what they knew—the skills they had developed. For these
137 first Native American immigrants it was hunting and tracking
138 skills, knowledge of fire, and tools of stone and bone.

139   They also had language. After thousands of years of separa-
140 tion from their relatives in Siberia, the languages of the Native
141 Americans throughout the western hemisphere became greatly
142 varied, with little resemblance to each other, and none with
143 that of Siberia.

---

[1]*nomadic* Wandering; nomadic tribes are not settled and move from place
to place usually in search of food or to find food for their animals.

144   In spite of this separation, it is interesting to note that the
145 descendants of these earliest inhabitants living in Siberia and
146 North America developed similar ways of dealing with their
147 environment. At a museum of the native peoples in Irkurst,
148 Siberia, in Russia, you can see snow shoes and leather moccasins
149 very much like those developed by Native Americans. It is
150 doubtful that the idea for these items came to America with the
151 first nomads, but peoples in similar circumstances developed
152 similar ideas to deal with their environment.

153 ## Differing Cultures
154   All immigrants have had to adapt
155 to their new environment. As the   *Native Americans*
156 nomadic bands spread out to different   *develop different*
157 parts of the two continents, they   *cultures.*
158 changed their ways of living and slowly
159 developed different cultures. By 5,000 years ago the beginnings
160 of many such cultural groupings could be identified in the
161 Americas, and several of these developed into highly complex
162 civilizations. The most famous of these are the Aztec and
163 Mayan civilizations in Mexico and Central America, and the
164 Inca civilization in Peru. In the United States there were many
165 different Native American cultures[2]. The Pueblo culture of the
166 southwest (Arizona, New Mexico, and Colorado), and the
167 Algonquian culture of the northeast are significant examples. In
168 each of these geographic areas, the Native Americans developed
169 cultures and patterns of behavior that allowed for highly suc-
170 cessful ways of life.

171 ## Mayan, Aztec, and Inca
172   Mayan civilization was in decline
173 by the time Spanish explorers arrived   *Mayan, Aztec,*
174 in the 16th century (1500s). It was an   *and Inca cultures*
175 urban culture with cities dominated by   *are all city based*
176 large stone pyramid-temples. Large   *civilizations.*
177 tracts of land were cultivated. Mayans
178 had invented writing and a system of mathematics. The Aztecs,
179 a more warlike civilization, had come to dominate Mexico and

---

[2]*culture* A set of beliefs and patterns of behavior developed by a group of
people. These appear in their religious, artistic, social, and political attitudes and are supported by their material productions.

180 most of the areas of Mayan civilization by 1500. Their capital,
181 Tenochtitlan, (Mexico City is built on the site) was one of the
182 great cities of the age. The gold and silver of the empire was
183 collected there. In Peru the Incas had a flourishing urban-
184 based civilization that controlled large areas of the Andes.

185 These civilizations, while extremely important for under-
186 standing the history of Mexico and all of the Americas, are not
187 as directly related to United States history as the cultures of
188 the Pueblos and Algonquians.

189 ## Pueblo

190 The culture of the Pueblos revolved around their villages.
191 Pueblos are villages of multi-storied buildings and were built
192 with defense in mind. Some, such as Pueblo Bonito, stand in
193 valleys as large isolated structures with windowless solid walls
194 facing out. Connected houses and
195 rooms built against these outside walls
196 face a yard where outdoor life centered
197 safe from attack. Other pueblos were
198 built on the sides of cliffs or, as with
199 the Hopis, on mesas[3].

Pueblo dwellers evolve very complex political, social, and religious organizations.

200 Often hundreds of people lived within one pueblo. Pueblo
201 dwellers were dependent on agriculture, and not hunting, for
202 survival. Men did this work while the women prepared the food
203 and cared for children. Politically each pueblo was independent
204 and was run by a man's council.

205 Religion centered around the cultivation of crops and there
206 were elaborate ceremonies and rituals, often with dancing, to
207 celebrate planting, harvesting, and to bring rain. Many of
208 these ceremonies continue today as part of the rich culture of
209 the various tribes who still live in pueblos in the southwest,
210 and outsiders may attend these religious ceremonies.

211 As you watch the religious dances of, for instance, the Hopis,
212 you are struck by the intricacy of the ritual, by the soberness
213 and deep feelings of the participants, and by their great need
214 for favorable conditions for their agriculture.

---

[3]*mesas* Flat plateaus with steep sides.

215   You can also appreciate how different these traditions
216 seemed to the Spanish who entered the Southwest after 1500.
217 Even today, when TV exposes us to all the cultures of the
218 world, we often find it difficult to accept what is different. It is
219 this experience of being different that all immigrants experience.
220 The Spaniards found it difficult to accept the culture of the
221 Pueblo peoples, yet it was a highly developed culture long before
222 they came. That many pueblos still exist is a credit to the peoples
223 of this earlier civilization in what became the United States.

224 ## Algonquian

225   The Native Americans who greeted the Europeans on the
226 Atlantic coast also lived in villages. The villages of those tribes
227 in the Algonquian language group were built of wood and
228 other perishable materials, and only archaeological evidence
229 remains of them. The villages were often surrounded by wooden
230 posts forming a wall for defense. An extended family lived in
231 a single house. The female members remained in the home in
232 which they were born, and males joined their wife's families.
233 This arrangement is referred to as matrilineal.

234   The way societies form families—matrilineally or patrilin-
235 eally—is important because it reveals how important males
236 and females are within the society, how social power is distrib-
237 uted, and often how political and economic power is held. For
238 instance, Algonquian women did the agricultural work for the
239 tribe, could become political leaders of the tribe, and often
240 were the religious leaders.

241   The religious beliefs of the Algonquians, as is natural with
242 any agricultural people, focused on the crops. They worshipped
243 the forces of nature involved with
244 planting and harvesting. The Native   *The Algonquians live*
245 Americans had an understanding of a   *in a close relationship*
246 close relationship between humans   *with nature.*
247 and their natural environment.

248   One Iroquois chief—the Iroquois are a tribe of the Algonquian
249 group—remarked that the Iroquois planned for the "seventh
250 generation," and not just for the next year or two. Planning
251 for the seventh generation suggests a realization that actions
252 have long range effects that must be considered. As we face
253 environmental crises, some scholars suggest we could have

254 learned much if we had tried to understand the religious
255 teachings of the agriculturally based Native American societies
256 of the northeast, or of the Pueblos.

257   The Europeans did not understand, or appreciate, the
258 complexity and significance to the Native Americans of their
259 religious beliefs. The two cultures came into conflict, as often
260 happens when two cultures meet or when immigrants from
261 a different cultural tradition arrive. Usually the minority is
262 persecuted by the intolerant majority, but as we shall see in
263 the case of the Europeans coming to the Americas, the minority
264 view triumphed. This was due to many factors, and has meant
265 the loss to us of ideas from which we might have learned.

266 Evidence of Pre-Columbian Contacts

267   There is now evidence to support the idea that many Native
268 American cultures had contacts with Africans and Europeans long
269 before the "discovery" of America by Christopher Columbus.
270 These contacts appear to have been peaceful. There is no evidence
271 for continual trade. What ideas were exchanged is not clear,
272 but the appearance of clay figurines with distinctly Negroid
273 features in Aztec art before 1500 AD, and of inscriptions in
274 Egyptian hieroglyphs and Celtic writing in New England,
275 prove there were contacts.

276   Another bit of information that is difficult to account for,
277 except in terms of contact with Europe, is the fact that the
278 arrangement of stars we call the Big Dipper was referred to as
279 the Great Bear by the ancient Greeks, the Romans, and the
280 Native Americans of New England. This is attested to by Cotton
281 Mather, a minister in Boston in colonial days, who asked the
282 natives in Boston what they knew of navigation. In their
283 explanation they referred to the Big Dipper as the Bear, and
284 described how they used the North Star and the Great Bear (Big
285 Dipper) in finding direction. We can understand how different
286 people would use the North Star but what makes this remark-
287 able, and supports the idea of contacts, is the fact the stars in
288 the Big Dipper are not arranged to look like a Bear except by the
289 greatest stretch of the imagination.

290 KEY POINT TO REMEMBER

291 Native American peoples had developed sophisticated civiliza-
292 tions long before the arrival of European settlers or explorers.

293 LINKS FROM THE PAST TO THE PRESENT

294 1. All Americans or their ancestors share the immigrant expe-
295   rience, giving us all something in common.
296 2. Native American religious beliefs provide insights that can
297   be helpful in the environmental crisis.

298 DATES

299 50,000 years ago—ancestors of Native Americans crossed from
300   Siberia to North America.
301 5,000 years ago—Native Americans developed urban-based civi-
302   lizations.
303 c.[4] 300–900 AD[5] Mayan culture developed in southern Mexico.
304 c. 1500 AD—Aztec culture flouished in Mexico; Inca culture
305   thrived in Peru.

306 QUESTIONS

307 *Identify each of the following:*

308 Mayan   Pueblo
309 Aztec   Algonquian
310 Inca   Pueblo Bonito

> Use the following questions to help determine what information you need to learn in the previous subsections, which contain the answers to these questions.

311 *True or False:*

312 1. The Mayans had conquered the Aztecs before
313   the first Europeans arrived.
314 2. As we face environmental crises, we realize we
315   could have learned how to treat our environ-
316   ment better from the Algonquians.

---

[4]*c.* An abbreviation for circa (about); it is used before a date to indicate the date is approximate and not exact.

[5]*AD* Designation of time in the Christian calendar, which begins counting with the birth of Jesus Christ. Thus, AD stands for the Latin *Anno Domino*—"in the year of our Lord."—Many nations today accept this system of dating even when not practicing Christians. The letters CE, standing for the Common Era, are sometimes used in place of AD.

3. All Americans or their ancestors came to America as immigrants either voluntarily or under force.

4. Before the arrival of European immigrants, no cities were built by Native Americans.

Multiple Choice:

1. The Pueblos of the southwestern United States were built
   a. high up on mountains.
   b. on islands.
   c. on mesas and cliffs and in valleys.

2. The first Native American immigrants to the Americas brought with them
   a. only the ability to communicate.
   b. fur clothing, hunting tools and baskets, hunting skills, fire, and communication.
   c. their relatives and their tents and packages.

3. The religious beliefs of both the Pueblos and the Algonquians centered on
   a. the forces of nature involved in the production of crops.
   b. successful hunting expeditions.
   c. witchcraft involved in matrilineal descent.

4. The fact the Big Dipper is called the Great Bear by both Europeans and Algonquians suggests
   a. the Big Dipper can be seen by both groups at night.
   b. the North Star is important for navigation.
   c. there was contact between Europe and America before Columbus.

ANSWERS

| True or False: | 1. F | 2. T | 3. T | 4. F |
| Multiple Choice: | 1. c | 2. b | 3. a | 4. c |

346 II. EUROPEAN IMMIGRANTS

347   The first European immigrants to the New World, of whom
348 we have any clear evidence, came from Northern Europe. They
349 are usually referred to as the Vikings or Norsemen, and their
350 visits and small settlements in Greenland, Nova Scotia, and
351 New England are dated about 1000 AD. Contacts between the
352 Norsemen and the Algonquian groups
353 lasted for the next 400 years. Recently   *The Celts and*
354 evidence has been found that long   *Vikings make contact*
355 before the Vikings, immigrants from   *with the New World.*
356 the Celtic[1] lands of Europe had settled
357 in the area of New England.

358 The Celts

359   Two questions the historian would immediately ask on
360 reading this last sentence are "What is the evidence?" and
361 "Why is this information important?" The best way to answer
362 the second question is to answer the first.
363   Evidence of settlements during the period of the Roman
364 Republic (509–31 BC) by the Celtic peoples comes from inscrip-
365 tions found at a number of locations
366 in the northeast, from Algonquian   *Celtic peoples visit*
367 tales of ancestors who came from   *the New World*
368 "across the sea" rather than on the   *during the period of*
369 overland bridge, from circles of stones   *the Roman Republic.*
370 in North America that are similar to
371 Stonehenge in England, and from the facial features of the
372 Algonquians, which are as much like European features as they
373 are like the features of the western Native American tribes.
374   The latter point suggests that the Algonquians were a mixed
375 group and not pure descendants of those who came across the
376 land bridge from Siberia. They probably exchanged ideas with
377 other peoples when both were at an early stage of civilization.
378 The Algonquians may well have learned about navigation and
379 the use of the North Star and of the Great Bear from the Celts.

---

[1]*celtic* Civilization found in Western France, Southern England, and Ireland
about 1000 BC. Stonehenge in England was built by the Celts.

380 **The Vikings**

381   The story of the Vikings or Norsemen is more likely to be
382 known by Americans than that of the Celts. It is often included
383 in history textbooks because there is more evidence for their
384 visits and settlements. There are written references to travel to
385 North America in the archives[2] of Denmark.

386   Eric the Red, who was exiled from Iceland, founded a
387 settlement in Greenland about 1000 AD. According to the *Sagas*
388 or old stories of Scandinavia, his son, Leif Ericson, explored the
389 coast of North America. Several settle-
390 ments were established, with some
391 evidence suggesting the Norsemen
392 penetrated as far as Minnesota either
393 coming down from Hudson Bay or
394 going west through the Great Lakes.

A Norseman, Leif Ericson, explores the coast of North America, and colonies are established.

395   Contacts with the Northeast continued for many years. A
396 Danish court record states that in 1354 a search party was sent
397 to locate a settlement on the coast of Greenland. Apparently
398 the settlement had been destroyed, or there had been no contact
399 with it for some time. After that time, contacts between the
400 Norse settlements in North America and Europe appear to have
401 ceased, and the next immigrants came from southern Europe.

402 **Why Was Contact Lost?**

403   Why did these contacts cease, and
404 why weren't they widely known
405 throughout Europe? We do not know
406 for certain, but historians have offered
407 many hypotheses. These include the
408 growth of new ideas during the
409 Renaissance[3] and the rise and spread of Islam[4]. There is, how-
410 ever, no general agreement. Thus the answer, as so often in
411 history, is hidden in mystery.

Historians offer different hypotheses as to why contact was lost.

---

[2]*archives* Official government records.

[3]*Renaissance* The period of time in Europe between the Middle Ages and the
    Modern Era. The time of the Renaissance varied in different parts of Europe.

[4]*Islam* The religion of which Mohammed is the prophet. Mohammed lived
    and heard the word of God in Mecca and Medina, Saudi Arabia. From
    there the faith of Islam was spread by conquests from Spain to Indonesia.
    It is still the major faith in North Africa, the Near East, Pakistan, and
    Indonesia and is widespread throughout the world.

412 Re-establishing Contact

413   Slowly conditions changed and new views developed as
414 they always do. The period we call the Renaissance replaced
415 the Middle Ages. The Renaissance began in Italy around 1300
416 AD and slowly spread to Northern and
417 Western Europe. Among the many   *Renaissance attitudes*
418 philosophical ideas of the Renaissance,   *encourage new*
419 new attitudes toward the individual,   *explorations.*
420 and the concept of a secular[5] nation
421 state were most important. The former encouraged individual
422 initiative, manifested in the individual exploits of discoverers,
423 explorers, and conquerors. The latter encouraged the growth
424 of what we consider a modern nation.

425   The Renaissance provided impetus for the explorations of
426 the Portuguese and provided ideas and new sailing techniques,
427 which Christopher Columbus used on his voyages. Another
428 impetus to Portuguese exploration was a response to new
429 economic conditions brought about by both the earlier Crusades
430 and the Renaissance.

431   The Crusades had directed attention away from Northern
432 Europe towards the eastern Mediterranean. Although the
433 Crusades failed, and Christian Europe could not dislodge the
434 followers of Mohammed from the eastern Mediterranean, they
435 did introduce new ideas and new goods from Asia to Europe.
436 The Italians of Venice and Genoa traded with the Islamic peoples
437 for goods like silks and spices, and devel-
438 oped a near monopoly[6] of the trade.

439   After 1400 the Portuguese rulers   *Portuguese explorers*
440 began to look for a route to Asia along   *sail around Africa to*
441 the African coast, but they had no idea   *establish a sea route*
442 as to how large Africa would be.   *to Asia.*

443   New instruments—the magnetic compass and the astro-
444 labe, which allows the sailor to determine latitude—helped
445 navigators on these explorations. They were also aided by the
446 development of a new type of ship, the caravel, which could
447 sail against the wind.

---

[5]*secular* Having to do with worldly as opposed to spiritual or religious concerns.

[6]*monopoly* Exclusive possession of anything; control of the supply of any
   commodity or service in a given market or area that permits the holder
   of the monopoly to set prices.

448 As so often in history, inventions helped create change.
449 Prince Henry the navigator, son of King John I of Portugal, is
450 given credit for beginning these explorations, which became
451 very profitable as the Portuguese brought African products to
452 Europe. They introduced the first black slaves into Europe,
453 thus beginning the era of Black Slavery. Eventually, in 1488
454 Bartolomeu Dias rounded the southern tip of Africa, and in
455 1498 Vasco da Gama sailed around Africa to India.

456 The Portuguese had found a new route to the riches of
457 Asia. But this was not the only possible route. Christopher
458 Columbus had another idea.

459 ## Christopher Columbus

460 Christopher Columbus was born in or near the Italian
461 town of Genoa. His parents were wool weavers, but Columbus
462 became a sailor and developed a vision that changed the
463 course of history. Columbus' idea had been rejected by the
464 Portuguese by whom he had been employed as a sailor. They
465 were not interested in financing an expedition across the ocean
466 because they were finding success along the African coast.
467 Columbus therefore went to Ferdinand and Isabella of Spain.

468 After several years, the rulers of
469 Spain agreed to help finance a voyage
470 westward from Spain to Japan and on
471 to India. The result is the famous first
472 voyage of Christopher Columbus and
473 his three sailing ships, the *Nina*, *Pinta*,
474 and *Santa Maria*. He touched land, probably in the Bahamas,
475 and named the first island he touched San Salvador.

Ferdinand and Isabella of Spain agree to finance a voyage by Christopher Columbus.

476 While many others had already come to the Americas, his
477 trip was followed by an ever increasing number of voyages, the
478 stories of which spread throughout Western Europe. Soon, the
479 rapidly developing nation states of Western Europe—Spain,
480 France, and England—were involved in a race to find a way
481 through the Americas and on to Asia.

482 To the Europeans it seemed that Columbus had "discovered
483 a new world." It changed history. We know, however, that
484 many immigrants and discoverers had already come to this new
485 world of the Americas. It had already been "discovered" many
486 times. Columbus came at a time in which many technical

487 developments in sailing techniques
488 and communication made it possible
489 to report his voyages easily and to
490 spread the word of them throughout
491 Western Europe. It was also at a time of
492 growing economic rivalries between the
493 developing nation states. They were all
494 seeking new wealth, and this eventually
495 led to a rivalry for the establishment of
496 colonies in the Americas.

Columbus is often credited with "discovering a new world," but he merely encountered what was already discovered by Native Americans and others.

497 Spanish Explorers

498   Columbus made four voyages to
499 the west, and explored the Caribbean
501 and Latin American area extensively.
502 He died in 1506, still certain he had
503 arrived at the coast of Asia, and his Spanish settlement in Santo
504 Domingo became the base for many expeditions.

Spaniards explore the Americas and sail around the world.

505   Two important Spanish expeditions were those led by Ponce
506 de Leon, who conquered Puerto Rico in 1508–9 and explored
507 Florida in 1513, and by Vasco Nunez de Balboa, who crossed the
508 Isthmus of Panama and saw the Pacific in 1513. After extensive
509 explorations along the coast, the Spanish began the conquest
510 of Central and South America.

511   In 1519 Ferdinand Magellan, a Portuguese sailing for Spain,
512 started on an expedition around the world. Although Magellan
513 was killed, the expedition returned to Spain in 1522. Magellan's
514 expedition proved that the earth was round, and that the lands
515 visited by Columbus were not Asia.

516 John Cabot

517   The first voyage west not sponsored
518 by Spain was that of John Cabot, an
519 Italian who lived in Bristol, England.
520 His two voyages, in 1497 and 1498,
521 were supported by English merchants

English claims to North America are established by voyages of John Cabot.

522 and by an agreement with the English King, Henry the VII.
523 John Cabot sailed along the coasts of Newfoundland and New
524 England as far south as Delaware Bay, claiming this territory
525 for England and providing the basis for English claims to
526 North America.

Summary

After the voyages of Christopher Columbus reacquainted the Europeans with the Americas, the nations of Western Europe undertook many voyages to this "New World." Based on these expeditions, England, France, Spain, and the Netherlands all laid claim to large areas of the Americas in spite of the fact that the areas claimed were inhabited by Native Americans whose ancestors had come to the Americas as immigrants thousands of years before Columbus. The historian when writing history must create hypotheses based on evidence to explain the past. Evidence such as the shared experience as immigrants by the ancestors of all Americans needs to be included if the hypotheses are to be judged adequate.

> Use the important summary information that follows to help determine what is essential for you to learn from this unit.

KEY POINT TO REMEMBER

Christopher Columbus did not "discover" America. It had been discovered by the Native Americans and had been known to the Celtic peoples and Vikings. His voyages reacquainted Europeans with the American continent.

LINKS FROM THE PAST TO THE PRESENT

1. The Renaissance inspired individualism, which has been a hallmark of American society.
2. Throughout history, inventions, ranging from the plow to the stirrup to the atomic bomb, have led to major historical changes.

PEOPLE TO REMEMBER

Christopher Columbus Italian explorer; re-established regular contact between Europe and the Americas. His voyages from Spain to the Caribbean started in 1492.

559 **DATES**

560 Before 31 BC—Celts visited Americas.

561 c. 1000 AD—Norsemen visited Americas.

562 1492—First voyage of Columbus.

563 1519—Magellan's expedition circled the world.

564 **QUESTIONS**

565 *Identify each of the following:*

566 Crusades   Vasco de Gama

567 Middle Ages   Ferdinand and Isabella

568 Renaissance   Christopher Columbus

569 Islam   John Cabot

570 *True or False:*

571 1. The Portuguese were not interested in Christopher Columbus'

572   ideas of sailing west because they were pursuing a route to

573   India around Africa.

574 2. Sagas are the great stories of exploration written by the Celts.

575 3. The Portuguese introduced the first black slaves into modern

576   Europe.

577 4. Ponce de Leon conquered Puerto Rico.

578 5. Ferdinand Magellan sailed around the world and reported

579   to Ferdinand and Isabella that the world was round.

580 *Multiple Choice:*

581 1. Evidence of Celtic settlement in North America includes

582   a. facial features of the Algonquians and inscriptions.

583   b. circles of stones like Stonehenge in England.

584   c. both of the above.

585 2. Viking contacts with America

586   a. lasted for many years.

587   b. were very limited.

588   c. came only on the island of Greenland.

589 3. Portuguese explorations were helped by
590   a. the Italians of Genoa and Venice.
591   b. African slaves who sailed the ships.
592   c. new instruments—the compass and astrolabe—and a
593   new ship design—the caravel.

594 4. The rulers of Spain agreed to
595   a. finance Christopher Columbus' voyage westward.
596   b. repay Christopher Columbus for any expenses he had
597   on his voyage.
598   c. send immigrants to America.

599 5. News of Christopher Columbus' voyages spread through-
600   out Europe because of
601   a. the invention of the steamship.
602   b. the conquest of Western Europe by Islam.
603   c. recent inventions in communication and the ideas of
604   the Renaissance.

605 ANSWERS
606   True or False: 1. T   2. F   3. T   4. T   5. F
607 Multiple Choice: 1. c   2. a   3. c   4. a   5. c

PRACTICE READING 8: WORLD LITERATURE

THE FALL OF ROME AND THE RISE OF CHRISTIANITY

THE DECLINE OF CLASSICAL CULTURE

The power of the Roman Empire, which had given political stability to the Western World (the *Pax Romana*), had also insured a cultural unity for many centuries because of its adoption in essence of Greek religious, literary, and philosophical traditions. But from the high point of the Augustan or Golden Age (30 B.C.–14 A.D.), which had produced Virgil, Horace, Livy, and Ovid, and the somewhat dimmer glories of the Silver Age (14–117), whose literary lights were Seneca, Martial, Tacitus, Juvenal, and Epictetus, a slow decline of Roman preeminence took place. Roman bureaucracy became increasingly inefficient, and emperors who fancied themselves more and more in the roles of oriental despots were in the main unable to make headway against barbarian inroads at the borders of the empire and against social and economic unbalance within. Recognizing the growing power of Christianity and perhaps hoping that it would act as an integrating force, the Emperor Constantine gave up the Roman imperial pretensions to divinity, put the Christian monogram on the banners of his troops, and thus in the year 330 made Christianity the official Roman religion. He did indeed succeed in reuniting the Empire, which had been split into Eastern and Western segments in 284, but his placing the capital at Byzantium on the Bosphorus was in itself indicative of a waning power.

> Scan the entire chapter, paying special attention to the bold-faced sub-headings. What are the general topics covered in this unit? Are any of them familiar to you? Are they interesting? Are they challenging? Look for any special features that indicate that information is especially important for you to focus on, such as boxes surrounding the material.

31   The final abandonment of the West by the Roman Empire
32 in 476 left Europe in a chaotic state with a shifting population
33 organized only in barbaric tribal units, in remnants of old
34 Roman civic groups, or in the growing religious centers of
35 Christianity. The common people sought, wherever possible,
36 the protection of a local ruler, bishop, city official, or tribal
37 chief. The resulting division of civilization into small units
38 ruled by an overlord, together with the inevitable alliances
39 made by the members of the ruling class, created the feudal
40 system with its innate disposition to oppose any possible
41 political unification into nationhood and its sharply drawn
42 distinction between nobleman and serf.

43   From the sixth to the eighth century, organized scholarship,
44 education, law, government, and the other accoutrements of
45 civilization seemed to have disappeared, but there remained
46 nevertheless a few individuals and groups who preserved and
47 handed down the classical tradition of the past. Frowned upon
48 by the Church, pagan books and pagan scholarship gradually
49 disappeared, and in such an uncertain world the impetus to
50 original creation lapsed. But stories, such as the legends of
51 Homer, remained alive in human memories to be written
52 down later in medieval romances; and the dream of the
53 restoration of the Roman Empire haunted the European mind
54 until well past the Renaissance.

55   During this interval of turmoil, the Church was mainly
56 responsible for the preservation of the formal learning of the
57 past. Although repudiating pagan knowledge, Churchmen
58 were forced to rely on the heritage of Greece and Rome as the
59 only educational training available. Consequently, it was classical
60 training that nurtured the organizing talent of the Church,
61 and Christians whose natural bent was toward scholarship
62 compiled encyclopedic works that were uncritical compendiums
63 of pagan learning dressed in Christian clothes. When formal
64 education reasserted itself, principally within the Church, the
65 typical curriculum followed the guide of the Neoplatonist
66 Capella in dividing the fields of knowledge into the *trivium*
67 (grammar, rhetoric, dialectic) and the *quadrivium* (geometry,
68 arithmetic, astronomy, music). In his *Marriage of Philology and*
69 *Mercury*, Martianus Capella (5th C.) presented this material in

70 the favorite medieval form of an allegory in which the seven
71 liberal arts are figured as presents to the bride. For other text-
72 books, the early Middle Ages relied on Boethius (c. 480–520),
73 who translated much of Aristotle and wrote commentaries on
74 arithmetic, geometry, music, and logic. Cassiodorus (c. 490–
75 c. 583) compiled Church history, commentaries on scripture,
76 and theological treatises that owe much to the spirit of Aristotle's
77 organizing talent. Around 530, Benedict of Nursia founded at
78 Monte Cassino a library of both secular and religious works.
79 Members of monastic orders laboriously copied such books
80 and became the principal publishers of the Middle Ages.

81   Of the many classical works so preserved, only a few appear
82 to have been generally known, but they remained safe until
83 their rediscovery by the humanists of the early Renaissance.
84 The most popular medieval encyclopedia was compiled by
85 Isidore of Seville (d. 636), a Christian bishop who organized a
86 voluminous mass of pagan and Christian learning, often from
87 the least reliable sources, into a series of books, of which the
88 *Etymologies* became the first essential of all libraries for centuries
89 to come.

90   The survival of Platonism also played its part in the vigor-
91 ous movement known as Neoplatonism. The essential idea of
92 this half-philosophy, half-religion is best expressed in Plato's
93 *Symposium*:

94   And the true order of going, or being led by
95   another, to the things of love, is to begin from the
96   beauties of earth and mount upwards for the sake of
97   that other beauty, using these as steps only, and from
98   one going on to two, and from two to all fair forms,
99   and from fair forms to fair practices, and from fair
100   practices to fair notions, until from fair notions he
101   arrives at the notion of absolute beauty, and at last
102   knows what the essence of beauty is.

103   Plato held that ultimate reality resides in absolute ideals
104 like truth and beauty, earthly truths and beauties being but
105 transitory shadows from which a glimpse of the absolute may
106 be caught. The chief distinction of Neoplatonism, as well as

107 the many Gnostic creeds of the time, was the sense of mystic
108 rapture to be experienced in climbing the ladder of love from
109 earthly things to the vision of Essence, and in the elaborate
110 mystical symbolic details with which the stages of approach
111 into the heart of the mystery were decorated. The Pythagorean
112 doctrine of numbers was also enlisted to illustrate the essential
113 abstraction of the doctrine. The number *one*, represented geo-
114 metrically by the point, is the essence of abstraction. *Two*, rep-
115 resenting the line, possesses the earthly quality of length but,
116 having no thickness, is still in the domain of the abstract. The
117 number *three* symbolizes the triangle or first plane figure. *Four*
118 is the elementary number of solids. As the numbers progress
119 they image the multiple earthly reflections of the Divine Idea,
120 which is unity. Neoplatonism became known in Christian
121 Europe mainly through the Greek Porphyry (c. 233–c. 304) who
122 was the devoted disciple of Plotinus, chief among the founders
123 of Neoplatonism. Much of the Platonic spirit also survived in
124 Christianity itself.
125   Later, another source of learning became available at the
126 periphery of Christian Europe in the rise and expansion of
127 Moslem power. Islam conquered most of what was left of the
128 Roman Empire of the East, dominated the eastern Mediter-
129 ranean for part of the seventh century, and had control of all
130 Spain to the Pyrenees by the eighth century. Assimilating and
131 retaining through Syrian translations much of the Hellenism
132 that remained in the Eastern or Byzantine Empire, the Arabs
133 revived and expanded the scientific and rational attitude of
134 Greece, and added a great deal that was peculiarly their own,
135 such as their attainments in mathematics and medicine. One of
136 the greatest of Moslem schools at Cordova in Spain disseminated
137 its influence throughout the Christian world through students
138 who came there to study, and, particularly in the later Middle
139 Ages, through Averroës (1126–1198) and Avicenna (980–1037)
140 whose treatises made Aristotle the preeminent authority in
141 European thought in the twelfth and thirteenth centuries.
142   Within Christian Europe, scholarship and the intellectual
143 attitude were stimulated by Rhabanus Maurus (c. 776–856),
144 whose *De Universo* enlarges on Isidore of Seville mainly through
145 amplification of Christian learning; by Walafrid Strabo (806–849),

146 who assembled past authorities to interpret the scriptures; by
147 Alcuin (735–804), who was retained by Charlemagne to found
148 his Palace School; by Gerbert of Aurillac (c. 950–1003), who
149 became Pope Sylvester II and whose teachings include Latin
150 writers and Arabic learning; by
151 Fulbert of Chartres (c. 960–1028),
152 who founded at Chartres a school
153 of liberal learning that became
154 the outstanding educational insti-
155 tution of the time; and by John
156 Scotus Erigena (c. 810–875), who
157 interpreted Christian theology
158 in Neoplatonic terms. With the
159 renewed intellectual vitality of
160 the later Middle Ages, intense
161 theological debates and the
162 founding of scholasticism were
163 to place Aristotelian thought and
164 method in a dominant position.

> Create an outline describing the flow of information described on the previous pages. Keep your outline simple by just indicating the main points made in the text. Remember the brain learns quicker by learning the general flow of information and then linking the specific details to that flow.

165 Aristotle's Influence

166   Aristotle (384–322 B.C.), perhaps the greatest and certainly
167 the most influential of the Greek philosophers, was looked
168 upon as a final authority in many areas of thought, from logic
169 to empirical science to ethics and poetics. Even today his writ-
170 ings continue to influence scholars of philosophy, literature,
171 biology, and other disciplines. Thanks in part to his father, a
172 physician with connections in the Macedonian court, Aristotle
173 joined Plato's famed Academy in Athens in 367 B.C., first as a
174 student and later as a teacher. After Plato's death, Aristotle
175 worked in several royal courts, including that of Philip II,
176 where he became the tutor to the young Alexander the Great.
177 Aristotle returned to Athens in 335 B.C. to found the Lyceum,
178 his own school, which pursued a much broader range of subjects
179 than the Academy. He died in Chalcis in 322 B.C.
180   Although the establishment of an authentic *Corpus*
181 *Aristotelicum* is in some ways impossible, much effort has been
182 made to reconstruct the original form of Aristotle's writings.
183 The body of his work is normally divided into three groups:

184 logic, physics, and ethics. Two of Aristotle's most important texts
185 (especially in connection with the humanities), the *Metaphysics*
186 and the *Rhetoric and Poetics*, do not fit easily into any one of
187 these groups.

188   The *Rhetoric* outlines, in a theoretical manner, some of the
189 traditional methods used in the Greek schools of philosophy, as
190 well as in the political arena. Aristotle insists on the importance
191 of the creative element in an orator's formation of an argument.
192 The *Poetics* is often called the first work of literary criticism/
193 theory. Only a fragment of the complete text remains today,
194 but in it one finds a wealth of insight into the nature of poetry.
195 Contradicting Plato's criticism of poetry as imitative and
196 mimetic, Aristotle sees the poetic creation as ultimately imagi-
197 native, presenting ideal truths that rival the records of history
198 and the discoveries of science. Furthermore, poetry, in the
199 Aristotelian conception, should not be judged by the morality
200 of its subject. The much-disputed view that tragedy produces
201 a catharsis or purging in the spectator is also presented in this
202 text. Of course, it is unclear what influence this treatise may
203 have exerted on medieval poets, but we know that much of
204 the early structure of European institutions of higher learning
205 was based on the teachings of Aristotle. Neoclassical writers,
206 and especially dramatists such as
207 Racine and Corneille, often con-
208 sulted the work of Aristotle as a
209 guide to their theoretical concep-
210 tions of drama and verse form.
211 The *Poetics* continues to be at the
212 base of many modern literary
213 theories, including structuralism
214 and the neo-Aristotelian critics.

> Describe Aristotle's influence on philosophy as described in this unit. Think about his famous works listed in this unit and their significance.

215 **Classical Ancestors of Literary Genres**
216   It should be noted that most literary genres in Western litera-
217 tures have their roots in classical predecessors and models. In
218 drama, the tragedies of Aeschylus (525 B.C.–456 B.C.) such as
219 *Prometheus Bound* and *Oresteia* and those of Sophocles (496 B.C.–
220 406 B.C.), including *Antigone* and the *Oedipus* plays, established
221 dramatic principles and themes that continue to influence

222 playwrights and audiences to the present day. The comedies of
223 Aristophanes (450 B.C.–385 B.C.), such as *Clouds* and *Lysistrata*,
224 led the way toward dramatic art as an entertaining form of
225 social commentary and reform.
226   The epics of Homer, the *Iliad* and the *Odyssey* (composed
227 perhaps as early as the tenth century B.C.), were vastly influen-
228 tial on Roman epics such as Virgil's *Aeneid* and the traditions
229 of heroic narrative generally. In poetry, the lyric and ode owe
230 their early development to such poets as Pindar (522 B.C.–
231 443 B.C.) and Sappho (c. 600 B.C.). The elegy—a reflective poem
232 typically treating such topics as the loss of youth, the death of
233 a loved one, or a similarly serious contemplation—stems from
234 such early Greek poets as Callinus (seventh century B.C.),
235 Mimnermus (c. 630 B.C.), and Solon (c. 600 B.C.). Iambic and
236 satiric verse, popular throughout virtually all periods of most
237 Western literatures, took early form in the biting lampoons of
238 Archilochus (c. 650 B.C.) and Hipponax (c. 550 B.C.) Greek
239 historians established prose styles and, more generally, set
240 forth rhetorical patterns with which to assert and support an
241 argument. Herodotus (484 B.C.–424 B.C.) and Thucydides
242 (460 B.C.–400 B.C.) wrote prose histories that, in their aesthetic
243 design, rose to the stature of literature. In philosophy, the dia-
244 logues of Plato remain unsurpassed models for literary artistry.
245 The treatises of Protagoras, Prodicus, and Hippias proved influ-
246 ential for the development of prose works in the
247 fields of ethics and political science. Finally, in the
248 area of oratory, the elaborate rhetorical systems
249 evident in the speeches of Antiphon, Isocrates,
250 and the great Demosthenes have provided models
251 and a theoretical basis for the art of public speak-
252 ing and rhetorical analysis up to the present.

> Picture the classical ancestors of literary genres and their important works.

253 **The Barbarian Invaders**
254   Although barbarian only in comparison with the high civ-
255 ilizations of Greece and Rome, the term "barbarian invaders"
256 is commonly used to describe the tribes that swept over
257 Europe during the fourth and fifth centuries, bringing with
258 them traditions foreign to the Mediterranean world and con-
259 stituting the nuclei from which the modern European nations
260 were formed.

261   The largest of the national groups was referred to by Caesar
262 and Tacitus as the Germans. Migrating from the west shore of
263 the Baltic Sea, this vigorous tribal group had reached the
264 shores of the Rhine at the time of Caesar and had occupied all
265 of modern Germany and the low countries.

266   The most belligerent of the German tribes, the Goths, had
267 pushed south as far as the southern Danube basin and the Black
268 Sea by 200 A.D. Divided by the Dniester River into Ostrogoths
269 (East Goths) and Visigoths (West Goths), they were actually
270 two independent groups speaking a common language and
271 possessing a common cultural heritage. Under pressure of the
272 Huns, the Visigoths began a series of migrations that carried
273 them through Greece, Italy (where they sacked Rome in 410),
274 and finally into Spain, where they built up a strong kingdom
275 and assimilated the Roman culture already established there.
276 Their rule continued until the early parts of the eighth century,
277 when they were defeated by the Moslems and became part of
278 the mixed elements that make up the Iberian peninsula. The
279 Ostrogoths, under similar pressure, settled in Italy (Theodoric
280 the Ostrogoth became King of Italy in 493) until they were
281 defeated by the Emperor Justinian and absorbed into the
282 Byzantine Empire in 555.

283   The best integrated and least migratory of the Germans,
284 the Franks, remained close to their homes in the western
285 Rhineland, imitated the Romans in government and military
286 organization, and gradually took over Gaul as the Roman
287 occupation dwindled in strength. Their leader Clovis, who
288 ruled from 481 to 511, drove the Romans out of northern
289 France and then continued his aggression against the Ostrogoths
290 until he controlled all the territory between the Rhine and the
291 Pyrenees. After a period of internal conflict, Charles Martel,
292 son of that Pepin who had reunited all the Franks, stopped the
293 Moslem advance between Tours and Poitiers in 732. His son,
294 also named Pepin, united Franco-Germany and handed down a
295 consolidated empire to his son Charlemagne. Under the banner
296 of Christianity, Charlemagne drove the Moslems from the
297 Pyrenees as far as Barcelona and extended the boundaries of
298 the Frankish Empire south into Italy and north into Brittany.
299 Through him the tradition of the Roman Caesar was revived

300   when, in keeping with the spirit of Augustine's *City of God*, he was
301   crowned in 800 by the Pope as ruler of the Holy Roman Empire.
302   Actually, the Empire did not outlast Charlemagne's son. In 987
303   the kingdom of France passed into the hands of Hugh Capet,
304   who founded a new dynasty. But the legal line of Holy Roman
305   Emperors passed to Otto I, King of Germany, and continued
306   intermittently until 1804 as a symbol of an unrealized dream.

307   These various tribes brought with them their own legends
308   and traditions. In contrast to the Greek love of light, beauty,
309   and moderation, the Germans appear to have exalted such
310   ideals as physical vigor, courage, and loyalty. Their religions,
311   derived mainly from nature myths and an awareness of a
312   world of deprivation and danger, were based upon the cold and
313   joyless nature of both heaven and earth, and upon the endless
314   struggle of good against overpowering evil. The Christian proffer
315   of a Redeemer and the promise of a blissful immortality made
316   ready converts of a people who must also have been impressed
317   by the superior civilization of the Christian missionaries. In 341
318   Bishop Ulfilas came as a missionary to the Goths, translated
319   parts of the Bible into Gothic, and won converts even before
320   Christianity became the official religion of Rome. Other tribes
321   were converted by later contact with Christian Romans. In this,
322   as in many other ways, the Mediterranean and the northern
323   civilizations commingled, so that, by 700 "Roman" meant the
324   region around Rome; in Gaul the Franks were speaking Gallic-
325   Latin or French; in Italy Lombards and Goths modified Latin
326   into the various Italian dialects; and in Spain and Portugal
327   Latin was becoming Spanish and Portuguese. Latin, which
328   continued to be the language of the Church and the language
329   of learning (almost synonymous phrases in the Middle Ages),
330   became less rigorous, more fluid, and simpler in construction.
331   Meanwhile, the very folklore of the various barbarian tribes
332   became infused with morals and concepts obviously Christian
333   in origin.

334   **A Revised View of the Dark Ages**

335   In some traditional treatments of world history, the period
336   from the decline of the Roman Empire to the Crusades (c. 1200)
337   is described as a cultural midnight of sorts—eight hundred

338 years during which nothing of particular note happened in
339 art, music, literature, religion, or politics. This view, however,
340 misrepresents important cultural developments not only in
341 the rest of the world but in Europe as well.

342   During the supposedly "dark" ages the Mayan Indians
343 developed an advanced civilization in Central America and
344 Mexico (beginning about 300). They perfected calendars,
345 developed new mathematical and astronomical techniques,
346 built architectural wonders, and forged new mythologies and
347 religions. Not long after (320), India began its Golden Age
348 under the Gupta dynasty. In the mid-500s, the Byzantine
349 Empire reached its greatest extent and influence under Emperor
350 Justinian I (a period of cultural history idealized by Yeats in his
351 later poetry). Roman law was codified during this time, as was
352 Judaic law in the compilation of the Talmud (c. 600). In 622
353 Mohammed fled from Mecca to Medina, his "Hegira," marking
354 the beginning both of the Islamic calendar and the founding
355 of a world-wide religion. From 700 to 1000, the first great
356 black empire in Western Africa, the Ghana Empire, flourished
357 as a trading state. Entire new civilizations emerged during this
358 period, with Muslim Arabs in Africa conquering an immense
359 empire extending as far as west-central France, where they
360 were turned back by Charles Martel and the Franks in 732.

361   In Europe, Huns invaded the Baltic region about 400, driving
362 Gothic tribes before them into the far western reaches of the
363 continent and, eventually, to England. There, Patrick, Columba,
364 and Columban were responsible in the fifth and sixth centuries
365 for establishing a strong monastic tradition. Monasteries became
366 repositories for both classical and Christian learning. Celtic
367 mythology was recorded for the first time in these monastic
368 centers, and a new decorative art style was developed, as evi-
369 denced in book illumination (such as the Lindisfarne Gospels
370 and the Book of Kells, both eighth century). In contemporary
371 France and Germany, the feudal system developed under the
372 Merovingian kings. A mini-Renaissance occurred during the reign
373 of Charlemagne and the intellectual influence of the Anglo-Latin
374 scholar Alcuin (c. 732–804).

375   In the Arab Empire, a brilliant cosmopolitan civilization
376 emerged with the founding of Baghdad in 762. Lyric poetry

377 was reborn, and surviving libraries of Greek, Persian, Syrian,
378 and Sanskrit manuscripts were translated into Arabic. Baghdad,
379 Cordova, and Cairo became important centers of science,
380 medicine, and mathematics by the 900s.
381   In sum, therefore, the phrase "dark ages" should
382 not be interpreted as a blanket judgment on all
383 intellectual and cultural development during the
384 first millennium A.D. In fact, the use of the phrase
385 may stem more from ignorance of other cultures
386 and traditions than from an actual lack of cultural
387 activity during the period.

> Why according to this text should we revise our view of the dark ages? Do you agree or disagree with this? Why?

388 **The Rise of Christianity**
389   With the decline of the official and essentially lifeless
390 Roman pagan religion, mystical and highly emotional religious
391 cults from the East became increasingly popular in the Roman
392 Empire. By the second century, Phrygia, Syria, Egypt, and Persia
393 had all contributed ceremonials and rituals designed to cleanse
394 the initiate of sin and prepare him for an eternal life of beatitude.
395 Amid a welter of mystical beliefs and Neoplatonic creeds, the
396 simple teachings of Jesus of Nazareth stand out in bold relief.
397 It was not long, however, before the followers of Jesus, the
398 architects of Christianity, had adopted the solid historical
399 background of Hebraism, borrowed rituals from Greek mystery
400 cults, allied themselves philosophically with Neoplatonism,
401 and stressed the hope of immortality that was offered by the
402 competing Persian religions of Mithraism and Manichaeism.
403 From Persia, too, came the dominant Christian duality of light
404 and darkness, heaven and hell, salvation and sin, together
405 with the date chosen for Christmas and many rites and rituals.
406 Combining the intellect of Greece, the organizing talent of Rome,
407 the rich tradition of the Hebrews, the mysticism of the East,
408 and the powerful personal appeal of its founder, Christianity
409 quickly became a kind of all-inclusive religion that, in spite of
410 official Roman attempts at suppression, was easily, by the third
411 century, the most popular of religions.
412   Like its only serious rival, Mithraism, it provided ceremonies
413 by which the initiate received the emotional experience of
414 achieving salvation through mystical union with a risen

415 redeemer. The Christian was also in possession of a body of
416 doctrine or "mystery" that was understandable only to those who
417 had been purified and were worthy to partake of the sacramen-
418 tal rites. Apparently satisfying the religious instinct more than
419 any of the other mystery cults of the time, Christianity built a
420 solid organization throughout the Roman Empire. In the third
421 century each local capital was presided over by a bishop. Arch-
422 bishops controlled the larger provinces, and at the head of the
423 Church were the patriarchs in Rome, Constantinople, Jerusalem,
424 and Alexandria. Under Constantine, Christianity was proclaimed
425 the official state religion. In 451, Leo I, a Roman bishop, asserted
426 that the Bishop of Rome was the successor of Peter, the founder
427 of the church, and set up the Papacy at Rome as the supreme
428 and undisputable head of the Church. Meanwhile, learned men
429 within the Church had settled their many disagreements largely
430 through the persuasion of the then still pagan Constantine,
431 who presided over the Council of Nicaea in 375, and had built
432 a solid body of doctrine. Wealthy converts provided a sound
433 financial backing. The Church also possessed a document
434 known as the "Donation of Constantine" (proved to be a
435 forgery in 1440) by which the Emperor Constantine suppos-
436 edly conferred upon Pope Sylvester I sovereignty over the
437 western portion of the Roman Empire.

438   When Roman power declined in the West, the Church
439 became its inevitable successor. As the heir to Greek and
440 Roman culture, it possessed an intellectual superiority over the
441 semicivilized tribes of Europe. Its organization was superior to
442 that of any other power, ecclesiastical or temporal. Taking
443 advantage of the "Donation of Constantine," it held itself
444 always exempt from civil control, and succeeded at intervals
445 in actually ruling over various cities in Italy. By destroying or
446 relegating to oblivion Greek and Roman books with their
447 references to other deities and other religious and moral out-
448 looks on life, it came close to establishing itself as the sole rep-
449 resentative of God on earth. Simultaneously it established a
450 near monopoly on education, so that learning became possible
451 only through the channels of Christian education. Persecution
452 of nonbelievers eliminated opposition, and the threat of excom-
453 munication (removal from Christian salvation), though seldom

454 put into effect, acted as a cogent weapon to coerce individuals
455 and governments. As the greatest single power in Europe, the
456 Church often tended to become more concerned with earthly
457 affairs than with spiritual salvation, and attracted to itself
458 unscrupulous seekers of power whose personal lives were
459 sometimes blatantly scandalous. It also educated many
460 learned men. It was both the destroyer and preserver of classical
461 culture, destroying books that would have continued a pagan
462 tradition, but preserving many of the elements of Greek and
463 Roman learning in a world that was being overwhelmed by
464 the inroads of barbarians.

465   As opposed to the increasing worldliness of the official
466 Church, many deeply religious men renounced entirely earthly
467 pleasures to live in solitude and self-mortification. By the
468 fourth century these individual hermits or anchorites also
469 began to succumb to the organizing power of the Church and
470 formed the monastic orders with well-defined rules of com-
471 munal living. The most famous monastic regimen was the
472 work of Benedict of Nursia (c. 480–550), who founded the
473 monastery of Monte Cassino where a daily schedule
474 of routines of prayer and work, together with
475 explicit regulation of food and clothing, was put
476 in force. The monasteries, scattered throughout
477 Europe, not only acted as the most striking symbol
478 of the Christian ideal of the saintly and contem-
479 plative life but also provided a refuge where learn-
480 ing and literature could survive. Each monastery
481 had its *scriptorium*, where ancient books were
482 stored and copied and where the great majority of
483 Christian religious writings originated. Closely
484 connected with the Benedictine monasteries were
485 the schools that became, through the years, the
486 medieval universities.

> Describe the impact of the emergence of Christianity upon early literature. Are there any important people or places mentioned in this section that should be remembered? Why? What memory tool would work best for learning this material?

487 THE EARLY CHRISTIAN WRITERS

488   The official literature of Christianity begins with the records
489 of Christ and his apostles set down by the early converts to the
490 new religion. Four of the accounts of the life of Christ, known

491 as the "gospels" or "glad tidings," together with the book describ-
492 ing the *Acts of the Apostles*, the inspirational and doctrinal letters
493 written by St. Paul, and the visionary book of *Revelations*, were
494 collected by a council into the Canon known as the *New*
495 *Testament.* These "scriptures" together with all the riches of the
496 *Old Testament* formed the basis for elaboration, commentary,
497 and the creation of an intricate theology by a long line of
498 learned Churchmen known as the Church Fathers. The earli-
499 est of these patristic writings were mainly defenses of the faith
501 and attacks on rival religions, but soon turned to elaborations
502 of matters of theology and doctrine. Following the lead of Philo,
503 a devout Jew of the first century who found Neoplatonic doc-
504 trines concealed in the texts of Hebrew scriptures, various of
505 the Fathers began to write figurative interpretations of pas-
506 sages from both the *Old* and the *New Testament*, and thereby
507 not only made allegory a favorite medieval form but set the
508 tone of the kind of thinking that was to dominate the period.
509 From that time, speculation proceeded always on the basis of
510 past authority, advances being made in compiling more and
511 more interpretations of what was often originally intended as
512 the literal story of the Hebrew patriarchs. Argument similarly
513 proceeded mainly along the allegorical tradition of pointing out
514 analogies. For example, a genealogical record of ten generations
515 is explained as a veiled reference to the Ten Commandments.

516 **Origen**
517   Origen (c. 185–253) held that scripture contained a three-
518 fold meaning: corporeal (literal), psychic (applying to the soul),
519 and pneumatic (a kind of ultimate spiritual meaning). He
520 added that some passages do not contain a corporeal sense but
521 are meaningful only when interpreted figuratively, illustrating
522 by reference to the six waterpots, containing two or three
523 firkins apiece, which figure in the story of the marriage in
524 Cana (John 2:6):

525   And perhaps on this account the water-vessels
526   containing two or three firkins apiece are said to be for
527   the purification of the Jews, as we read in the Gospel
528   according to John: the expression darkly intimating,

529　with respect to those who [are called] by the apostle
530　the 'Jews' secretly, that they are purified by the word
531　of the Scripture, receiving sometimes two firkins: i.e.,
532　so to speak, the 'psychical' and 'spiritual' sense; and
533　sometimes three firkins since they have, in addition
534　to those already mentioned, also the 'corporeal' sense,
535　which is capable of [producing] edification. And six
536　water-vessels are reasonably [appropriate] to those
537　who are purified in the world, which was made in six
538　days. (*De Principiis*, IV, 1.)

539 **Ambrose**

540　Ambrose (c. 340–397) found symbolic meanings everywhere
541 and, by showing similitudes between Christian scriptures and
542 both pagan practices and the world of nature, he did much to
543 fuse pagan culture with Christian doctrine. His *Physiologus* is the
544 earliest Christian bestiary that, allegorically, teaches moral and
545 religious truths by illustrations from the animal kingdom, each
546 beast symbolizing a moral or religious truth. His *Hexameron*, a
547 series of sermons on the six days of Creation as the prototype of
548 universal history, became one of the basic Christian authorities.

549 **Jerome**

550　Jerome (c. 340–420) was converted from devotion to clas-
551 sical culture by the appearance of a visionary figure saying,
552 "You are a Ciceronian, not a Christian." A remarkable linguist,
553 scholar, and imaginative creative writer, he produced many
554 works, the most prominent being a translation of the *Old
555 Testament* into easy Latin (the *Vulgate*), a series of brief biogra-
556 phies of prominent Christians (*De Viris Illustribus*), and the
557 Lives of the Saints (*Vitae Sanctorum*). Composed for the purpose
558 of providing popular literature of an edifying nature, these
559 stories of the saints had numerous successors, which appealed
560 strongly to the imaginations and emotions of all classes of
561 people and culminated, in the thirteenth century, in the *Golden
562 Legend* by Jacopo da Voragine.

563 **AUGUSTINE (354–430)**

564 IMPORTANCE

565 Towering above these earlier writers, synthesizing the
566 doctrine of his predecessors, and creating a massive struc-
567 ture of dogma, Aurelius Augustinus remained the greatest
568 Christian authority until the thirteenth century. His rest-
569 less mind, packed with wide and varied knowledge, was
570 brought to the service of a religion in which he passion-
571 ately believed. The result was a series of extraordinary
572 writings that combine the idealism of Plato, the organiz-
573 ing impulse (if not the talent) of Aristotle, the rhetorical
574 eloquence of Cicero, and a depth of insight and feeling
575 that was peculiarly his own. He also gave the final stamp
576 of approval to allegory as a literary device and as a path-
577 way to truth, explaining that by such investigation man
578 may discover the mysteries of God which are set down in
579 scripture, and simultaneously derive a keen esthetic satis-
580 faction, for "the most hidden meanings are the sweetest."
581 He also gave impetus to the increasing use of number
582 symbolism among Christian thinkers. There being no better
583 earthly medium of expressing abstraction (and hence the
584 Divine Idea) than the relationships of numbers, the Divine
585 Plan, as indicated by the Trinity, was understood to have
586 been based on an archetypal numerical scheme whose
587 physical expression was observable in the mundane world.

588 *The Confessions*

589 Of Numidian stock, Augustine was born in northern Africa
590 of a pagan father and a Christian mother. This combination of
591 circumstances gave him an unusual opportunity for intellectual
592 and religious exploration, the extent of which is mirrored in his
593 autobiography, *The Confessions (Confessiones)*, composed around
594 397, shortly after he became a bishop. His title is employed in
595 the sense of the Christian confession of the glory of God.
596 Intended for the comfort and salvation of all mankind, this
597 volume is unusual for its period because of its highly personal
598 and frank revelations of the author's inner life. It is also
599 indicative of the important part played by Christianity in the

600 inward turning of modern literature in contrast to the objec-
601 tivity of classical literature. Ecstatic and devout in tone, inter-
602 larded with scriptural quotations, more concerned with
603 spiritual struggles than literal external fact, the *Confessions*
604 makes use of autobiography as inspiration for others to turn
605 from evil and misguided ways to the True Life. It is also a highly
606 dramatic narrative because of the long and bitter struggle it
607 unveils between Augustine's propensity for paganism and sen-
608 suality, in which he was encouraged by his father, and his
609 soul-searching spiritual and intellectual straining toward
610 Christianity and chastity, the dream of his devout and somewhat
611 overpowering mother.

612   His early years in the relatively small town of Thagaste are
613 conveyed to the reader as the accumulation of the normal
614 growing apperceptions of ordinary boyhood, to which was
615 coupled a childish unthinking faith in God instilled in him by
616 his devoted mother, Monica. His innate powerful masculinity
617 which made him rebellious and recalcitrant in his studies he
618 calls a sin against his spiritual Mother (the Church) and the
619 mother of his flesh. His father Patricius, on the other hand, was
620 apparently delighted with the indications of a potent sexual
621 nature that he had observed in the growing boy. Baptism, almost
622 administered on one occasion when he seemed mortally ill,
623 was withheld possibly because of the parental conflict in the
624 household. His father seems to have had ambitions for his son
625 to become a professional rhetorician, to which end the boy
626 was sent to the nearby city of Madaura for study.

627   The age of sixteen, although described in very vague terms in
628 the autobiography, was clearly a critical period in Augustine's
629 life. A tightening of family finances forced him to return home
630 for a year of idleness during which he "wallowed" in licentious-
631 ness, possibly including homosexuality, and joined a group of
632 "lewd young fellows" whose crimes he sought to emulate. One
633 specific account is given, together with a searching and acute
634 examination of his own motives, of the stealing of some pears,
635 a minor theft that becomes in his account a symbol of the
636 "attractiveness of beautiful bodies, in gold and silver, and all
637 *things*." He was probably alluding to this period when he refers
638 in Book VIII to his youthful prayer, "Give me chastity and con-
639 tinency, only not yet!"

640   Meanwhile, he gave sufficient promise as a student for his
641 father to send him to Carthage at the age of seventeen to con-
642 tinue his studies. During his first year he took a mistress or
643 concubine who bore him a son the next year. The child was
644 named Adeodatus, "the gift of God," and was baptised together
645 with Patricius five years later. The irregular but at that time not
646 uncommon family appears to have been a stabilizing factor in
647 Augustine's high-strung and libidinous nature. He declares
648 that he was entirely faithful to his unnamed concubine during
649 the many years they lived together. He became a teacher at
650 Carthage and found himself leaning toward the doctrines of
651 Manichaeism which, based on a principle of two opposing
652 forces of good and evil, seemed to correspond to the reality of
653 his own nature. At one time he was sought out by a Christian
654 bishop at the behest of his mother, whose prayers for her son's
655 salvation were unceasing. The bishop very wisely determined
656 to allow Augustine to find his own salvation, assuring Monica
657 that her piety would ensure the ultimate good of her son. In
658 time, Augustine became an active Manichean and remained in
659 Carthage where, until the age of twenty-eight, he studied the
660 esoteric doctrines, mainly astrological, of the East. In his twenty-
661 ninth year he met the Manichean bishop Faustus whose far-
662 famed skill in disputation proved such a disappointment to
663 Augustine that he gradually lost faith and renounced the religion.
664   Becoming disgusted as well with the licentiousness of the
665 students at Carthage, he traveled to Rome where he accepted
666 an invitation to teach rhetoric at Milan. There his mother
667 joined him and he listened eagerly to the famous Christian
668 bishop Ambrose whose sermons stimulated in him a desire to
669 attain the concept of a purer life. His approach to Christianity
670 was further hastened by reading the Pauline Epistles in which
671 Paul's own fear of the flesh clearly struck a sympathetic chord.
672 Together with his friend Alypius he studied the writings of
673 Paul and writhed in torment during a long struggle between
674 flesh and spirit. At the same time a kind of practical wisdom
675 caused his mother to arrange what must have been a finan-
676 cially and socially profitable marriage with a girl still two years
677 too young for the ceremony. Augustine apparently concurred in
678 the plans even though they forced him to send his concubine

679 back to Africa after fourteen years; "torn from him," he says.
680 She took the vow of celibacy; Augustine kept the child with
681 him. He describes his anguish, and he also confesses that, soon
682 after, he took another concubine.

683   At the age of thirty-one, he completely rejected Manichaeism
684 but was unable to accept the Christian doctrine of the cause of
685 evil until his reading of the Neoplatonists convinced him of
686 the ultimate reality of the Divine Idea, of which the physical
687 world is an imperfect copy. But the doctrine of the incarnation
688 of Christ continued to perplex him until continued study of
689 the Scriptures made him understand the role of the Son as the
690 Mediator between Divine Reality and corporeal imperfection.

691   His personal struggle with fleshly desires continued into
692 his thirty-second year, when he was strengthened by the story
693 of St. Anthony and by the conversion of Victorinus, translator
694 of the Neoplatonists Plotinus and Prophyry. At the height of
695 an intense struggle, a childish voice from a nearby house
696 repeated, "Take up and read." Interpreting this as a command
697 of God, Augustine returned to Alypius, opened the volume of
698 Paul at random, read the admonition in *Romans* XIII, 13–14,
699 to put off the flesh and to put on the Lord Jesus Christ, and
700 rushed in to his mother to tell her that her prayers had at last
701 been answered. After his miraculous conversion, in the year
702 386, he gave up his profession and sought seclusion in the
703 country to prepare himself for baptism. He was baptised at
704 Easter in his thirty-third year and joined the Church together
705 with his friend Alypius and his son Adeodatus.

706   Returning to Africa with his mother, he was with her at her
707 death at Ostia in her fifty-sixth year, receiving her dying
708 admonitions, burying her body, and finding himself secure in
709 the knowledge that she was "not altogether dead." This extra-
710 ordinary human and mystical drama is concluded in the tenth
711 book by a confession of faith, an examination of the faculty
712 of memory, and a discussion of the ways by which God is
713 known to man. Here is to be found some of Augustine's most
714 eloquent rhetoric, particularly in the magnificent paragraphs
715 beginning, "But what do I love, when I love Thee?" and con-
716 cluding, "I asked the earth and it answered me, 'I am not He'
717 . . . and I replied unto all the things which encompass the door

718 of my flesh, 'Ye have told me of my God, that ye are not He,
719 tell me something of Him.' And they cried out with a loud
720 voice, 'He made us.' " The three last books, XI–XIII, omitted in
721 some editions, elaborate on one of Augustine's favorite subjects:
722 the six days of Creation in which were allegorically disclosed the
723 mystery of the Trinity (the factors of six being one, two, three)
724 and the archetypal pattern of the Universe (whose history is
725 composed of six ages). Thus the act of Creation gave substance
726 and form to the Divine Idea.
727   The remaining years of Augustine's life began with the for-
728 mation of a monastic community in his native city where he
729 resided for three years. Then on a visit to Hippo he was per-
730 suaded by the Christians there to accept a vacant post as pres-
731 byter, from which he advanced to become Bishop. From then
732 until his death in 430, he was entirely engaged in ecclesiastical
733 duties, including the composition of voluminous works on
734 Christian doctrine and in defense of Christianity against rival
735 religions and heretical creeds, a career which brought him into
736 a controversy with Faustus in which his own previous knowl-
737 edge of Manichaeism served him in good stead.

738 *The City of God*
739   Augustine's greatest vindication of Christianity and his
740 most brilliant theological work was a labor of thirteen years
741 between 413 and 426. *The City of God (De Civitate Dei)*, as its
742 title signifies, is the new Christian state that is to take the
743 place of the decaying pagan Roman Empire. The work was
744 composed in the shadow of the terrifying event of the sack of
745 Rome in 410. At a time when Christianity was still contending
746 with paganism, Gnosticism, Neoplatonism, and the many
747 mystical faiths of Eastern origin, this invasion of the ancient
748 and almost holy city seemed to many a clear sign of punish-
749 ment by the gods for the official acceptance of Christianity.
750   Begun as an answer to such criticism, the first ten books are
751 mainly concerned with citing the misfortunes of Rome under
752 pagan gods. But in contrasting the temporal nature of Rome
753 and the Christian promises of eternity, Augustine discovered a
754 great theme in a reworking of his personal conflict between
755 flesh and spirit. This same conflict that makes a drama of his

756 *Confessions* is broadened in *The City of God* into the universal
757 conflict between the City of Man and the City of God, a struggle
758 that courses throughout all human and Divine history. He
759 therefore devotes the last twelve books to a contrast between
760 human and Divine history. His plan divides these latter books
761 into three groups of four apiece. (The number twelve, Augustine
762 explains elsewhere, is the symbol of the apostles preaching the
763 Trinity through the four parts of the world.) The first four
764 books describe the origin of the two cities in the nature of
765 Adam, the second four relate their earthly history from Cain
766 and Abel to the time of Christ, the third four predict their ulti-
767 mate conclusions at the Last Judgment.

768   The book is fascinating in its insights into the spiritual,
769 philosophical, and political turmoil of the period. It is estheti-
770 cally magnificent in its grand design, and intellectually
771 absorbing in its many intricate and ingenious arguments. It is
772 penetratingly true in its analysis of the moral conflict in all
773 human nature. It falls just short of ultimate greatness because
774 of Augustine's fatal weakness for digression on topics which
775 particularly excite his interest, most of which he treats at
776 length in his other writings and which constantly interrupt
777 the course of his main argument and the flow of his great
778 human drama. From a purely historical viewpoint, *The City of*
779 *God* is a wonderful first-hand commentary on the status of
780 early Christianity at the time of a
781 crumbling civil authority, clearly
782 indicating the dependence of
783 Christian doctrine on Platonism
784 and the uphill struggle to create
785 a solid core of doctrine amidst
786 innumerable conflicting religions
787 and philosophies.

> Who are some of the famous early Christian writers and what were their influences on literature?

---

788 ANCIUS MANLIUS SEVERINUS BOETHIUS
789 (c. 475–525)

790   Actually more a survivor of Graeco-Roman learning than
791 a member of the group of Church writers, Ancius Manlius
792 Severinus Boethius was easily the outstanding purveyor of

793 pagan knowledge to the medieval Christian world. The last of
794 the pagan philosophers, he was canonized by the Church with
795 the result that his writings became an effective bridge between
796 the two worlds. As Cassiodorus put it, with more eloquence
797 than strict precision:

798   Through your translations the music of Pythagoras
799   and the astronomy of Ptolemaeus are read by the
800   Italians; the arithmetic of Nicomachus and the geo-
801   metry of Euclid are heard by the Westerns; the theol-
802   ogy of Plato and the logic of Aristotle dispute in the
803   language of Quirinus; the mechanical Archimedes
804   also you have restored in Latin dress to the Sicilians;
805   and whatever discipline or arts fertile Greece has pro-
806   duced through the efforts of individual men, Rome
807   has received in her own language through your single
808   instrumentality.

809 Boethius was born in Rome around the year 475 under the
810 last of the Roman emperors. He grew up under King Odoacer
811 as an unusually studious lad, possibly guided by his father
812 who became consul in 487. After his father's death, he was
813 cared for by men of noble families, married the daughter of a
814 senator, and had two sons. When Theodoric the Ostrogoth
815 succeeded Odoacer, the talents and ability of Boethius made
816 him a favorite of the monarch. He became consul in 510 and
817 his two sons were made consuls in 522, an event that the
818 father describes as the height of his felicity. There is no reason
819 for not accepting his own statement that his passion for justice
820 was the cause of the misfortunes which soon followed. Towards
821 the end of the reign of Theodoric he was accused of conspiring
822 against the king in attempting to maintain the integrity of the
823 senate and restore liberty to Rome. He was condemned, sent to
824 prison where he wrote his famous *Consolation of Philosophy* (524),
825 and was executed in 525. Although there is no real evidence
826 that Boethius was a practicing Christian, succeeding centuries
827 came to regard him as a martyr who had been persecuted
828 because of his opposition to the Arian heresy held by Theodoric.
829 He was canonized as Saint Severinus, his prison became a

830 shrine, and in 996 his bones were moved to a beautiful marble
831 tomb in the Church of Saint Augustine.

832   It was the ambition of Boethius to translate all of Aristotle
833 and Plato in an attempted reconciliation of the two philoso-
834 phies. He did translate some of Aristotle, wrote commentaries
835 on works of Aristotle, Porphyry, and Cicero, and was the
836 author of several books on logic and school books on the
837 *quadrivium* (arithmetic, music, geometry, and astronomy), which
838 remained basic texts throughout the Middle Ages.

839 ### *The Consolation of Philosophy*

840 | **IMPORTANCE**
841 | Boethius's best known and most original literary
842 | composition, *The Consolation of Philosophy (Philosophiae*
843 | *Consolationis)*, comes nearest to his desire to harmonize
844 | the philosophies of the past, combining Aristotle, Plato,
845 | Stoicism, and even a faint trace of the impact of the
846 | Christian attitude. Quiet and gentle in tone, unpretentious
847 | in content and simple in exposition, the *Consolation* remains
848 | a great humanistic document, examining into truth with
849 | humility and upholding the highest moral ideals with
850 | conviction. The work, divided into five books, is an allegory,
851 | written alternately in prose and verse, and imitating the
852 | form of Capella's *Marriage of Philology and Mercury*.

853   Book I begins with a verse lament for his many sorrows. As if
854 in answer to his complaint, a woman whom he comes to recog-
855 nize as his guardian, Philosophy, comes to comfort him. From
856 his answers to her questions, she discovers that Boethius knows
857 that the world is ruled by God but that he has forgotten his
858 destiny as a man, and that this lack of self-knowledge is the
859 cause of his distress.

860   In Book II, Philosophy introduces Fortune who describes to
861 him the many blessings he has enjoyed and explains the tran-
862 sitory and uncertain nature of Fortune's gifts.

863   In Book III, Philosophy promises to lead him to true happi-
864 ness which is in God, since God, the highest good, and true
865 happiness are synonymous. It follows that real evil cannot
866 exist since it is not the wish of the omnipotent Deity.

867   In Book IV, Boethius asks the reason for the existence of
868 evil and for the apparent fact that the evil are often rewarded
869 and the virtuous punished. Philosophy explains that this is
870 true only in appearance, that actually vice is always punished
871 and virtue rewarded, and the Divine Providence is always good.

872   Book V examines the problem of the apparent logical con-
873 flict between human free will and Divine foreknowledge. It is
874 concluded that the knowledge of an event is not the cause of
875 an event, and that for God time does not exist; therefore God
876 sees past, present, and future at once as an eternal present in
877 which evil is punished and goodness is rewarded. "Wherefore
878 fly vice, embrace virtues, possess your minds with worthy
879 hopes, offer up humble prayers
880 to your highest Prince. There is,
881 if you will not dissemble, a great
882 necessity of doing well imposed
883 upon you, since you live in the
884 sight of your Judge, who behold-
885 eth all things."

> How did Boethius integrate pagan works into Christianity? What influence did this have on early literature?

886 # THE MEDIEVAL BIBLE

887   During the Middle Ages, the *Vulgate* was the Bible used in
888 churches, though rarely owned or read by common folk. This
889 translation of the Bible into "easy" or common Latin was pre-
890 pared by Jerome about the year 400. Jerome's version separated
891 the generally accepted books of the Bible (such as *Genesis*,
892 *Exodus*, *Leviticus*, and so forth) from the "Apocryphal" books
893 (including *Tobit, Baruch, Judith, I and II Maccabees*, and others),
894 which Jerome regarded as proper for spiritual growth but not
895 for use as authoritative Scripture. In 1516, Erasmus completed
896 his Greek *New Testament*, with Latin annotations. This erudite
897 approach to translation inspired other Biblical scholars to
898 undertake English translations of the Bible. In 1526, William
899 Tyndale moved to Germany to accomplish the two-volume
900 English translation of the Bible forbidden by English religious
901 authorities (and thereafter banned by the Bishop of London).
902 Tyndale as well as those involved in the printing of his Bible
903 were savagely persecuted, with eventual imprisonment and
904 execution for Tyndale himself.

905 Simultaneously in England, King Henry VIII had befriended
906 Biblical translators, and the Coverdale Bible appeared in 1535
906 with an extended dedication to the King. A later version of this
907 Bible, printed in Paris, showed in a prefacing plate the King
908 handing the Word of God to his adoring people. In 1611, the
909 King James Bible was the result of a conference of religious
910 scholars called by King James in 1604. He appointed fifty-four
911 scholars, working in six groups, to prepare the "authorized"
912 version for use in the Church of England. That version remains
913 a primary scripture of the Protestant churches to the present.

914 **The Influence of Biblical Materials on Literature**
915 For both educated and uneducated people through the
916 Middle Ages and into the Renaissance, the plots, characters,
917 and themes of the *Old* and *New Testament* were better known
918 than any competing literature. Although few readers had
919 direct access to scripture (in the form of the *Vulgate*) prior to
920 the Reformation, the stories of the Bible were told and retold
921 in religious services and, graphically, in the brilliant religious
922 imagery appearing in stained glass windows and sculpture
923 within cathedrals. Any list of the traditional "matters" of liter-
924 ature—the Matter of Britain, the Matter of France, and the
925 Matter of Spain—must include, as an underlying foundation,
926 the Matter of Scripture. It is not unfair to assert, in fact, that most
927 of the literature of the Middle Ages and much Renaissance
928 literature would have been inconceivable apart from the avail-
929 ability of Biblical materials for the writer's use. Dante's *Divine
930 Comedy*, for example, relies not only on Biblical themes and
931 characters but, just as important, on the reader's familiarity
932 with the implication of Biblical symbols and allegories. Even
933 non-Biblical narratives, such as Tasso's *Jerusalem Delivered*,
934 make frequent use of Biblical allusions and symbols, as do
935 autobiographies such as Augustine's *Confessions*.
936 For a modern-day secular audience, it may be difficult to
937 conceive of a set of stories so pervasive and respected in their
938 cultural influence that relatively trivial details can be used by
939 authors to engage rich associations on the reader's part. The
940 phrase "water into wine," for example, from one of Jesus's
941 miracles, would likely recall for a medieval audience not only

942 the entire New Testament story but also the allegorical signifi-
943 cance attached to that story by the Church—for example, the
944 use of wine in communion as
945 the blood of Christ. Biblical
946 materials, in short, were used as
947 a shorthand of sorts by which
948 both secular and religious writers
949 drew into play a shared world, or
950 language, of spiritual meaning.

> **Describe the influences of the Bible on literary works described in this unit.**

PRACTICE READING 9: BUSINESS MATH

1 ADDITION IN BUSINESS

2 Unit 1 Addition Skills

3 Addition is the most frequently used mathematical
4 operation in business. In the course of maintaining
5 business records and carrying out business trans-
6 actions, the employee has to use addition and be
7 accurate in such calculations.

8   Invoices, purchase orders, stock records, and
9 time cards require the use of addition. Moreover,
10 most business transactions involve money, so you
11 will be doing many calculations involving the
12 addition of dollars and cents.

13 *REVIEW OF ADDITION*

14 Addition involves combining two or more numbers
15 called **addends** to obtain the **sum**, or **total**, of the
16 group. Note that you will always be adding numbers
17 with the same label—dollars and dollars, hours and
18 hours, gallons and gallons. You *cannot* add dollars to
19 hours or gallons to miles or minutes to pounds.

> Skim this entire chapter and become aware of its structure. Notice the use of units to subdivide this chapter into smaller divisions of information. Pay careful attention to the use of charts, columns, boxes, and practice problems to make this chapter easier to learn. Think about the most efficient way you can put this information to use during your reading of the unit.

20 $45.75 ⎫
21   8.35 ⎬ ← Addends $45.75 + $8.35 + $1.58 = $55.68
22 + 1.58 ⎭   Sum (Total)
23 $55.68 ← Sum (Total)   Addends

24 PROCEDURE: To find the sum of two or more decimal numbers:

25   1. Arrange the numbers in column form so that digits with
26   the same place value are directly under each other. The
27   numbers should be written so that the decimal points line
28   up vertically.

29   2. We always add from right to left, so the right-hand column of
30   digits is added first to get the first partial sum. The right-hand
31   digit of this partial sum is written under the right-hand
32   column of digits, and the remaining digit (or digits) is carried
33   to the next column.
34   3. This procedure is continued for each column of digits.
35   4. The decimal point is placed in the answer under the column
36   of decimal points in the addends.

37 **EXAMPLE 1**
38 Find the total of $23.45 and $38.28.

39 STEP 1. $23.45   Write the numbers in a column, with the
40   +38.28   decimal points aligned.

                   1
41 STEP 2. $23.45   Add the right-hand column of figures,
42   +38.28   putting the right-hand digit under the
43   3   column and carrying all other digits to the
44   next column.

              1   1
45 STEP 3. $23.45   Continue for the remaining columns of
46   +38.28   digits.
47   61 73

48 STEP 4. $23.45   Insert the decimal point in the answer under
49   +38.28   the decimal points of the addends. Place the
50   *Answer* $61.73 $ sign with the total, and label your answer.

51 *Note:* Whole numbers are a special case, as the decimal point
52   does not appear. With whole numbers, the decimal point
53   is always understood to be to the right of the digits.

54 **EXAMPLE 2**
55   234 = 234.
56 1,386,934 = 1,386,934. } (The decimal point is understood.)
57   3 = 3.

58 **EXAMPLE 3**

59 Add $234 and $3.78.

60 STEP 1. $234.00   Place the decimal point to the right of the

61   + 3.78   whole number, and align the decimal points.

62   Note that $234 has .00 cent.

63 STEP 2. $234.00   Add the numbers according to the

64   + 3.78   procedure given.

65 *Answer* $237.78

66 *Note:* Many forms use a line instead of a decimal

67   point to separate dollars and cents.

68 **EXAMPLE 4**

69                    $237.78 = $237 | 78

What is the basis for addition? Did you need to use the practice problems offered in this unit, or were they testing information that is already familiar to you?

70 ## *CHECKING ADDITION*

71 Accuracy is very important in business, because a mistake may

72 cost a business concern thousands of dollars. It is good practice

73 *always* to check the accuracy of your arithmetic in order to

74 avoid mistakes.

75 HINT: The best way to check addition is to add the numbers

76   again in a *reverse direction*. If you originally added the

77   numbers *down*, check your addition by adding *up*.

78 **EXAMPLE 5**

79   To add: To check:

80   367   7,289

81   2,428   367

82   58   Add down.   2,428

83   572   58

84   3,864   572   Check up.

85   7,289   3,864

86   7,289 = 7,289

87 *Exercises*

88 **Exercise A** Solve the following problems, indicating zero cent
89 where necessary, and check your answers:

90 **1.** $63.75 + $28.15 + $35.82 + $73.47

91 **2.** $472 + $3,428.75 + $35.60 + $25

92 **3.** $232.43 + $364 + $472.10 + $527

93 **4.** $4,620 + $28.75 + $473.58 + $39

94 **5.** $607.75 + $28 + $327.85 + $215

95 **6.** $78 + $3,420.75 + $215.05 + $325

96 **7.** $48.73 + $2,070 + $628.47 + $372

97 **8.** $2,105.80 + $63 + $472.98 + $65.75

98 **9.** $35 + $347.80 + $8,923

99 **10.** $68 + $5,255 + $347.75 + $78.63

100 **11.** $4,623.49 + $793.78 + $93 + $78.50

101 **12.** $415.09 + $5,168.35 + $368 + $3.68

102 **13.** $649.57 + $84 + $5,627.26 + $10,738.47

103 **14.** $4,628.63 + $8,418.97 + $12,657.35 + $18,721.62

104 **15.** $6,327.56 + $14,246.76 + $976 + $18,648.95

105 **16.** $17,984 + $864.77 + $9,458.67 + $25,638.29

106 **17.** $6,456.36 + $49,275.49 + $876 + $9,786.68

107 **18.** $19,753.68 + $8,372.56 + $27,419 + $678.55

108 **19.** $5,458.63 + $7,568 + $43,786.17 + $596.56

109 **20.** $28,705 + $827 + $5,947.66 + $18,572.98

110 **Exercise B** Find the total for each of the following forms, and
111 check your answers:

112 **21.**

Expense Records Week of 9/19		
Salesperson	Amount	
Anderson, B.	$63	50
Bates, G.	71	68
Berger, M.	94	32
Carter, J.	87	55
Chambers, V.	74	19
Total		

22.

Expense Records Week of 9/26		
Salesperson	Amount	
Anderson, B.	$72	61
Bates, G.	68	24
Berger, M.	87	57
Carter, J	76	42
Chambers, V.	83	81
Total		

122 **23.**

Expense Records Week of 10/3		
Salesperson	Amount	
Anderson, B.	$88	50
Bates, G.	91	50
Berger, M.	84	82
Carter, J.	77	44
Chambers, V.	64	29
Total		

24.

Expense Records Week of 10/10		
Salesperson	Amount	
Anderson, B.	$82	31
Bates, G.	78	45
Berger, M.	67	70
Carter, J.	76	36
Chambers, V.	83	87
Total		

132 **25.**

		Date: September 3	
Salesperson	Sales		Commission
Anderson, B.	$15,685	75	$1,568	58
Bates, G.	13,856	80	1,385	68
Berger, M.	18,560	44	1,856	04
Carter, J.	14,375	86	1,437	59
Chambers, V.	15,963	45	1,596	35
Total			

141 **26.**

		Date: October 3	
Salesperson	Sales		Commission
Anderson, B.	$14,888	93	$1,488	89
Bates, G.	15,958	55	1,595	86
Berger, M.	21,060	66	2,106	07
Carter, J.	24,395	89	2,439	59
Chambers, V.	45,964	45	4,596	45
Total			

150 **27.**

Inventory	
Item	Quantity
25-watt Bulbs	75
40-watt Bulbs	123
60-watt Bulbs	115
75-watt Bulbs	98
100-watt Bulbs	135
Total	

28.

Inventory	
Item	Quantity
8 × 10 Frames	1,327
11 × 14 Frames	864
12 × 16 Frames	649
16 × 20 Frames	2,115
18 × 24 Frames	1,923
Total	

29.

Inventory	
Item	Quantity
Men's Ties #62	2,478
Men's Ties #68	987
Men's Ties #71	3,628
Men's Ties #74	5,870
Men's Ties #78	697
Men's Ties #81	874
Men's Ties #85	1,320
Men's Ties #90	2,054
Total	

30.

Inventory	
Item	Quantity
Vinyl Tiles #608	648
Vinyl Tiles #715	8,627
Vinyl Tiles #312	963
Vinyl Tiles #077	4,738
Vinyl Tiles #347	763
Vinyl Tiles #920	817
Vinyl Tiles #516	5,078
Total	

Find the subtotal and the total for each of the following forms:

31.

HANDY & SONS

March 28 19--

SOLD TO _P. Griffiths_

ADDRESS _1031 Brookfield Ave._

CLERK *M.N.* DEPT *33* AMT REC'D $*105*

QUAN.	DESCRIPTION	AMOUNT	
3	*Sport Shirts*	$26	85
6	*Pairs of Socks*	11	70
2	*Ties*	18	00
1	*Pair of Shoes*	36	95
	Subtotal		
	8% Sales tax	7	48
	Total		

POSITIVELY NO EXCHANGES MADE UNLESS
THIS SLIP IS PRESENTED WITHIN 3 DAYS.

174 32.

```
┌─────────────────────────────────────────┐
│         OFFICE SUPPLIES, INC.             │
│              March 30  19--               │
│                                           │
│  SOLD TO   J. Mendez                      │
│  ADDRESS   628 Amboy Road                 │
│  ┌──────────┬────────────┬─────────────┐  │
│  │ CLERK J.R.│ DEPT  6    │ AMT REC'D $/20│ │
│  ├──────────┼────────────┼──────┬──────┤  │
│  │ QUAN.    │ DESCRIPTION │   AMOUNT    │  │
│  ├──────────┼────────────┼──────┼──────┤  │
│  │ 6 reams  │ Typing Paper│ $29 │ 10   │  │
│  │ 12       │ Ribbons     │  33 │ 75   │  │
│  │ 12       │ Ko-rec-type │  22 │ 20   │  │
│  │ 5 doz.   │ #2 Pencils  │  19 │ 75   │  │
│  │          │ Subtotal    │     │      │  │
│  │          │ 8% Sales tax│   6 │ 29   │  │
│  │          │ Total       │     │      │  │
│  └──────────┴────────────┴──────┴──────┘  │
│   POSITIVELY NO EXCHANGES MADE UNLESS     │
│   THIS SLIP IS PRESENTED WITHIN 3 DAYS.   │
└─────────────────────────────────────────┘
```

Why is it important to check your answers? Are all these examples necessary for you to practice? If not, could your reading time become more efficient by skimming these examples and only performing those that appear challenging or unfamiliar to you? Learn to use your reading time more efficiently by not getting involved with information that you already understand, or by using assistance that is unnecessary for your understanding.

175 **Word Problems**

176 Word problems are easier to solve if you watch for key phrases.

177 For instance, key phrases indicating addition are:

178   "Find the total."

179   "What is the cost of . . . ?"

180 Use addition if you are given a set of numbers in the same units
181 (money, hours, parts, etc.) and are asked for the *total*, the *sum*,
182 or the *(total) cost*.

183 **Exercise C** Solve the following problems:

184 **33.** A company bought two typewriters for $1,525 each, a desk
185   for $785.90, a chair for $124.75, and an adding machine for
186      $1,250.95. Find the total amount of the purchases.

187 **34.** Last week you made the following sales: Monday, $529.50;
188 Tuesday, $327.85; Wednesday, $98.25; Thursday, $705.80;
189 Friday, $615.75. What were your total sales for the week?

190 **35.** The Taylor Building Company deposited the following
191 checks: $315.80, $475.60, $115.28, $287.60, $330.50, and
192 $98.15. What was the total amount of the deposit?

193 **36.** The Ace Real Estate Company estimates the monthly cost
194 of maintaining its office as follows: rent, $1,325; electricity,
195 $175; telephone, $165; supplies, $145; miscellaneous
196 expenses, $170. Find the estimated total cost of running
197 the office for a month.

198 **37.** Sam Steinfeld has the following deductions from his weekly
199 pay check: federal withholding tax, $42.50, Social Security,
200 $12.75; state tax, $14.10; city tax, $8.75; medical insurance,
201 $2.40. Find the total of his payroll deductions.

202 **38.** Marcia Rice had the following travel expenses for the week
203 of June 14: hotel, $301; food, $117.25; entertainment,
204 $63.85; car rental, $289.68; and telephone, $38.90. What
205 were her total expenses for that week?

206 **39.** The breakdown of the Alvarez family's monthly mortgage
207 payment is as follows: reduction of principal, $98.75; inter-
208 est charges, $138.63; escrow for real estate tax, $113.78; and
209 mortgage insurance premium, $13.52. How much is the
210 total monthly payment?

211 **40.** The sales by department for the Buy-Rite Supermarket for
212 November 8 were as follows: grocery, $9,468.75; meat,
213 $5,627.93; deli, $4,193.43; produce, $4,248.65; and nonfood,
214 $6,374.60. What were the total sales for that day?

215 **41.** Sharon earns part of her salary from commissions based on
216 sales. Last week she earned the following commissions:
217 $35.63, $41.50, $23.78, $47.83, and $38.35. She also earns
218 a base salary of $125, to which the commissions are added.
219 What was Sharon's total salary last week?

220 **42.** Frank made the following credit card purchases for the
221   month of June: $28.95, $15.63, $89.78, and $53.27. Find
222   his total credit card purchases for the month.

223 # Unit 2 Horizontal Addition

224 Many business forms are designed with sums to be added across
225 the page and totaled in the right-hand column. Most often,
226 these forms record income or expenses over a period of time
227 or by a number of categories.

Department Sales

Week of 6/17

Department	Cash		Charges		C.O.D.		Total	
Ladies' Wear	$3,425	65	$2,315	78	$3,478	58	——	——
Men's Wear	2,975	40	1,848	37	2,264	37		
Children's Wear	1,563	90	987	35	1,2			
Appliances	2,562	76	4,628	74				
Furniture	3,782	35						

Weekly Sales by Department

Date: 1/15

Dept.	Mon.		Tues.		Wed.		Thurs.		Fri.		Sat.		Sun.		Total	
Grocery	$1,821	72	$1,763	15	$1,948	65	$2,163	47	$2,065	38	$1,918	42	$1,621	40	——	——
				43	1,163	70	1,485	72	1,391	72	1,268	34	1,020	65	——	——
							1,583	45	1,465	68	1,371	52	1,169	37	——	——
									1,315	10	1,219	05	1,129	15	——	——
											872	38	784	19	——	——

228   With such forms, you should learn to add each line *horizon-*
229 *tally* across the page. This method is quicker and avoids mistakes
230 sometimes made in copying the numbers into a column.

231 ## *REVIEW OF HORIZONTAL ADDITION*

232   Horizontal addition is less familiar to most of us than verti-
233 cal addition and hence takes practice to master. Try to train your
234 eye to move from number to number, each time concentrating
235 on the digit with the same place value so that you will not be
236 adding, for example, tens to hundreds.

237 **EXAMPLE 1**

238 Horizontally add $23.45, $33.57, and $43.22

239 STEP 1. $23.45 + $33.57 + $43.22 = $ 4

240 STEP 2. $23.45 + $33.57 + $43.22 = $ .24

241 STEP 3. $23.45 + $33.57 + $43.22 = $ 0.24

242 STEP 4. $23.45 + $33.57 + $43.22 = $100.24

243 ## *CHECKING HORIZONTAL ADDITION*

244 As in vertical addition, you should check your accuracy by
245 adding the numbers in the reverse direction.

246 **EXAMPLE 2**

247   To add:

248   Add to right.

249                    $32 + 53 + 84 + 27 = 196$

250   To check:

251   Check to left.

252          $196 = 32 + 53 + 84 + 27 = 196$

253                          $196 = 196$

254 *Note:* Many forms that require horizontal addition also require
255   vertical addition. This is an automatic check on your
256   accuracy.

257 **EXAMPLE 3**

258 STEP 1. Add each of the lines across.

Weekly Sales by Department															Date: 1/15
Dept.	Mon.		Tues.		Wed.		Thurs.		Fri.		Sat.		Sun.		Total
Grocery	$1,821	72	$1,763	15	$1,948	65	$2,163	47	$2,065	38	$1,918	42	$1,621	40	$13,302 19
Produce	963	54	907	43	1,163	70	1,485	72	1,391	72	1,268	34	1,020	65	8,201 10
Dairy	1,461	70	1,368	50	1,485	61	1,538	45	1,465	68	1,371	52	1,169	37	9,869 83
Meat	1,235	85	1,173	85	1,345	57	1,478	45	1,315	10	1,219	05	1,129	15	8,897 02
Deli	863	50	743	78	968	43	1,019	25	982	15	872	38	784	19	6,233 68
Nonfood	734	68	715	93	853	19	916	42	868	58	753	62	642	35	5,484 77
Totals															**Grand Total**

259 STEP 2. Add each of the columns down (including the Total
260 column).

Weekly Sales by Department															Date: 1/15
Dept.	Mon.		Tues.		Wed.		Thurs.		Fri.		Sat.		Sun.		Total
Grocery	$1,821	72	$1,763	15	$1,948	65	$2,163	47	$2,065	38	$1,918	42	$1,621	40	$13,302.19
Produce	963	54	907	43	1,163	70	1,485	72	1,391	72	1,268	34	1,020	65	$ 8,201.10
Dairy	1,461	70	1,368	50	1,485	61	1,538	45	1,465	68	1,371	52	1,169	37	$ 9,869 83
Meat	1,235	85	1,173	85	1,345	57	1,478	45	1,315	10	1,219	05	1,129	15	$ 8,897 02
Deli	863	50	743	78	968	43	1,019	25	982	15	872	38	784	19	$ 6,233 68
Nonfood	734	68	715	93	853	19	916	42	868	58	753	62	642	35	$ 5,484 .77
Totals	$7,080	99	$6,672	64	$7,765	15	$8,601	76	$8,088	61	$7,403	33	$6,367	11	$51,979.59
															Grand Total

261 STEP 3. As a final check, add the bottom line across, and com-
262 pare it with the *grand total* in the lower right corner. If
263 the two totals do not agree, you have made a mistake
264 in addition.

265 $7,080.99 + $6,672.64 + $7,765.15 + $8,601.76
266 + $8,088.61 + $7,403.33 + $6,367.11 = $51,979.59

267 $51,979.59 = $51,979.59

268 *Exercises*

269 **Exercise A** Find the sum of each set of numbers by adding hor-
270 izontally. Check your answers.

271 **1.** $8 + 5 + 3 + 2 + 8 + 9 =$
272 **2.** $6 + 8 + 9 + 5 + 3 =$

3. 32 + 45 + 13 + 72 + 63 =

4. 68 + 75 + 93 + 84 + 48 =

5. 53 + 61 + 94 + 68 + 47 =

6. 372 + 593 + 625 + 853 + 729 =

7. 3,427 + 5,628 + 7,964 + 4,943 =

8. 5,925 + 8,615 + 4,457 + 2,815 =

9. 23,472 + 47,065 + 17,528 =

10. 63,067 + 42,971 + 33,461 =

11. 94,128 + 21,072 + 15,735 =

12. 72,361 + 54,135 + 24,715 =

13. 96,725 + 63,420 + 15,823 =

14. 37,621 + 49,268 + 10,674 =

15. 19,432 + 27,419 + 31,620 =

16. 73,128 + 25,625 + 43,119 =

17. 50,623 + 18,972 + 21,682 =

18. 46,721 + 27,632 + 58,119 =

19. 23,125 + 48,575 + 63,945 + 15,075 =

20. 68,475 + 73,243 + 54,972 + 85,925 =

Exercise B Find the totals on the following forms, and check your answers:

21.

	Hours Worked					Week of 10/17
Employee	Mon.	Tues.	Wed.	Thurs.	Fri.	Total Hours
Adams, C.	8	8	12	12	10	——
Adman, M.	9	9	13	4	10	——
Burke, W.	8	8	10	8	7	——
Curtis, A.	8	6	12	8	10	——
Dellman, A.	12	8	6	12	6	——
Evans, P.	8	10	8	8	12	——
Totals	+	+	+	+	=	Grand Total

22.

	Hours Worked					Week of 10/24
Employee	Mon.	Tues.	Wed.	Thurs.	Fri.	Total Hours
Adams, C.	8	7	11	9	12	———
Adman, M.	9	8	12	7	10	———
Burke, W.	10	8	7	12	9	———
Curtis, A.	8	7	11	9	10	———
Dellman, A.	11	8	9	12	7	———
Evans, P.	9	11	7	8	12	———
Totals	+	+	+	+	=	Grand Total

23.

	Payroll Deductions											Week of 3/23	
Employee Card No.	Federal Tax		FICA Tax		State Tax		City Tax		Pension		Health Plan		Total	
01	$35	15	$12	25	$ 8	79	$5	18	$7	35	$2	15	—	—
02	43	70	13	47	9	16	5	78	8	38	3	21	—	—
03	42	61	14	18	9	83	6	10	8	74	3	47	—	—
04	38	61	13	17	8	91	5	83	7	84	2	65	—	—
05	53	26	19	25	12	42	7	86	9	24	3	81	—	—
06	51	80	18	72	12	39	7	47	9	18	3	34	—	—
07	45	73	16	37	9	72	6	19	7	49	2	73	—	—
08	57	20	19	38	13	24	8	86	9	42	3	68	—	—
09	38	90	13	41	8	64	5	93	7	92	2	71	—	—
10	55	30	18	15	13	05	8	74	8	19	3	42	—	—
Totals	+		+		+		+		+				=	Grand Total

24.

					Stock # 6178	
	Articles Sold					
					Week Ending 4/13	
Salesclerk	Mon.	Tues.	Wed.	Thurs.	Fri.	Total
Bohlen, D.	417	378	392	365	453	———
Brown, C.	325	465	353	328	437	———
Cortez, A.	364	405	428	429	349	———
DeMato, J.	378	372	364	347	391	———
Keelman, W.	427	437	415	328	467	———
Gonzalez, J.	394	364	371	412	368	———
Totals	+	+	+	+	=	Grand Total

25.

	Weekly Sales by Department									Date: 1/8	
Dept.	Mon.		Tues.		Wed.		Thurs.		Fri.		Sat.		Sun.		Total	
Grocery	$1,943	16	$1,948	65	$1,863	41	$2,158	17	$1,984	53	$1,928	31	$1,730	09	——	—
Produce	983	75	973	18	867	38	968	38	828	16	793	82	834	15	——	—
Dairy	1,575	68	1,562	84	1,471	35	1,420	93	1,420	93	1,341	72	1,286	94	——	—
Meat	1,316	37	1,347	19	1,285	64	1,241	63	1,241	63	1,163	58	1,092	66	——	—
Deli	965	53	860	93	763	28	738	40	738	40	629	40	643	19	——	—
Nonfood	847	19	784	52	654	32	635	19	635	19	515	15	553	55	——	—
Totals		+		+		+		+		+		+		+		= Grand Total

26.

	Weekly Sales by Department									Date 1/15	
Dept.	Mon.		Tues.		Wed.		Thurs.		Fri.		Sat.		Sun.		Total	
Grocery	$1,743	87	$1,901	94	$1,941	28	$1,876	70	$2,132	13	$1,970	66	$1,740	89	——	—
Produce	985	86	970	52	847	24	920	40	943	09	794	77	818	18	——	—
Dairy	1,427	93	1,518	18	1,459	64	1,347	58	1,496	75	1,581	29	1,362	74	——	—
Meat	1,508	10	1,484	53	1,389	99	1,475	33	1,397	16	1,284	43	1,171	88	——	—
Deli	813	27	875	06	773	26	798	18	852	28	806	11	723	35	——	—
Nonfood	641	32	799	17	683	38	661	65	647	03	539	12	528	05	——	—
Totals		+		+		+		+		+		+		+		= Grand Total

27.

	Department Sales						Week of 6/17	
Department	Cash		Charge		C.O.D.		Total	
Ladies' Wear	$3,425	65	$2,315	78	$3,478	58	——	——
Men's Wear	2,975	40	1,848	37	2,264	37	——	——
Children's Wear	1,563	90	987	35	1,287	50	——	——
Appliances	2,562	76	4,628	74	3,768	87	——	——
Furniture	3,728	35	5,947	39	4,215	95	——	——
Toys	1,584	72	867	48	1,367	58	——	——
Totals			+		+		= Grand Total	

369 **28.**

370

371

372

373

374

375

376

377

378

Employee	Payroll									Week of 8/19	
	Mon.		Tues.		Wed.		Thurs.		Fri.		Total
Carter, G.	$43	65	$39	75	$47	38	$36	15	$38	19	—— ——
Cerbin, M.	37	48	41	62	32	75	46	72	31	27	—— ——
Cobury, F.	42	35	37	28	38	74	34	63	43	19	—— ——
Dean, J.	34	72	42	67	36	19	42	72	39	38	—— ——
Dejur, C.	39	68	43	50	38	63	39	74	45	28	—— ——
Grant, L.	42	90	36	42	38	63	41	53	36	82	—— ——
Totals		+		+		+		+		=	Grand Total

What is horizontal addition? How does it differ from the type of addition you performed earlier? Are all these examples helping you to understand horizontal addition better, or are they wasting your time?

PRACTICE READING 10: LAW

1 LAW AND THE LEGAL SYSTEM

2 Nature and Origin of Law

3   The origin of law is obscure.
4 In its most primitive form, law
5 rested on brute power —the abil-
6 ity of one individual to control
7 others through strength. Then,
8 the *lex talionis*, the law of retalia-
9 tion (an eye for an eye, a tooth
10 for a tooth), arose from injured
11 individuals' impulse for revenge.
12 As society progressed, however,
13 it became necessary to create
14 rules governing both the behav-
15 ior of individuals toward one
16 another and the conduct of indi-
17 viduals toward society as a whole.

> Skim this chapter and pay careful attention to the use of type fonts and bold-faced type to offset important information. Use the unit questions at the end of this chapter to focus on the new definitions and information that are most relevant in this chapter.

18   Laws therefore were enacted for different purposes:
19 • **Public law** prohibits certain kinds of behavior that society
20   finds objectionable. It includes constitutional, administra-
21   tive, and criminal law. Public law concerns *an individual's*
22   *relationship with society*.
23 • **Private law** is intended to compensate an injured party and
24   to prevent or end disputes. Thus, private law includes tort
25   law, the law of private injury, and contract law. Private law
26   governs *an individual's relationship with another individual*.

27 Jurisprudence (The Science 28 or Philosophy of Law)

29   One school of thought, sometimes referred to as "legal
30 realism," defines law as that which a judge will decide con-
31 cerning issues brought to him or her. However, there are other

32 schools of thought with very different views on the law. "Legal
33 positivism" defines law as simply a command from a sovereign
34 (e.g., a king's decree, a legislature's statute, a judge's order).
35 "Natural law" theorists believe that absolute moral rules can be
36 found in a higher law and that any human law to the contrary
37 is not law at all.

38   There is a close relationship between law and morality, and
39 conduct that a reasonable person deems moral and right is
40 unlikely to collide with law. Thus, since law reflects morality,
41 strict control over all members of society should not be necessary.
42 (Most people follow the law because it is in keeping with their
43 own moral philosophy.)

44 Systems of Law

45   There are currently two major legal systems in use in the
46 Western world:

47 1. **Civil Law (Code law—found in most of Europe and Latin**
48   **America)**: The main goal of Civil Law (whose origins can
49   be traced to the Roman Empire) is to establish a body of
50   legal rules in one systematic code. In this system judicial
51   decisions (case law) are not a source of law, although they
52   may be useful to judges in deciding cases.
53 2. **Common law (Case law—found in most English-speaking**
54   **countries)**: England did not follow Civil Law. Instead, English
55   judges resolved disputes on a case-by-case basis, using
56   precedents set in similar previous cases as their guide. Since
57   the United States was a British colony, an understanding of
58   English common law is vital to the study of American law.

59   Sir William Blackstone's *Commentaries*, published just before
60 the American Revolution, is considered the best text on English
61 law as it existed when the United States gained its independence.
62 According to Blackstone, common law is an "ancient collection
63 of unwritten maxims and customs." American common law
64 contains not only this collection inherited from England, but
65 also all subsequent case law as it has developed over time.

66   As common law developed, judges followed precedents
67 when confronted with new cases. The requirement that courts
68 follow their own precedents is based on the legal principle of

69 *stare decisis* or "stand by the decision." *Stare decisis* binds all of
70 the lower courts of a jurisdiction to judgments rendered by the
71 highest court in that same jurisdiction. *Stare decisis* is not
72 absolute; a decision of the highest court can be amended
73 either by that court changing its mind or by legislative mandate.
74 In the absence of a precedent, a court may follow its own sense
75 of justice or fairness, with due regard for prevailing custom or
76 morality.

77 Unless changes are constitutionally prohibited, the legisla-
78 ture may enact laws known as *statutes* to modify the common
79 law. These statutes, subject to judicial interpretation, are col-
80 lected into codes. Along with case law, the codes form the law
81 that courts generally apply. (Common law codes should not be
82 confused with Civil Law codes. In common law, a code is
83 merely the collection of statutes passed by the legislature; a
84 Civil Law code is intended to be a comprehensive statement of
85 the entire law.)

86 After England's conquest by William the Conqueror (A.D.
87 1066), Norman kings created—alongside the developing
88 common law—an independent, but parallel, system of justice
89 known as *equity*. Based on concepts of fair play, equity cases
90 have no juries, and the equity system covers injunctive relief
91 (court-ordered restraining orders), specific contract perfor-
92 mance, contract modification, and parts of family law.
93 Though the equity system no longer exists as a separate system
94 of justice, many of the principles and maxims of equity have
95 been merged into the common law.

96 SUBSTANTIVE AND PROCEDURAL LAW

97 It is crucial to any study of law, including American business
98 law, to be able to distinguish between two types of law:

99 1. **Substantive law** defines legal rights and obligations in
100 regard to a specific subject, such as contracts, torts, crimes,
101 or property.
102 2. **Procedural law** is concerned with the enforcement of sub-
103 stantive law in a court of law. Rules of procedure are
104 intended to promote justice.

105 Theoretically, there would be 50 bodies of law (combined
106 case and statutory law) among the 50 states in the United States.

107 Actually, however, there is great interdependence,
108 conscious parallelism, and a disciplined effort to
109 develop uniform legislation among the states. The
110 *Uniform Commercial Code (UCC)*, adopted in 49
111 states and partly in Louisiana, is the most success-
112 ful of the proposed uniform laws. However, even
113 the UCC has not completely achieved uniformity.
114 State legislatures can make changes, and courts are
115 free to give independent and varying interpreta-
116 tions of existing laws.

> Describe and differentiate the different systems of law. What are some of the advantages and disadvantages to each system?

117 # Courts

118   There are two main court systems in the United States: the
119 federal and the state systems. The hierarchical structure of
120 federal courts is comparable to that of the various state court
121 systems. Therefore, as an example, we will look at the federal
122 judiciary.
123   At the bottom rung are the U.S. *district courts*, which are trial
124 courts. In each state there is at least one federal district court.
125 If a party wishes to appeal the district court's judgment, he or
126 she brings the case before the *appeals court*, which is the circuit
127 court for that district. Each circuit court generally covers the
128 federal district courts in several states. (The one exception is
129 Washington, D.C., which, because of its heavy volume of
130 work, has its own circuit.)
131   Lastly, appeals from circuit court decisions (or from holdings
132 of the highest court of a state) *may* be heard by the *U.S. Supreme
133 Court*. In a few cases, a party has an absolute right of appeal.
134 In most cases, though, it is solely up to the Supreme Court
135 whether to hear an appeal. Usually the case must involve a
136 federal question (e.g., about the U.S. Constitution or a federal
137 statute).
138   There are other types of specialized courts, too, such as
139 federal bankruptcy courts, state landlord-tenant courts, and state
140 small claims courts. However, the general trial courts, with juries
141 available, remain the main arena for most important cases.
142   The power of a court system to hear and decide a case is
143 called *jurisdiction*. The federal courts are limited to hearing

144 cases specifically placed within their power by the U.S.
145 Constitution or other laws. *Subject-matter jurisdiction* is the
146 judicial power to decide the issues in a case. Federal courts decide
147 *federal questions*, which are cases involving the federal
148 Constitution, statutes, or treaties. In such cases, federal court
149 jurisdiction is *exclusiv*e, but in some areas it is *concurrent*, that
150 is, state courts can also hear cases on these subjects.

151   In addition to federal questions, Congress has provided
152 another form of subject-matter jurisdiction to the federal courts:
153 *diversity jurisdiction*. This means that when opposing parties in
154 a civil lawsuit are citizens of different states, a matter based on
155 state law (and normally brought before a state court) can be
156 heard in a federal court *if* one of the parties requests it *and if*
157 the amount of the controversy exceeds $50,000. Corporations
158 are treated as "citizens" of both their place of incorporation
159 and their principal business location; for partnerships, however,
160 courts look to the citizenship of each general partner.

161   If a defendant wishes to transfer a case from one state to
162 another, or from state court to federal court, his request will be
163 for *removal*. Such requests must be made at the beginning of
164 the case and are only granted if the correct jurisdiction lies in
165 another court. State courts are generally open to hear any type
166 of case, unless it is precluded by the U.S. Constitution or federal
167 statutes or treaties. *Most common law areas*—such as torts,
168 contracts, crimes—*tend to be brought before state courts*.

169   In addition to subject-matter jurisdiction, for each particular
170 case, a court needs jurisdiction over the litigants themselves.
171 *Personal (in personam) jurisdiction* is the judicial power over the
172 parties in a case. By filing a lawsuit, the *plaintiff* voluntarily
173 submits to the court's personal jurisdiction. Personal jurisdiction
174 over the *defendant* requires that the defendant work or live in
175 the state in which the lawsuit was filed, or have other clear-cut
176 ties to the state. In addition, states have passed "long-arm
177 statutes," which extend personal jurisdiction for the courts over
178 people or corporations in certain specified circumstances.

179   When a court has authority over the subject matter and
180 parties of a lawsuit, it has jurisdiction. However, there still may
181 be problems with *venue*, the place (usually the county) where
182 the case will be tried. Proper venue is defined by statute and is

183   usually based on the notion of convenience to the parties,
184   especially the defendant.

185   Obviously, the law varies from state to state. The doctrine of
186   *stare decisis* does not require one state to follow another state's
187   precedents. When disputes arise of transactions occurring in
188   more than one state, the issue is covered by a body of law
189   known as *conflict of laws* (or choice of laws). Thus, while a
190   court will almost always apply its own procedural law, it must
191   look to conflict-of-laws principle and choose between differ-
192   ent substantive laws:

193   • For *torts* (e.g., accident cases), the applicable law is usually
194   that where the injury occurred.
195   • For *contracts*, courts generally look to the law intended
196   (expressly or implicitly) by the parties to the contract.
197   • In *criminal cases*, courts apply their own substantive and
198   procedural laws regardless of where the acts were commit-
199   ted; however, almost all criminal prosecutions take place in
200   the same state where the alleged crime occurred.

201   Once a court renders a judgment, the U.S. Constitution's
202   "full faith and credit" clause requires that other states recognize
203   the validity of that judgment as it specifically affects
204   the rights and parties subject to that judgment.

What are the different types of courts and how do their roles differ?

205   This does not mean that other states must adopt
206   the reasoning on which a decision is based; one
207   state's precedents are *not* binding on another state.
208   The clause simply means that the judgment must
209   be honored by other states' courts.

210 # Attorneys

211   Modern attorneys operate in two main areas: the law office
212   and the courtroom. All practicing attorneys must have a general
213   command of legal principals. In addition, attorneys must be
214   *able to find specific and detailed application of legal principles*
215   within the large body of case law and statute law. Thus, as a
216   business law student, you must become familiar with the
217   kinds of research materials that exist.

218   *Statutory law* is found in a state code or in the federal code.
219   These codes are cross-referenced to other statutes and key
220   cases interpreting and applying the same statute in question.

221 *Case law* is collected in the opinions of the appellate courts
222 of the states and the United States. Opinions of trial courts are
223 usually not published, except for federal trial courts. Case law
224 may also be found in legal encyclopedias, textbooks, and com-
225 puter data banks such as WESTLAW and LEXIS.

226 Businesses rely on attorneys not only when they are sued,
227 but also to prevent problems. The hope is to improve business
228 practices and thus reduce the risks of lawsuits and other fines
229 or legal expenses.

230 A lawyer has several functions: investigator, drafter, nego-
231 tiator, advisor, and advocate. A lawyer has a duty to advise
232 against illegal actions, but also must maintain confidences
233 shared during the course of an attorney/client relationship.

234 Except for in-house counsel (lawyers who are employees of a
235 business, perhaps in a company's legal department), the business-
236 person usually contacts an attorney rather than vice versa. The
237 *attorney/client privilege* permits clients to keep matters discussed
238 with their attorneys confidential. This privilege can be waived
239 by a client; for example, the client may divulge attorney/client
240 communications to a third party. Also, because the attorney/
241 client privilege depends on *confidential* communications, it does
242 not extend to statements made in the presence of, or letters sent
243 to, persons besides the attorney and the client.

244 Each state has ethical codes of conduct governing lawyers.
245 In general, the attorney must:

246 1. only take cases that he or she can handle competently;
247 2. zealously advocate the client's cause, while remaining faithful
248   to the attorney's own obligation as an officer of the court
249   not to undermine the overall purposes of the system;
250 3. keep the client reasonably informed (e.g., concerning
251   settlement offers);
252 4. abide by the attorney/client privilege; and
253 5. take measures to protect the client when withdrawing from
254   a case.

255 Occasionally, attorney/client conflicts stem from what the
256 attorney believes are her ethical obligations. Frank discussions
257 between the attorney and the client are usually necessary and
258 may resolve such differences.

259   The businessperson's basic knowledge of the
260 legal system can play an important role in the
261 lawyer's attempts to resolve problems. There is no
262 substitute for professional advice, but the business-
263 person's limited knowledge can help him realize
264 when the services of a lawyer are necessary, and
265 what assistance the attorney and the client can
266 mutually provide to one another.

267 # Litigation

268   Procedural law is very complicated and varies
269 from court to court. There are federal rules of pro-
270 cedure, and each state court system also has its
271 own rules. Appellate courts have different rules
272 from trial courts, and even courts in the same
273 jurisdiction may have different local rules.
274 Furthermore, criminal and civil cases follow differ-
275 ent rules. Nevertheless, most cases follow a gener-
276 al pattern of procedure.

277   The person who initiates the lawsuit is called
278 the *plaintiff*. The person sued is the *defendant*. In
279 equity cases, the parties are instead called the
280 *petitioner* and the *respondent*, respectively. In a criminal case
281 there is no plaintiff; instead, the criminal defendant is opposed
282 by the state itself, often referred to as the "the prosecution" or
283 "the people."

284   The papers required to bring the issues in a lawsuit before
285 the court are termed the *pleadings*. To begin the action, the
286 plaintiff's lawyer files a *complaint* with the clerk of a trial court
287 with the proper jurisdiction and venue. The complaint contains
288 a brief description of the facts, the basis of the suit, and a
289 request for remedies.

290   An official then serves a *summons* and a copy of the com-
291 plaint on the defendant. An affidavit is usually filed attesting
292 to the fact that the defendant received the summons and com-
293 plaint. The summons notifies the defendant that he or she
294 must file an *answer* to the complaint with both the court and the
295 plaintiff's attorney within a certain time period. The summons

What are two main areas that an attorney operates within? Describe the ethical codes of conduct governing lawyers. What would be a good memory system to use for memorizing these details?

Pay careful attention to the use of boldface and type size to offset different levels of importance in this section. Pay close attention to italics to locate important terms of vocabulary.

296 also tells the defendant that failure to file an answer will lead
297 to a judgment by default for the plaintiff.

298   An answer, however, is not the defendant's only choice. He
299 may file a *motion to dismiss*, sometimes called a *demurrer*, in
300 which he contends that, even if the plaintiff's allegations are
301 true, there is no legal basis for finding the defendant liable.

302   The answer generally admits or denies each of the various
303 allegations set forth in the complaint. It may include *affirmative*
304 *defenses*, that is, allegations of facts that, if proved by the
305 defendant, defeat the plaintiff's claim. Generally, a complaint
306 or answer may be amended unless a statute or rule specifically
307 prohibits such amendment, or unless the amendment is made
308 at such a later date that its acceptance as a new pleading would
309 be grossly unfair to the other party.

310   When answering the complaint, or shortly thereafter, the
311 defendant may file a *counterclaim*, which is a reverse complaint:
312 one by the defendant against the plaintiff. Two other claims
313 are (1) *cross claims*, brought by a plaintiff against one or more
314 co-plaintiffs, or more likely, by a defendant against one or
315 more co-defendants; and (2) *third-party claims*, whereby a
316 defendant brings a new party into a lawsuit. In addition, large
317 numbers of plaintiffs may join together in a *class action*.

318   Besides the motion to dismiss, many other types of *motions*,
319 or requests to the court, may be made before the case goes to
320 trial. The most important motion is the motion for *summary*
321 *judgment*. It may be filed at any time by either the plaintiff or
322 the defendant. Summary judgment is to be awarded if the
323 judge decides that: (1) there is no genuine issue as to material
324 (potentially determinative) facts; and (2) when the law is applied
325 to these facts, one party is clearly entitled to a verdict in her
326 favor. Summary judgment may be granted on all or part of a
327 lawsuit. The summary judgment may also be used to limit or
328 eliminate certain types of damages, such as punitive damages.

329   Before there is a trial, each party is entitled to obtain
330 information from other parties and other potential witnesses.
331 These pretrial procedures are know as *discovery*.

332   Discovery may serve several purposes:

333 1. By providing parties with access to evidence that might
334   otherwise be hidden, it prevents surprises at the trial.

335   2. It may narrow the issues at the trial (i.e., some questions may
336   be resolved).
337   3. It preserves witnesses' testimony prior to trial (important
338   witnesses may be unavailable at trial, their memories may
339   fade, or their testimony may change).
340   4. It may place the case in a position for summary judgment.
341   5. It may lead to pretrial settlement, as both parties see their
342   strengths and weaknesses.
343   The main methods of discovery are depositions, interrogato-
344 ries, requests for admissions, and the production of documents.

345 ### Depositions

346   A *deposition* is sworn testimony by one of the parties or any
347 other witness, usually recorded and transcribed by a notary
348 public. The testimony is ordinarily taken in response to oral
349 questions from the parties' attorneys, although it can be in
350 response to written questions.

351 ### Interrogatories

352   *Interrogatories* are written questions to be answered in writing,
353 and under oath by another party (generally the opposing party).
354 Unlike depositions, interrogatories can be directed only toward
355 the parties themselves. Their usefulness is further reduced by
356 the fact that the answering party's attorney can prepare the
357 answers. However, interrogatories usually cost less than deposi-
358 tions, and the scope can be broader.

359 ### Requests for Admissions

360   *Requests for admissions* are, like interrogatories, made and
361 answered in writing and can be directed only to another party.
362 The requesting party asks the other side to admit particular
363 facts or acknowledge that certain documents are genuine.
364 Admissions are conclusive. Thus, this method can save trial
365 time because the parties have already agreed on some matters.

366 ### Production of Documents

367   Parties may be required to produce, for inspection and copy-
368 ing, all their documents that may be relevant to the case. A depo-
369 sition may include document production by the witness as well.

370 ***Trial***

371   The trial issues can be narrowed via a *pretrial conference*.
372 Although judges may use these conferences to encourage
373 settlement, the main purpose is to ensure that the trial will
374 proceed as smoothly as possible: Witnesses, exhibits, areas of
375 dispute, and agreed upon facts are all identified ahead of time.

376   The next step is the trial itself. A jury trial is available in
377 criminal cases and in most civil lawsuits. The major exceptions
378 are (1) certain cases (e.g., divorce) that are historically based
379 on equity, and (2) administrative agency proceedings.

380   The plaintiff or the defendant can ask for a trial by jury;
381 this right is usually waived if not requested in the plaintiff's
382 complaint or the defendant's answer.

383   A jury trial involves a *petit jury* (usually 12 members,
384 though some states allow as few as six). The petit jury decides
385 whether the defendant is guilty in criminal cases, or liable in
386 civil cases. In federal courts and most state courts, the jury's
387 decision must be unanimous. The federal courts and most
388 states also have *grand juries* (approximately 18 to 24 jurors),
389 which, under the guidance of prosecutors, decide whether an
390 individual should be charged with a crime (indicted).

391   In *jury selection*, the first step in the trial, prospective jurors
392 are questioned by the attorneys for both sides and by the
393 judge. This examination is known as *voir dire*. Any number of
394 potential jurors can be kept off the panel *for cause* (e.g., bias),
395 and the attorneys for each side also have the right to reject a
396 few (generally about three) without offering a reason, i.e., by
397 *peremptory challenge*.

398   After the jury has been selected, the next step is the presen-
399 tation of *opening statements*, where each attorney presents what
400 he or she expects to prove.

401   The *plaintiff's* case is then presented. Witnesses, called by
402 the plaintiff's attorney, testify in response to the questions:
403 first *direct examination* by the attorney who called them, and
404 then *cross-examination* by the opposing attorney. Other evidence
405 that could help the plaintiff's case is offered at this time. At the
406 end of the plaintiff's case, the defendant may move for dismissal
407 of the case, or for a *directed verdict*. The directed verdict will be
408 granted by the judge if the plaintiff has failed to prove one or

409 more elements of her case. If the judge grants the motion, the
410 jury is instructed by the judge to find for the defendant.

411   If the trial continues, the next step is the *defendant's case*.
412 This follows the same procedure as the plaintiff's case, but offers
413 witnesses and evidence for the defense. When the defendant's
414 case is complete, the plaintiff may move for a directed verdict
415 in his favor. Also, in jury trials, this may be the proper time for
416 the defendant to request a directed verdict.

417   Finally, in the *summation*, each attorney has the opportunity
418 to review the testimony and other evidence and make closing
419 arguments.

420   Throughout the trial, the judge makes legal rulings on
421 evidence and other matters. Generally, only after the summa-
422 tions does he instruct the jury concerning the law that is
423 applicable to the case and the various verdicts that the jury
424 may render.

425   The jury then retires and tries to resolve all the *fact* (not legal)
426 issues. As stated before, in federal courts and in most states, it
427 is only when all members agree that the jury renders a *verdict*.
428 In a nonjury trial, the judge makes the decision.

429   In reaching a verdict, consideration of evidence is governed
430 by the *burden of proof* (persuasion). This refers to:

431   • A party's obligation, when asserting fact, to *come forward*
432   with evidence establishing this fact.

433   • The necessity for one party to *persuade* the trier of fact (the
434   judge or jury) that his or her contentions are supported by a
435   *preponderance of the evidence*—that his or her version of the
436   facts is, at the very least, slightly more believable than the
437   opposition's. However, other allegations demand a higher
438   standard of persuasion than a preponderance of the evidence
439   (e.g., in a criminal case, the prosecution must prove the
440   defendant's guilt beyond a reasonable doubt). If both sides
441   are equally as believable, then the defendant generally wins.

442   Even after the jury returns its verdict, the losing party may
443 ask the judge to enter judgment for her, *notwithstanding* the
444 verdict for the other side. This is a motion for judgment *non*
445 *obstante veredicto*, or *judgment notwithstanding the verdict*
446 *(J.N.O.V.)*. This is a rare and serious measure, and the judge's
447 interpretation of the evidence at trial must meet very high
448 standards.

449 Either attorney can request that the trial court grant a *new*
450 *trial*, usually for one or more of the following reasons:
451 1. erroneous interpretations of the substantive law,
452 2. erroneous admission or exclusion of evidence,
453 3. insufficient evidence or a verdict contrary to law,
454 4. excessive or inadequate damages award,
455 5. jury misconduct or other irregularities, and
456 6. newly discovered evidence.
457 Often these grounds, particularly (1) through (4), serve as
458 the basis for an appeal requesting reversal or a new trial.

459 ### *Appeal*

460 Each party to a lawsuit generally is entitled to one *appeal*,
461 held in an appellate court. Consideration of further appeals is
462 discretionary. Appellate courts do not hold trials; there are no
463 witnesses or juries. The court simply reviews the record of the
464 trial and the briefs submitted by the parties' attorneys. A *brief*
465 is a written argument supported by citations of prior court
466 decisions, statutes, or other authorities.

467 The attorneys may present short oral arguments of key
468 points. They must also answer searching questions from the
469 judges. When the court reaches a decision, it issues a written
470 opinion that can provide future
471 guidance in similar cases.

472 Opinions, in whole or in
473 part, may affirm the original
474 judgment (the most frequent
475 result), reverse the judgment,
476 instruct the lower court to issue a
477 new judgment, or remand (i.e.,
478 send back) the case to the lower
479 court for further proceedings.
480 Decisions other than to affirm
481 are almost always based on a trial
482 court's errors of law. Mere belief
483 that the jury or judge did not
484 draw the correct factual conclu-
485 sions is insufficient grounds for
486 reversal.

> Outline and describe the various points made regarding litigation. Consider a hypothetical lawsuit and ask yourself how these points might apply to that situation. Remember putting information into a context helps to make it more relevant, easier to recall, and improves comprehension.

487 Alternative Dispute Resolution

488 The vast majority of disputes are settled out of court. Most
489 do not even reach the point where a suit is filed. If a complaint
490 is filed, settlement usually occurs before trial. Several factors
491 may spur compromise, such as (1) anxiety about going to court,
492 (2) the time and expense of lawsuits, (3) concern about bad
493 publicity, (4) the need for a quicker resolution, (5) uncertainty
494 as to the outcome, and (6) a desire to maintain good business
495 or personal relationships with the other party.

496 Alternative Dispute Resolution (ADR) is becoming a very
497 popular option in order to avoid going to court. The two most
498 frequently used out-of-court dispute resolution methods are
499 mediation and arbitration. Both involve neutral third parties
500 who are often familiar with, or even experts in, the disputed
501 subjects.

502 In *mediation*, a third party (mediator) helps the disputing
503 parties settle the case. Mediators cannot impose a settlement
504 on the parties, but often can effect compromise. Mediation is
505 increasingly used in settling labor disputes and in resolving
506 consumer complaints, and some laws mandate mediation.

507 However, mediation cannot accomplish very much when the
508 parties are unwilling to compromise. In such cases, *arbitration*
509 may be more useful. *Unlike a mediator, an arbitrator has the*
510 *power to make a final, binding decision.*

511 A dispute usually goes to arbitration because a contract
512 either requires it or permits a party to request it. In certain
513 instances, a law may mandate arbitration. Parties seeking to
514 avoid arbitration usually will not be able to because of enforce-
515 ment by both state and federal legislation. Arbitration is often
516 a shorter, cheaper, and less formal version of litigation.

517 *Once arbitration is completed, grounds for appeal are extremely*
518 *limited.* Courts are to overturn an arbitration award only if
519 (1) it went beyond the matters submitted to the arbitrator(s),
520 or (2) the arbitrator(s) failed to follow statutory requirements,
521 or (3) the award arose out of fraud or corruption. *Clearly, an*
522 *arbitration award is even less susceptible to reversal than is a court*
523 *judgment.* Because arbitration usually saves money and time,

524 often promotes less hostile rela-
525 tions than litigation, and can,
526 when necessary, submit complex
527 issues to experts, arbitration
528 agreements are routinely placed
529 in many business contracts.

> Skim the questions on the following pages and determine if you need to practice answering these questions or if you already possess an understanding of this topic and are ready to learn new material.

530 **_Questions_**

531 _Identify each of the following:_

532 affirmative defenses	discovery	pleadings
533 alternative dispute	district courts	pretrial conference
534 resolution	equity	private law
535 answer	"federal questions"	procedural law
536 appeal	jurisdiction	production of
537 appeals court	"full faith and	documents
538 arbitration	credit" clause	public law
539 attorney/client	grand jury	removal
540 privilege	interrogatories	requests for
541 attorneys	J.N.O.V.	admissions
542 brief	jurisdiction	respondent
543 burden of proof	jurisprudence	_stare decisis_
544 case law	legal positivism	statutes
545 Civil Law	legal realism	statutory law
546 class action	_lex talionis_	subject-matter
547 common law	long-arm statutes	jurisdiction
548 complaint	mediation	substantive law
549 concurrent	motion to dismiss	summary
550 jurisdiction	natural law	judgment
551 conflict of laws	opening statement	summation
552 counterclaim	peremptory	summons
553 cross claims	challenge	Supreme Court
554 cross-examination	personal	third-party claims
555 defendant	jurisdiction	Uniform
556 depositions	petit jury	Commercial Code
557 direct examination	petitioner	venue
558 directed verdict	plaintiff	_voir dire_

559 *Answer These Review Questions:*

560   1. How does common law differ from Civil Law?

561   2. Why should a definition of law emphasize enforcement?

562   3. Why is it difficult to make law "uniform" by enacting
563   uniform statutes?

564   4. Is substantive law more important than procedural law?

565   5. What are the three main levels of courts in the federal
566   judiciary?

567   6. State the difference between the functions of a trial court
568   and an appellate court.

569   7. What is the key constitutional question concerning "long-
570   arm" personal jurisdiction?

571   8. Distinguish jurisdiction from venue.

572   9. What state's substantive laws usually govern a tort case?

573 10. What are the four main methods of discovery?

574 11. Who usually has the burden of persuasion?

575 12. Name at least five reasons why disputes are compromised.

576 *Apply Your Knowledge:*

577   1. If, after you lose at trial, your lawyer forgets to file your
578   appeal within the required period of time, is that the end of
579   your substantive rights in the case?

580   2. Jenny Jones wants to sue Bob Breach for breach of contract.
581   Jenny lives in New York, and Bob lives in California. The
582   contract was signed at a business meeting in Los Angeles.
583   Bob has not left California for years, nor has he ever done
584   any business elsewhere.

585   (a) In what court can Jenny sue Bob?

586   (b) In what court does Jenny's right to sue depend on the
587   amount in controversy?

588   (c) Why is it unlikely that Jenny can sue anywhere else?

589   (d) What happens if the contract states that it is to be gov-
590   erned by New York law? Discuss both personal jurisdiction
591   and conflict of laws.

592   (e) Assume that New York gives defendants a longer time to
593   answer a complaint than does California. Which time
594   period can Bob use to try to have the case thrown out as
595   being too late?

596   3. Bob refuses to answer Jenny's complaint. Jenny obtains a
597   judgment, including a damages award, by default. Bob moves
598   to another state, one which generally does not enforce the
599   type of contract that Jenny and Bob had. May Jenny use the
600   new state's courts to collect her money (damages award)
601   against that state's new resident, Bob?
602   4. Bob does not leave California. He answers the complaint and
603   files a motion for summary judgment, with an affidavit that
604   says he has never met anyone named Jenny Jones, that there
605   was no contract, and that the signature on the contract is
606   not his. Will Bob win? What is the standard for granting a
607   summary judgment?

608 *Answers*

609 *Answers to Review Questions:*

610   1. Common law emphasizes precedent (past court decisions),
611   while Civil Law emphasizes the wording of statutes (the
612   code). Civil Law attempts to set forth the entire law on a
613   subject, but common law accepts that gaps in the law must
614   be filled by judicial interpretations of the law.
615   2. If law is not enforced, it has little effect on society. When
616   governments enact numerous laws but fail to enforce them,
617   citizens lose their respect for the law and social order is
618   weakened.
619   3. Each of the 50 states is a sovereign state with the right to
620   define and carry out its own laws, subject only to constitu-
621   tional limits. Even when so-called uniform laws are passed
622   by a legislature, judges may interpret those laws differently.
623   4. Yes, inasmuch as one needs to have substantive law in
624   order to "have a case." But procedural law is very important,
625   too. Incorrect or improper procedures can deprive a person
626   of the ability to have his or her substantive rights vindicated.
627   While procedural law usually is more flexible than substan-
628   tive law, that flexibility is limited. One usually must follow
629   the rules (procedure) in order to obtain justice (have one's
630   substantive rights upheld).
631   5. District courts, circuit courts, the U.S. Supreme Court.

632　　6. Trial courts hear witnesses and decide factual disputes. Both
633　　　　trial and appellate courts interpret the law, but usually it is
634　　　　only the appellate court whose interpretations may well be
635　　　　published and serve as precedent, or at least guidance, for
636　　　　other courts. Appeals courts review lower court decisions on
637　　　　the record established at trial (they do not hear new evidence),
638　　　　and their review is focused much more on the law than the
639　　　　facts. (Trial court *factual* findings are only overturned in
640　　　　extreme cases—where the higher court finds no basis what-
641　　　　soever for a factual determination.)

642　　7. Whether the defendant had enough "contacts" within the
643　　　　state so that requiring him or her to defend a lawsuit there
644　　　　does not violate due process of law.

645　　8. Jurisdiction involves a court's power over the issues (subject-
646　　　　matter jurisdiction) and parties (personal jurisdiction) in a
647　　　　case. Once jurisdiction has been established, venue is merely
648　　　　a matter of deciding whether a particular locale (e.g.,
649　　　　county) is a proper place to bring the lawsuit.

650　　9. The state where the injury occurred.

651　10. Depositions, interrogatories, requests for admissions, and
652　　　　production of documents.

653　11. The plaintiff.

654　12. (1) anxiety about going to court; (2) the time and expense of
655　　　　lawsuits; (3) concern about bad publicity; (4) the need for a
656　　　　quicker resolution; (5) uncertainty as to the outcome; (6) a
657　　　　desire to maintain good business or personal relationships
658　　　　with the other party.

659　*Answers to "Apply Your Knowledge":*

660　　1. Yes, in that you cannot force the court to hear your case
661　　　　simply because your authorized agent—your attorney—
662　　　　made a mistake. Cases must end at some point, and so the
663　　　　procedural law is rather inflexible about letting people open
664　　　　up a case after the time to appeal has already passed. (More-
665　　　　over, how fair would it be to the winning party if it could never
666　　　　be certain that in fact the case was now fully resolved?)

667　　　　Note, though, that you might have another, new case: a
668　　　　case against your attorney for legal malpractice. (See Chapter
669　　　　3 on negligence by professionals.)

2. (a) California State court. (b) Jenny can sue in the federal court in California if she contends that the damages from the alleged breach of contract were more than $50,000 (diversity jurisdiction). (c) It appears that Bob would not be subject to any other state's (e.g., New York's) long-arm jurisdiction; thus, no personal jurisdiction. (d) No probable effect on personal jurisdiction. Under basic conflict-of-laws principles, though, the California court must interpret the contract according to New York law, as that was the law intended by the contracting parties. (e) The time period for the state in which Bob is sued (California). Statutes of limitations are not substantive law, but are a matter of procedural law (so the court applies its own state law).

3. Yes. The prior judgment is entitled to "full faith and credit" in another state.

4. It is very unlikely that Bob will win his summary judgment motion. Such motions can be granted only if there is (1) no genuine issue about the material facts, and (2) entitlement to judgment on the law applicable to the material facts.

   Jenny's complaint probably sets forth enough facts to show that there is material factual dispute between the parties about whether there was a contract and whether Bob was a party to it. But because pleadings themselves (e.g., complaints) are not evidence in the way that an affidavit, testimony or other sworn statements are, Jenny should file her own affidavit counter to Bob's contentions or showing why his points are irrelevant (e.g., she acted through an agent and never met Bob). Another reason for Jenny to file is as a practical matter, to oppose all erroneous, potentially harmful claims by an opponent.

PRACTICE READING 11: ELECTRONICS

1 INTRODUCTION TO
2 ELECTRONICS

3   The Greeks are believed to have discovered
4 electricity in the process of conducting some of
5 their experiments. While working with a piece of
6 amber (the fossilized resin from an ancient species
7 of tree), which is translucent and golden in color,
8 they found that if the amber was rubbed briskly, it
9 would exhibit an attraction for tiny bits of light-
10 weight material. You have probably seen this happen
11 when you run a comb through your hair on a dry
12 day and pick up bits of paper with it. The Greeks
13 believed that the forces of amber were at work in
14 this phenomenon. Similarly, the Romans found that lignite (a
15 form of coal) could be rubbed and could produce, by friction,
16 the same reaction. However, it is the Greeks who have been
17 given credit for the first experiments that later led in 1600 to
18 the work of William Gilbert (an Englishman) with friction and
19 static electricity. Gilbert wrote a book on the substances with
20 which he had experimented. He showed that amber was not
21 the *only* such material that produced an attraction for the bits
22 of paper.

23   Gilbert is given credit for coining the word *electrics*. The
24 Latin word *electrum* is derived from the Greek *elektron*, which
25 in turn means "amber." Gilbert was influenced by the Latin
26 being studied at the time. In all probability this is how the
27 name worked its way into print and history.

28   Gilbert has been called the father of electricity since he was
29 the first to classify objects that would produce an electrostatic
30 field when rubbed. He called these substances *electrics*.

31   Electronics is the application of electrical principles. Elec-
32 trical principles are derived from the uses and generation of
33 electric energy. Therefore, electricity is necessary for the proper

> Skim the chapter and look for its structure. Pay attention to the summary and questions at the end of the unit to help you prioritize what information is most important for you to learn.

34 operation of electronic devices and electronic circuits. In order
35 to understand electronics it is first necessary to know how
36 electricity is generated, distributed, and put to work in circuits.

37 Basic Atomic Structure

38   *Electricity* is defined as the
39 flow of electrons along a conduc-
40 tor. A conductor is an object that
41 allows electrons to pass easily.
42 That means electrons must be
43 organized and pushed toward a
44 goal. This is done in a number of
45 ways. But first, we must know
46 what an electron is before we can
47 start working with it.

> Notice the diagram contained within this subsection. Study the diagram and form a mental picture of its contents. Notice how much easier it is to learn the information when you refer to your mental picture while reading the material.

48   Elements are the most basic
49 materials in the universe. There
50 are 106 elements including some
51 that have been made in the lab-
52 oratory. Elements such as iron, copper, gold, lead, and silver
53 have been found in nature. Eleven others have been made in
54 the laboratory. Every known substance — solid, liquid, or gas
55 — is composed of elements.

56   An electron is the smallest part of an atom. An atom is the
57 smallest particle of an element that retains all the properties of
58 that element. Each element has its own kind of atom. That is,
59 hydrogen atoms are alike, and they are different from the
60 atoms of all other elements. However, all atoms have certain
61 things in common. They all have an inner part, the nucleus.
62 The nucleus is composed of very small particles called *protons*
63 and *neutrons*. An atom also has an outer part, consisting of
64 other small particles. These very small particles are called *elec-*
65 *trons*. The electrons orbit around the nucleus (see Figure 2-1).

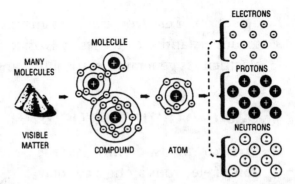

66 **Figure 2-1.** Molecular structure. The negative (–) particles are electrons.

67 ## *NEUTRONS*

68   Neutrons have no electric charge, but protons
69 are positively charged. Because of these charges,
70 protons and electrons are particles of energy. That
71 is, these charges form an electric field of force
72 within the atom. These charges are always pulling
73 and pushing one another; this action produces
74 energy in the form of movement.

> Continue to make full use of the diagrams in this unit.

75   The atoms of each element have a definite number of
76 electrons, and they have the same number of protons. A hydro-
77 gen atom has one electron and one proton (see Figure 2-2).
78 The aluminum atom has thirteen of each (see Figure 2-3A).

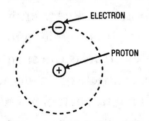

79 **Figure 2-2.** The hydrogen atom has one electron and one proton.

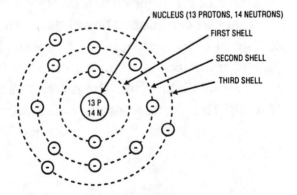

80 **Figure 2-3A.** The aluminum atom has 13 electrons.

81 The opposite charges—negative electrons and positive protons—
82 attract each other and tend to hold electrons in orbit. As long as
83 this arrangement is not changed, an atom is electrically balanced.
84   A closer look at the atom shows that the electron orbits the
85 nucleus in shells. A *shell* is made by an electron orbiting the
86 nucleus. An electron rotating around the nucleus makes a ring
87 around it, and, the ring may be elliptical in shape. At the same
88 time the *plane* of the electron shifts a few degrees, so that
89 another ring is produced, and then another and another, so
90 that finally there is an electron tracing the path of a complete
91 sphere or shell. Some electrons have a greater distance away
92 from the nucleus and they also shift their planes or orbits of
93 rotation. They are arranged in a similar fashion that forms a
94 second shell (see Figure 2-3B). The maximum number of shells
95 for any known element is *seven* (see Figure 2-3C). Shells are
96 labeled alphabetically from K through Q, starting with the
97 innermost shell. Each shell has a definite maximum limit as to
98 the number of electron orbits it can have. For instance, the K
99 *shell* has a maximum number of electrons of two. The second
100 shell, L, has eight, the third shell, M, 18, and so on. Copper has
101 29 electrons, so it has 2, 8, 18, and 1. The 1 electron sitting out
102 so far away from the holding force of the nucleus is easily
103 pushed along in various directions and can be moved into an
104 adjacent atom's orbit. Then that atom's electron is moved to the
105 next, and so on. This means there is a movement of electrons.
106 The flow of electrons is defined as electricity.
107   Keep in mind that the electrons sitting in the last shell are
108 called *valence electrons* and the electrical properties of a material
109 are dependent on the number of such electrons. A material
110 with eight valence electrons produces an inert material. Atoms
111 with fewer than four valence electrons tend to give up or move
112 electrons, and the fewer the valence electrons, the greater this
113 tendency. On the other hand, atoms with more than four elec-
114 trons in their orbits or last shell have a tendency to acquire
115 one or more additional electrons. In elements with atomic
116 valences of four, adjacent atoms form into a *crystal structure*
117 sharing their electrons in *covalent bonds*. Such bonds fill the
118 valence shell, and the material is electrically inert. This creates
119 the *semiconductor properties* that are the basis of solid state
120 (transistor) electronics.

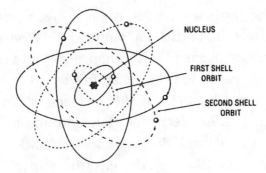

121 **Figure 2-3B.** Electron orbits and shells. Note how the rotation produces the
122   appearance of a shell.

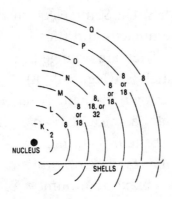

123 **Figure 2-3C.** Identification of atomic shells and the number of electrons in
124   each shell.

125 *FREE ELECTRONS*

126   Electrons in copper drift along in a random fashion when
127 at room temperature.

128   Heat is only one of the types of energy that can cause elec-
129 trons to be forced from their orbits. A magnetic field can also
130 be used to cause electrons to move in a given direction. Light
131 energy and pressure on a crystal are also used to generate elec-
132 tricity by forcing electrons to flow along a given path. When
133 electrons leave their orbits, they move from atom to atom at
134 random, drifting in no particular direction. Electrons that
135 move in such a way are referred to as *free electrons*. However, a
136 force can be used to cause them to move in a given direction.
137 That is how electricity (the flow of electrons along a conductor)
138 is generated. A conductor is any material that has many free
139 electrons by virtue of its physical makeup.

140 **Electric Energy**

141 So far you have read about electrons being very small. Just
142 how small are they? Well, electrons are incredibly small. The
143 diameter of an electron is about 0.000 000 000 000 22 (or 2.2
144 $\times 10^{-13}$) in. You may wonder how anything so small can be a
145 source of energy. Much of the answer lies in the fact that elec-
146 trons move at nearly the speed of light, or 186,000 miles per
147 second (mi/s). In metric terms that is 300 million meters per
148 second (m/s). As you can see from their size, billions of them
149 can move at once through a wire. The combination of speed
150 and concentration together produces great energy.

151 *CURRENT FLOW*

152 When a flow of electrons along a conductor occurs, this is
153 commonly referred to as *current flow*. Thus, you can see that
154 the movement of electrons is related to current electricity.

155 *CONDUCTORS*

156 A material through which electricity passes easily is called
157 a *conductor* because it has free electrons. In other words, a
158 conductor offers very little resistance or opposition to the flow
159 of electrons.

160 All metals are conductors of electricity to some extent.
161 Some are much better than others. Silver, copper, and aluminum
162 let electricity pass easily. Silver is a better conductor than
163 copper. However, copper is used more frequently because it is
164 cheaper. Aluminum is used as a conductor where light weight
165 is important.

166 Why are some materials good conductors? One of the most
167 important reasons is the presence of *free electrons*. If a material
168 has many electrons which are free to move away from their
169 atoms, that material will be a good conductor of electricity.

170 Although free electrons usually move in a haphazard way,
171 their movement can be controlled. The electrons can be made to
172 move in the same direction, and this flow is called *electric current*.

173 Conductors may be in the form of bars, tubes, or sheets.
174 The most familiar conductors are wire. Many sizes of wire are
175 available. Some are only the thickness of a hair. Other wire
176 may be as thick as your arm. To prevent conductors from

177 touching at the wrong place they are usually coated with a
178 plastic or cloth material. This covering on the conductor is
179 called an *insulator*.

180 *INSULATORS*

181   An insulator is a material with very few, if any, free electrons.
182 No known material is a perfect insulator. However, there are
183 materials that are such poor conductors that they are classified
184 as insulators. Glass, dry wood, rubber, mica, and certain plastics
185 are insulating materials.

186 *SEMICONDUCTORS*

187   So far you have looked at insulators and conductors. In
188 between the two extremes are semiconductors. Semiconductors
189 in the form of transistors, diodes, and integrated circuits or
190 chips are used every day in electronic devices. Now is the time
191 to place them in their proper category.

192   Materials used in the manufacture of transistors and diodes
193 have a conductivity halfway between that of a good conductor
194 and a good insulator. Therefore, the name semiconductor is given
195 them. Germanium and silicon are the two most commonly
196 known semiconductor materials. Through the introduction of
197 small amounts of other elements (called impurities) these
198 nearly pure (99.999 999%) elements become *limited* conductors.
199 The opposite of conductors is resistors. *Resistors* are devices
200 used to give a measured amount of opposition or resistance to
201 the flow of electrons. This opposition to current flow is measured
202 in ohms (Ω) and indicates the amount of resistance a piece of
203 material offers to the flow of electrons. Take a look at Figure 2-4
204 to see how these semiconductor materials are placed between
205 good conductors and poor conductors.

206 Voltage and Current

207   In order to be able to measure the movement
208 of electrons along a conductor, it is necessary to
209 have units of measurement. This is somewhat dif-
210 ficult since you cannot see, taste, smell, or hear
211 electricity. Feeling it is possible, but dangerous.
212 This means that some way must be devised to be

Place marks in the margin next to specific statistics that need to be memorized. Consider using index cards, music, and pegging systems to store and retrieve this information.

213 able to detect its presence, its direction of flow, and its magni-
214 tude. Before you can measure amount, you must have some
215 type of unit to measure electricity in. (Electricity is defined as
216 the flow of electrons along a conductor.)

217 *VOLTS*

218   We measure the difference of potential between two plates
219 in a battery in terms of volts (V). It is actually *electric pressure*
220 exerted on electrons in a circuit. A circuit is a pathway for the
221 movement of electrons. An external force exerted on electrons
222 to make them flow through a conductor is known as *electro-*
223 *motive force*, or emf. It is measured in volts. Electric pressure,
224 potential difference, and emf mean the same thing. The words
225 *voltage drop* and *potential drop* can be interchanged.

226 *CURRENT*

227   For electrons to move in a particular direction, it is necessary
228 for a potential difference to exist between two points of the
229 emf source. If 6,250,000,000,000,000,000 (or 6.25×10^{18}) elec-
230 trons pass a given point in one second, there is said to be one
231 *ampere* (A) of current flowing. The same number of electrons
232 stored on an object (a static charge) and not moving is called
233 a *coulomb* (C).

234   As mentioned above, current is measured in amperes.
235 However, in electronics it is sometimes necessary to use smaller
236 units of measurement.

237   The *milliampere* is abbreviated as mA. It is one-thousandth
238 (0.001) of an ampere. The *microampere* is abbreviated as μA. It
239 is one-millionth (0.000 001) of an ampere. Note the Greek let-
240 ter *mu* (μ) is used for micro.

241   You may want to become familiar with the Greek alphabet.
242 Table 2-1 defines the terms used in electricity and electronics
243 and their corresponding Greek letters.

244   Current flow is assumed to be from negative (−) to positive
245 (+) in our explanations here. Electron flow is negative (−) to
246 positive (+), and we assume that current flow and electron
247 flow are one and the same. It makes explanations simpler as
248 we progress into electronics. The *conventional* current flow is
249 the opposite or positive (+) to negative (−).

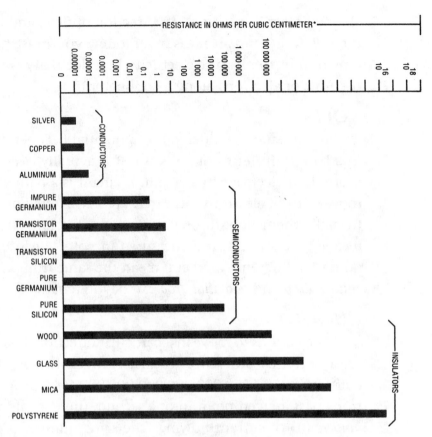

250 **Figure 2-4.** Location of insulators, semiconductors, and conductors in relation
251   to one another in terms of inherent resistance.
252   *A cubic centimeter (cm³) is one centimeter (0.3937 inches)
253   long, one centimeter wide and one centimeter high.

254   An ammeter is used to measure current flow in a circuit. A
255 milliammeter is used to measure smaller amounts, while the
256 microammeter is used to measure very small amounts of current.
257 (See Table 2-2 for metric prefixes.)
258   A voltmeter is used to measure voltage. In some instances
259 it is possible to obtain a meter which will measure
260 both voltage and current plus resistance. This is
261 called a *multimeter.* or *volt-ohm-milliammeter* (VOM).

If the information in the following tables is essential for you to remember then use the index card system to store and retrieve these numerous details.

TABLE 2-1

THE GREEK ALPHABET USED IN ELECTRICITY AND ELECTRONICS

Name	Capital	Small	Used to Designate
Alpha	A	α	Angles, area, coefficients, and attenuation constant.
Beta	B	β	Angles and coefficients.
Gamma	Γ	γ	Electrical conductivity and propagation constant.
Delta	Δ	δ	Angles, increment, decrement, and determinants.
Epsilon	E	ε	Dielectric constant, permittivity, and base of natural logarithms.
Zeta	Z	ζ	Coordinates.
Eta	H	η	Efficiency, hysteresis, and coordinates.
Theta	Θ	$\upsilon\theta$	Angles and angular phase displacement.
Iota	I	ι	Coupling coefficient.
Kappa	K	κ	
Lambda	Λ	λ	Wavelength.
Mu	M	μ	Permeability, amplification factor, and prefix *micro*.
Nu	N	ν	
Xi	Ξ	ξ	
Omicron	O	o	
Pi	Π	π	Pi = 3.1416.
Rho	P	ρ	Resistivity and volume charge density.
Sigma	Σ	$\sigma\varsigma$	Summation.
Tau	T	τ	Time constant and time-phase displacement.
Upsilon	Y	υ	
Phi	Φ	$\phi\varphi$	Magnetic flux and angles.
Chi	X	χ	Angles.
Psi	Ψ	ψ	Dielectric flux.
Omega	Ω	ω	Resistance in ohms and angular velocity.

291

TABLE 2-2

292 **METRIC PREFIXES AND POWERS OF TEN**

293 **Metric Prefixes**

294 Multiple	Prefix	Abbrev.	Multiple	Prefix	Abbrev.
295 10^{12}	tera	T	10^1	deci	d
296 10^9	giga	G	10^2	centi	c
297 10^6	mega	M	10^3	milli	m
298 10^4	myria	My	10^6	micro	μ
299 10^3	kilo	k	10^9	nano	n
300 10	deka	D	10^{12}	pico	p

301 **Scientific Notation (Powers of Ten)**

302 Large numbers can be simplified by using scientific notation (powers of ten).

303 For example, the multiples of 10 from 1 to 1,000,000, with their equivalents

304 in powers of ten are:

$$305 \quad 1 = 10^0$$
$$306 \quad 10 = 10^1$$
$$307 \quad 100 = 10^2$$
$$308 \quad 1\,000 = 10^3$$
$$309 \quad 10\,000 = 10^4$$
$$310 \quad 100\,000 = 10^5$$
$$311 \quad 1\,000\,000 = 10^6$$

312 Likewise, powers of ten can be used to simplify decimal expressions. The

313 submultiples of 10 from 0.1 to 0.000 001, with their equivalents in powers

314 of ten, are:

$$315 \quad 0.1 = 10^{-1}$$
$$316 \quad 0.01 = 10^{-2}$$
$$317 \quad 0.001 = 10^{-3}$$
$$318 \quad 0.000\,1 = 10^{-4}$$
$$319 \quad 0.000\,01 = 10^{-5}$$
$$320 \quad 0.000\,001 = 10^{-6}$$

321 Power

322   *Power* is defined as the *rate* at which work is done. It is

323 expressed in metric measurement terms of watts (W) for power

324 and joules (J) for energy or work. A *watt* is the power that gives

325 rise to the production of energy at the rate of one joule per

326 second (W = J/s). A *joule* is the work done when the point of
327 application of force of one newton is displaced a distance of
328 one meter in the direction of the force (J = N · m).
329   It has long been the practice in this country to measure
330 work in terms of horsepower (hp). Electric motors are still rated
331 in horsepower and probably will be for some time inasmuch
332 as the United States did not adopt the metric standards for
333 everything.
334   Power can be electric or mechanical. When a mechanical
335 force is used to lift a weight, *work* is done. The rate at which the
336 weight is moved is *power. Horsepower* is defined in terms of mov-
337 ing a certain weight over a certain distance in one minute (e.g.,
338 33,000 lb lifted 1 ft in 1 min equals 1 hp). Energy is consumed
339 in moving a weight or when work is done. The findings in this
340 field have been equated with the same amount of work done by
341 electric energy. It takes 746 W of electric power to equal 1 hp.
342   The horsepower rating of electric motors is arrived at by
343 taking the voltage and multiplying it by the current drawn
344 under full load. This power is measured in watts. In other words,
345 1 V times 1 A equals 1 W. When put into a formula it reads:

346 $$\text{Power} = \text{volts} \times \text{amperes} \quad \text{or} \quad P = E \times I$$

347 where E = voltage, or emf, and I = current, or intensity of elec-
348 tron flow.

349 **Kilowatt.** The kilowatt is com-
350 monly used to express the
351 amount of electric energy used
352 or available. The term *kilo* (k)
353 means one thousand (1000). A
354 kilowatt (kW) is one thousand
355 watts.
356   When the kilowatt is used in
357 terms of power dissipated or con-
358 sumed by a home for a month it
359 is expressed in kilowatthours.

Focus on the definitions and formula emphasized in this portion of the text. Mark them off with an asterisk and use one of your memory systems to store and retrieve them.

360 The unit kilowatthour is abbreviated as kWh. It is the equivalent
361 of one thousand watts used for a period of one hour. Electric

362 bills are figured or computed on an hourly basis and then read
363 in the kWh unit. The entire month's time is equated to one
364 hour's time.

365   Milliwatt is a term you will encounter when working with
366 electronics. The *milliwatt* (mW) means one-thousandth
367 (0.001) of a watt. The milliwatt is used in terms of some very
368 small amplifiers and other electronic devices. For instance, a
369 speaker used on a portable transistor radio will be rated as 100
370 milliwatts, or 0.1 W. Transistor circuits are designed in milli-
371 watts, but power line electric power is measured in kilowatts.
372 Keep in mind that *kilo* 1000 and *milli* means 0.001.

373 Resistance

374   Any time there is movement there is resistance. This resis-
375 tance is useful in electric and electronic circuits. Resistance
376 makes it possible to generate heat, control electron flow, and
377 supply the correct voltage to a device.

378   Resistance in a conductor depends on four factors: material,
379 length, cross-sectional area, and temperature.

380   **Material.** Some materials offer more resistance than others.
381 It depends upon the number of free electrons present in the
382 material.

383   **Length.** The longer the wire or conductor, the more resis-
384 tance it has. Resistance is said to vary *directly* with the length
385 of the wire.

386   **Cross-Sectional Area.** Resistance varies inversely with the
387 size of the conductor in cross section. In other words, the larger
388 the wire, the smaller the resistance per foot of length.

389   **Temperature.** For most materials, the higher the tempera-
390 ture, the higher the resistance. However, there are some excep-
391 tions to this in devices known as *thermistors*. Thermistors
392 change resistance with temperature. They *decrease* in resis-
393 tance with an increase in temperature. Thermistors are used in
394 certain types of meters to measure temperature.

395   Resistance is measured by a unit called the *ohm*. The Greek
396 letter omega (Ω) is used as the symbol for electrical resistance.

397 *RESISTORS*

398   *Resistors* are devices that provide measured amounts or
399 resistance. They are valuable when it comes to making sure the
400 proper amount of voltage is pre-
401 sent in a circuit. They are useful
402 when generating heat.

403   Resistors are classified as
404 either *wirewound* or *carbon-com-*
405 *position.* The symbol for a resis-
406 tor of either type is

407   Wirewound resistors are used
408 to provide sufficient opposition
409 to current flow to dissipate power
410 of 5 W or more. A watt is a unit of
411 electric power. A watt is equal to
412 one volt times one ampere.

413   Wirewound resistors are made
414 of wire that has controlled resis-
415 tance per unit length.

> **Before reading this section familiarize yourself with the diagrams. It will make this technical text much easier to understand. Consider chunking down the information contained here into a series of steps that are easy to picture and retain.**

416   Resistance causes a voltage drop across a resistor when
417 current flows through it. The voltage is dropped or dissipated
418 as heat and must be eliminated into the air.

419   Some variable resistors can be varied but can also be adjusted
420 for a particular setting. Resistors are available in various sizes,
421 shapes, and wattage ratings.

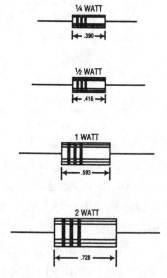

422 **Figure 2-5.** Wattage ratings of carbon-composition resistors.
423   All measurements shown here are in inches.

424 Carbon-composition resistors are usually found in electron-
425 ics devices. They are of low wattage. They are made in $^1/_8$-W,
426 $^1/_4$-W, $^1/_2$-W, 1-W, and 2-W sizes. The physical size determines
427 the wattage rating or their ability to dissipate heat (see Figure
428 2-5).

429 Carbon-composition resistors are usually marked according
430 to their ohmic value with a *color code*. The colors are placed on
431 the resistors in rings (see Figure 2-6).

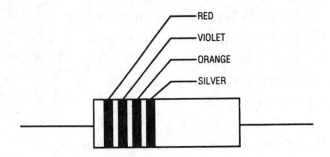

432 **Figure 2-6.** A 27,000-ohm (Ω) resistor.

433 Table 2-3 shows the values for reading the color code of
434 carbon-composition resistors.

435   **TABLE 2-3**

436   **RESISTOR COLOR CODE**

437 0 Black	5 Green
438 1 Brown	6 Blue
439 2 Red	7 Violet
440 3 Orange	8 Gray
441 4 Yellow	9 White

442 Take a close look at a carbon-composition resistor. The
443 bands should be to your left. Read from left to right. The band
444 closest to one end is placed to the left so you can read it from
445 left to right. The first band gives the first number according to
446 the color code. In this case (Figure 2-6) it is red, or 2. The second
447 band gives the next number, which is violet, or 7. The third
448 band represents the multiplier or divisor.

449 If the third band is a color in the 0 to 9 range in the color

450 code, it states the number of zeros to be added to the first two
451 numbers. Orange is 3; so the resistor in Figure 2-6 has a value
452 of 27,000 Ω of resistance.

453   The 27,000 Ω is usually written as 27 kΩ. The k stands for
454 thousand; it takes the place of three zeros. In some cases,
455 resistors are referred to as 27 MΩ (which means 27,000,000, or
456 27 million Ω), because the M stands for *mega*, and that is the
457 unit for million.

458   If there is no fourth band, the resistor has a tolerance rating
459 of ±20 percent (± means plus or minus). If the fourth band is
460 silver, the resistor has a tolerance of ±10 percent. If the fourth
461 band is gold, the resistor has a tolerance of ±5 percent.

462   Silver and gold may also be used for the *third* band. In this
463 case, according to the color code, the first two numbers
464 (obtained from the first two color bands) must be divided by
465 10 or 100. Silver means divide the first two numbers by 100.
466 Gold means divide the first two numbers by 10. For example,
467 if the bands of the resistor are red, yellow, and gold, then the
468 value is 24 divided by 10, or 2.4 Ω. If the third band is silver
469 and the two colors are yellow and orange, then the 43 is divided
470 by 100 to produce the answer of 0.43 Ω. Keep in mind, though,
471 that the fourth band will still be either gold or silver to indicate
472 the tolerance.

473   Resistors marked with the color code are available in hun-
474 dreds of size and wattage rating combinations. Wattage rating
475 refers to the wattage or power consumed by the resistor.

476 Ohm's Law

477   A German physicist by the name of Georg Ohm discovered
478 the relationship between voltage, current, and resistance in
479 1827. He found that in any circuit where the only opposition
480 to the flow of electrons is resistance, there is a relationship
481 between the values of voltage, current, and resistance. The
482 strength or intensity of the current is directly proportional to
483 the voltage and inversely proportional to the resistance.

484   It is easier to work with Ohm's law when it is expressed in
485 a formula. In the formula, E represents emf, or voltage; I is the
486 current, or the intensity of electron flow; R stands for resistance.
487 The formula is $E = I \times R$. It is used to find the emf (voltage)

488 when the current and the resistance are known.

489   To find the current, when the voltage and resistance are
490 known, use

491 $$I = \frac{E}{R}$$

492

493   To find the resistance, when the voltage and current are
494 known, use

495 $$R = \frac{E}{I}$$

496 ## USING OHM'S LAW

497   Ohm's law is very useful in electrical and electronics work.
498 You will need it often to determine the missing value. In order
499 to make it easy to remember the formula take a look at Figure
501 2-7. Here the formulas are arrived at by placing your finger on
502 the unknown and the other two will have their relationship
503 displayed.

504   The best way to become accustomed to solving problems is
505 to start with something simple, such as:

506 1. If the voltage is given as 100 V and the resistance is 25 Ω, it
507   is a simple problem and a practical application of Ohm's
508   law to find the current in the circuit. Use circuit. Use

509 $$I = \frac{E}{R}$$

510   Substituting the values in the formula,

511 $$I = \frac{100}{25}$$

512   means 100 is divided by 25 to produce 4 A for the current.
513 2. If the current is given as 2 A (you may read it on an ammeter
514   in the circuit), and the voltage (read from the voltmeter) is
515   100 V, it is easy to find the resistance. Use

516 $$R = \frac{E}{I}$$

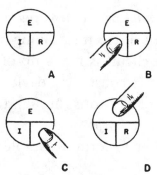

517 **Figure 2-7.** Ohm's law. Place your finger on the unknown value and the
518 remaining two letters will give the formula to use for finding the
519 unknown value.

520 Substituting the values in the formula,

521 $$R = \frac{100}{2}$$

522 means 100 divided by 2 equals 50 Ω for the circuit.
523 3. If the current is known to be 10 A, and the resistance is
524 found to be 50 Ω (measured before the circuit is energized),
525 it is then possible to determine how much voltage is
526 needed to cause the circuit
527 to function properly. Use

528 $$E = I \times R$$

529 Substituting the values in
530 the formula,

531 $$E = 10 \times 50$$

532 means 10 times 50 pro-
533 duces 500 or that it would
534 take 500 V to push 10 A
535 through 50 Ω of resistance.

> What is the significance of Ohm's law? How is it used? Can you solve problems using it? Did you need to use the practice problems to sharpen your under-standing of Ohm's law or did you understand the subject well enough to skip that section of the text?

536 # Circuits

537 There are a number of different types of circuits. Circuits are
538 the pathways along which electrons move to produce various
539 effects.

540   The *complete* circuit is necessary for the controlled flow or
541 movement of electrons along a conductor (see Figure 2-8). A
542 complete circuit is made up of a source of electricity, a con-
543 ductor, and a consuming device. This is the simplest of circuits.
544 The flow of electrons through the consuming device produces
545 heat, light, or work.

546   In order to form a complete circuit, these rules must be
547 followed:

548   1. Connect one side of the power source to one side of the
549   consuming device: *A* to *B*. (See Figure 2-8.)
550   2. Connect the other side of the power source to one side of
551   the control device, usually a switch: *C* to *D*. (See Figure 2-8.)
552   3. Connect the other side of the switch to the consuming
553   device it is supposed to control: *E* to *F*. (See Figure 2-8.)
554   When the switch is closed the circuit is complete.

555   However, when the switch is open, or not closed, there is no
556 path for electrons to flow, and there is an *open circuit* condition
557 where no current flows.

558   This method is used to make a complete path for electrons
559 to flow from that side of the battery with an excess of electrons
560 to the other side which has a deficiency of electrons. The battery
561 has a negative (–) charge where there is an excess of electrons

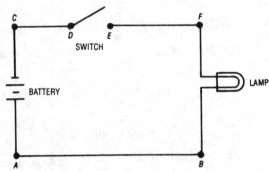

562 **Figure 2-8.** A simple circuit with a switch.

563 and a positive (+) charge where there is a deficiency of electrons.
564 Yes, you read it right: the – means excess and + means deficiency.
565 This is due to the fact that we are using the current flow and
566 electron flow as both the same and from – to + in the circuit.

567   A single path for electrons to flow is called a *closed*, or
568 *complete, circuit.* However, in some instances the circuit may

569 have more than one consuming device. In this situation we
570 have what is called a *series circuit* if the two or more resistors or
571 consuming devices are placed one after the other as shown in
572 Figure 2-9.

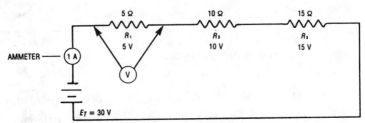

573   **Figure 2-9.** A series circuit with three resistors.

574 *SERIES CIRCUIT*

575   Figure 2-9 shows a series circuit. The three resistors are con-
576 nected in series, or one after the other, to complete the path
577 from one terminal of the battery to the other. The current
578 flows through each of them before returning to the positive
579 terminal of the battery.

580   There is a law concerning the voltages in a series circuit.
581 *Kirchhoff's voltage law* states that the sum of all voltages across
582 resistors or loads is equal to the applied voltage. Voltage drop
583 is considered across the resistor. Figure 2-9 shows the current
584 flow through three resistors. The voltage drop across R_1 is 5 V.
585 Across R_2 the voltage drop is 10 V. And, across R_3 the voltage
586 drop is 15 V. The sum of the individual voltage drops is equal
587 to the total or applied voltage of 30 V. E_T means total voltage.
588 It may also be written as E_A for applied voltage or E_S for source
589 voltage.

590   To find the total resistance in a series circuit, just add the
591 individual resistances or $R_T = R_1 + R_2 + R_3$. In this instance
592 (Figure 2-9) the total resistance is 5 + 10 + 15, or 30 Ω.

593 *PARALLEL CIRCUITS*

594   In a parallel circuit each resistance is connected directly
595 across the voltage source or line. There are as many separate
596 paths for current flow as there are branches (see Figure 2-10).

597   The voltage across all branches of a parallel circuit is the
598 same. This is because all branches are connected across
599 the voltage source. Current in a parallel circuit depends on the

600   **Figure 2-10.** A parallel circuit.

601   resistance of the branch. Ohm's law can be used to determine
602   the current in each branch. You can find the total current for
603   a parallel circuit by simply adding the individual currents.
604   When written as a formula it reads

605
$$I_T = I_1 + I_2 + I_3 + \ldots$$

606   The total resistance of a parallel circuit cannot be found by
607   adding the resistor values. Two formulas are used for finding
608   the total resistance (R_T). If there are *only two* resistors in paral-
609   lel, a simple formula can be used:

610
$$R_T = \frac{R_1 \times R_2}{R_1 + R_2}$$

611   If there are more than two resistors in parallel, you can use
612   the following formula. This formula may also be used with
613   two resistors in parallel. In fact it can be used for *any* number
614   of resistors.

615
$$\frac{1}{R_T} = \frac{1}{R_1} + \frac{1}{R_2} + \frac{1}{R_3} + \frac{1}{R_4} + \ldots$$

616   One thing should be kept in mind in parallel resistances:
617   The total resistance is always less than the smallest resistance.*

618   As branches are added to a parallel circuit, the voltage
619   across each branch is the same. However, the current divides
620   according to the resistance in the branch. The total current is

---

*   This is not true if one of the resistances is *negative*. The condition occurs
     only in active circuits, so for *most* applications the statement is true
     enough to be used for quick checks of your math.

621 equal to the sum of the individual currents. Inasmuch as current
622 and resistance are inversely related, that means if the currents
623 are added then the total or equivalent resistance of the parallel
624 circuit decreases with the increase in current. In order to
625 account for this decrease even though more resistance is added
626 to the circuit, the mathematical answer lies in the reciprocal
627 (1/R) formula. The reciprocal of the sum of the reciprocals of
628 the individual resistors in the circuit produces the desired
629 mathematical result and Ohm's law is satisfied when applied
630 to the total circuit values and when used for individual values
631 within the branch circuits.

632 *SERIES-PARALLEL CIRCUITS*

633   The series-parallel circuit is a combination of the series and
634 the parallel arrangement. Figure 2-11 shows an example of the
635 series-parallel circuit. It takes a minimum of three resistances
636 to make a series-parallel circuit. This type has to be reduced to
637 a series equivalent before it can be solved in terms of resistance.
638 The parallel portions are reduced to the total for that part of
639 the circuit, and then the equivalent resistance is added to the
640 series part to obtain the total resistance.

641   Total current flows through the first series resistor but
642 divides according to the branch resistances after that. There
643 are definite relationships which must be explored here before
644 that type of circuit can be fully understood. This will be done
645 in a later part of this book.

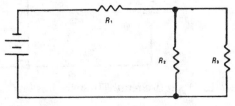

646 **Figure 2-11.** A series-parallel circuit.

647 *OPEN CIRCUITS*

648   An open circuit is an incomplete circuit. Figure 2-12 shows
649 an open circuit that will become a closed circuit once the
650 switch is closed. A circuit can also become open when one of
651 the leads is cut or when one of the terminals has the wire
652 removed. A loose connection can cause an open circuit.

653 *SHORT CIRCUITS*

654   The short circuit is something to be avoided because it can
655 cause a fire or overheating.

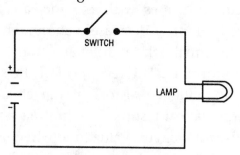

656 **Figure 2-12.** An open circuit produced by an open switch.

657   A short circuit has a path of low resistance to
658 electron flow. This is usually created when a low-
659 resistance wire is placed across the consuming
660 device (see Figure 2-13). The greater number of
661 electrons will flow through the path of least resis-
662 tance rather than through the consuming device.
663 A short usually generates an excess current flow
664 that can result in damage to a number of parts of
665 the circuit. If you wish to prevent the damage
666 caused by short circuits, use a fuse.

What are the different types of circuits? What causes a short circuit? Can you remember the important diagrams presented in this portion of the text? Where can you move your eyes to recall pictures that were seen and learned in the past?

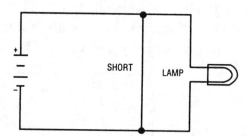

667 **Figure 2-13.** A short circuit. The wire has less resistance than the lamp.

668 *FUSES*

669   Fuses are available in a number of sizes and shapes. They
670 are used to prevent the damage done by excess current flowing
671 in a circuit. They are placed in series with the consuming
672 devices. Once too much current flows, it causes the fuse wire
673 inside the fuse case to melt. This opens the circuit and stops

674 the flow of current and prevents the overheating that occurs
675 when too much current is present in a circuit.

676   The symbol for a fuse is   . It fits into a circuit as
677 shown in Figure 2-14.

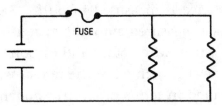

678 **Figure 2-14.** The location of the fuse in a circuit.

679 # SUMMARY

680   Electricity is defined as the
681 flow of electrons along a conduc-
682 tor. Electrons are the smallest part
683 of an atom. An atom is the small-
684 est part of an element which
685 contains all its properties. Elec-
686 trons can be directed along a
687 given path called a circuit by
688 means of magnetism, heat, light,
689 or pressure. Electrons that move
690 in a random motion are called
691 free electrons. These free electrons
692 when directed in a given direc-
693 tion make up what is called
694 electricity.

> Memorize the key facts covered in the summary using a memory tool. Consider using the index cards for specific details, playing music in the background to remain in peak learning state, and use emotional pegs to store and retrieve essential information.

695   Current flow is the flow of electrons along a conductor.
696 Current flow is from negative to positive.

697   A material through which electricity passes easily is called
698 a conductor. An insulator is a material with very few, if any,
699 free electrons. No known materials are perfect insulators.

700   The diameter of an electron is about 0.000 000 000 000 22
701 (or 2.2×10^{-13}) in. Materials used in the manufacture of tran-
702 sistors and diodes have a conductivity between that of a good
703 conductor and a good insulator.

704   Electricity is measured in terms of volts, amps, and ohms.

705 Meters are used to measure the flow of electrons, the voltage
706 drop across resistors, and the opposition put up to the flow of
707 electrons by certain materials.

708   Resistance is the opposition to the movement of electrons.
709 Resistance is measured in ohms. Resistors are devices which
710 provide measured amounts of resistance. There are two types
711 of resistors: wirewound and carbon-composition.

712   Power is defined as the rate at which work is done. Power
713 measured in terms of electrical energy is designated as watts.
714 The watt is one volt times one ampere for one second. The
715 kilowatt is one thousand watts. The kilowatthour is one thou-
716 sand watts for one hour.

717   It takes 746 watts to produce one horsepower. It takes a
718 mechanical horsepower defined in terms of 33,000 pounds lifted
719 one foot in one minute to equal one electrical horsepower
720 defined in terms of watts or 746 watts equal one horsepower.

721   Ohm's law states that the current in any circuit is equal to
722 the voltage divided by the resistance. It can also be substituted
723 so that the voltage is equal to the current times the resistance, or
724 the resistance is equal to the voltage divided by the current.

725   There are a number of types of circuits. The open circuit
726 does not have a complete path for electron flow from one ter-
727 minal of the voltage source to the other. A short circuit has a
728 resistance that is too small and therefore takes all the current
729 and bypasses it from the intended load. The series circuit con-
730 sists of resistors placed end to end. The parallel circuit consists
731 of resistors placed across the power source. The current in a
732 series circuit flows the same through all resistors. The current
733 in a parallel circuit divides according to the branch resistance.

734   A combination of series and parallel circuits can be made
735 with the use of at least three resistors.

736   Fuses are safety devices which protect circuits from overloads
737 and overheating. They open the circuit when overheated.

738 ## REVIEW QUESTIONS

739   1. Where does the word electricity come from?
740   2. What is an atom?
741   3. How does an electron fit into an atom?

742   4. Where do you find free electrons?

743   5. How big is an electron?

744   6. List five insulators.

745   7. What are the two most
746   common semiconductor
747   materials?

748   8. Define voltage and current.

749   9. What is the unit for measur-
750   ing electric power?

751   10. How much is a kilowatt?

752   11. How many watts are there
753   in one horsepower?

754   12. What is the symbol for
755   ohms?

756   13. What is the symbol for a resistor?

757   14. What type of resistor uses a color code?

758   15. How much is a kilo?

795   16. What is the term used to designate one million?

760   17. State Ohm's law.

761   18. State Kirchhoff's voltage law.

762   19. What is the formula used to find total resistance in a
763   parallel circuit?

764   20. What is the purpose of a fuse?

> Do you know the answers to these questions? If you followed my suggestion and memorized these questions before reading the material you would have known which material provided the answers.

PRACTICE READING 12: ANATOMY AND PHYSIOLOGY

1 # INTRODUCTION TO
2 # ANATOMY AND
3 # PHYSIOLOGY

4 The study of anatomy and physiology is essential to
5 understanding the human body. These disciplines
6 concern the body's structural framework and how
7 it works. What the body is able to do depends inti-
8 mately on how it is constructed, and the body's
9 construction gives a strong indication to what it
10 does. For example, the lungs are composed of
11 millions of air sacs with extremely thin walls. This
12 construction permits them to serve as a site for
13 exchanging oxygen and carbon dioxide gases.
14   The topic of anatomy has many subdivisions.
15 For example, **gross anatomy** concerns body struc-
16 tures examined by observation without the use of
17 a microscope. **Histologic anatomy** is the study of
18 cells, tissues, and organs as they are observed with
19 a microscope. **Developmental anatomy** deals with
20 the development of the individual from the fertil-
21 ized egg to the adult form.
22   Within the science of physiology, there are also
23 many subdivisions. For instance, **cytology** is the
24 study of cells and how they function; **neurophysiology** is the
25 study of nerve function; and **renal physiology** deals with the
26 excretory system and its activities. **Reproductive physiology**
27 is the study of reproductive organs and the methods for
28 reproduction.

> Skim Chapter 1 and pay careful attention to the use of different font sizes and typeface to highlight important details. Familiarize yourself with the charts and diagrams contained within this unit before reading the material. Finally, study the questions asked at the end of the unit to determine which information is essential for you to memorize and retain for peak learning performance.

29 Levels of Structure

30 The human body has several levels
31 of structural organization. At the
32 simplest level, the human body
33 is composed of **atoms**, the ultra-
34 microscopic building blocks of
35 matter. Atoms are typified by
36 oxygen, carbon, nitrogen, and
37 sodium. Atoms combine with
38 one another to form **molecules**.
39 Molecules are typified by water,
40 sodium chloride, proteins, carbo-
41 hydrates, and lipids (Figure 1.1).

Use the index card
method for mastering
the new vocabulary and
definitions in this text.
The index card method
is especially useful for
subjects like biology,
which require extensive
memorization.

42   The association of molecules with one another yields the
43 next level of organization, the **cell**. The cell is the fundamental
44 unit of living things. It has levels of subcellular structures such
45 as the nucleus, mitochondria, ribosomes, and lysosomes
46 (Chapter 3). Among the different cells in the body are nerve
47 cells, muscle cells, and blood cells.

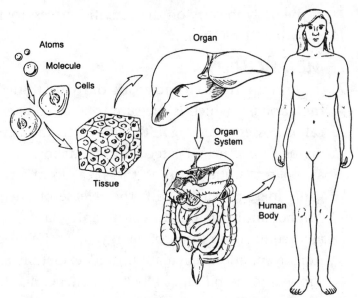

48   **FIGURE 1.1**   The levels of structure in the human body.

49   The next level of structural organization, the **tissue**, is a
50 group of cells of similar structure performing the same function
51 (Chapter 4). The body has four basic types of tissues: epithelial

52 tissue (such as in the organ linings), connective tissue (such as
53 blood and bone), muscle tissue, and nervous tissue. Each tissue
54 type plays a unique role in the body.

55   The next level of organization is the **organ**. An organ is
56 composed of two or more different kinds of tissues. The stomach,
57 for example, is an organ composed of epithelial tissue, muscle
58 tissue, nerve tissue, and connective tissue. An organ functions
59 as a specialized physiological center for a particular activity.

60   The final level of structural organization is the **organ system**,
61 composed of several organs with related functions. Organ
62 systems in the body include the digestive, respiratory, nervous,
63 and circulatory systems (Table 1.1). The systems operating
64 together form the **organism**, which is the highest level of
65 organization.

66 Characteristics of the Living Body

67 The human body, like other living things, has
68 certain characteristics distinguishing it from non-
69 living things. These characteristics enable the cells
70 of the body to carry on the activities necessary for
71 growth and survival.

72 *METABOLISM*

73   An important characteristic of living things is
74 **metabolism**, which is the sum total of all chemi-
75 cal processes occurring in the body. **Metabolism** is
76 divided into the subcategories of catabolism and
77 anabolism. **Catabolism** is the breakdown of or-
78 ganic matter, usually with the release of energy.
79 **Anabolism** is the buildup of organic matter, usu-
80 ally requiring an input of energy. Such life processes as diges-
81 tion, respiration, circulation, and excretion are adapted for
82 supplying the building blocks for metabolism and removing
83 the waste products of metabolism.

> Memorize Table 1.1 prior to reading the material in this subsection. Efficient use of tables can help you chunk down the details of a subject like biology into easy-to-remember key points, key points that easily can be linked to other extensive details.

84   **TABLE 1.1**   *Major Organ Systems in Humans*

85 Organ System	Physiological Role	Components
86 Integumentary 87	Covers the body and protects it	Skin, hair, nails, and sweat glands
88 Skeletal 89 90	Protects the body and provides support for locomotion and movement	Bones, cartilage, and ligaments
91 Nervous 92 93	Receives stimuli, integrates information, and directs the body	Brain, spinal cord, nerves, and sense organs
94 Endocrine 95	Coordinates and integrates the activities of the body	Pituitary, adrenal, thyroid, and other ductless glands
96 Muscular 97	Produces body movement	Skeletal muscle, smooth muscle, and cardiac muscle
98 Digestive 99 100 101	Absorbs soluble nutrients from ingested food	Teeth, salivary glands, esophagus, stomach, intestines, liver, and pancreas
102 Respiratory 103 104	Collects oxygen and exchanges it for carbon dioxide	Lungs, pharynx, trachea, and other air passageways
105 Circulatory 106 107	Transports cells and materials throughout the body	Heart, blood vessels, blood, and lymph structures
108 Immune 109 110 111	Removes foreign chemicals and microorganisms from the bloodstream	T-lymphocytes, B-lymphocytes, and macrophages; lymph structures
112 Urinary 113	Removes metabolic wastes from the bloodstream	Kidney, bladder, and associated ducts
114 Reproductive 115 116	Produces sex cells for the next generation of organism	Testes, ovaries, and associated reproductive structures

117 MOVEMENT AND OTHER CHARACTERISTICS

118 Another important characteristic is **movement**, the result of
119 contracting muscle cells. Movement can be voluntary, such as
120 occurs in the muscles of the skeleton, or it may be involuntary,

121 such as occurs in the lining of internal organs. The bones of
122 the skeletal system assist movement by providing attachment
123 sites for the muscles.

124   Another characteristic, **growth**, refers to an increase in the
125 size of body cells or the body itself. Growth is the process in
126 which an organism obtains materials from the environment
127 and forms more of itself. An increase in the number of cells,
128 the size of existing cells, or the substance surrounding the cells
129 constitutes growth.

130   A fourth characteristic is **conductivity**. Conductivity refers
131 to the ability of cells to receive stimuli and carry them from
132 one body part to another. This characteristic is associated with
133 nerve cells and muscle cells.

134   Still another important characteristic of the living body is
135 **reproduction**, the ability of the body to replicate itself.
136 Reproduction can refer to the formation of new cells for
137 growth, repair, or replacement, or the production of an entire-
138 ly new individual. Reproduction in humans involves the pro-
139 duction of sperm and egg cells and their union to form a
140 fertilized egg cell, which develops into a new individual. This
141 form of reproduction is known as **sexual reproduction**. It
142 compares to **asexual reproduction**—the duplication of a sin-
143 gle cell, which produces two identical daughter cells.

144   Other characteristics of living things include **irritability**,
145 the response of the body to an internal or external stimulus;
146 and **excretion**, the process of removing waste products from
147 the body.

148 ## *HOMEOSTASIS*

149 **Homeostasis** refers to the steady-state equilibrium existing in
150 the body and the maintenance of this state. It is associated
151 with the relative constancy of the chemical and physical envi-
152 ronment in the cells and in the organism itself. Such things as
153 water, nutrients, and oxygen are part of the chemical require-
154 ments to maintain homeostasis; a constant temperature and
155 atmospheric pressure are part of the physical requirements for
156 homeostasis.

157   The body is said to be in homeostasis when the needs of its
158 cells are met and its activities are occurring smoothly. All
159 organ systems play a role in homeostasis, and the composition

160 of fluids within the body is maintained precisely at all times.
161 Stress, such as heat, pain, or lack of oxygen, creates an imbalance
162 in the internal environment and disturbs the homeostasis of
163 the body.

164   Because internal conditions vary constantly, the body is
165 protected against extremes by self-regulating systems known
166 as **feedback systems**. With feedback systems the body sends
167 information back into the system to induce a response. The
168 **setpoint** of a feedback system is the normal value of a variable,
169 such as temperature. A sensor or **receptor** detects any deviation
170 from the setpoint, and a **control center** receives information
171 from various receptors to integrate and determine the response
172 to return to the setpoint. **Effectors** then implement the response
173 to return the body to homeostasis.

174   A feedback system is a **negative feedback system** when
175 the information decreases the system's output to bring the
176 system back to its setpoint. For example, the level of glu-
177 cose rises in the body after a meal, and the glucose stimulates
178 the release of insulin from the pancreas. Insulin facilitates the
179 passage of glucose into cells and reduces the glucose level.
180 The lowered glucose level then influences insulin-secreting
181 cells to decrease their output of insulin to maintain homeostasis.

182   Homeostasis may also be obtained by a **positive feedback**
183 **system**. In this situation, the information returned to the system
184 increases the deviation from the setpoint. For example, stimu-
185 lating a nerve cell membrane causes more sodium ions to flow
186 across the membrane into the cell, and the sodium flow
187 increases the membrane's passageways to encourage still more
188 sodium ions to flow inward. The result is a nerve impulse.

189 # Directional Terms

190 Directional terms are used in relation to one another to denote
191 where body parts are located. The point of reference for the
192 body is the **anatomical position**. In this position, the body is
193 erect with eyes forward, feet together, arms at the sides, and
194 palms up with the thumbs pointing away from the body (see
195 Figure 1.2).

196   In the anatomical position, the **anterior** aspect
197 of the body is toward the front of the body on the
198 belly side. Anterior is often used interchangeably
199 with the term **ventral** (even though ventral refers
200 to the belly side of a four-legged animal such as a
201 dog). The **posterior** aspect refers to the back side of
202 the human. This term is often used interchange-
203 ably with the term **dorsal**.
204   In the human body, the term **superior** refers to
205 the aspect toward the head or upper part of the
206 body. For example, the nose is superior to the
207 mouth. The terms **cephalic** and **cranial** are some-
208 times used instead of superior. The **inferior** aspect
209 of the body refers to a direction away from the
210 head or toward the lower part of the body. The term
211 **caudal** is an alternative expression. In this context,
212 the abdomen is inferior to the thorax.

> Directional terms and
> the planes covered in
> the next section are
> extremely important in
> biology, and it is essential
> that you remember
> each of these terms.
> Look at the diagram on
> the next page and make
> a mental picture of
> what each of these
> directional terms mean.
> Whenever these terms
> appear in the text you
> can use your mental
> pictures to understand
> how the material
> should be viewed.

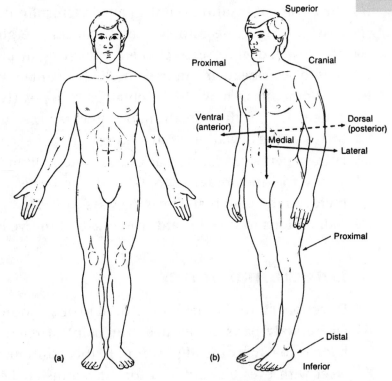

213 **FIGURE 1.2**   *The body and its directions. (a) The body in the anatomical posi-*
214   *tion standing with the feet together, arms at side, and palms up (b)*
215   *Several directional terms associated with anatomical structures of*
216   *the body.*

217   The term **medial** refers to a direction closer to the midline
218 of the body or to one of its structures—the nose is medial to
219 the eyes. The term **lateral** refers to a location off to the side
220 and away from the midline—the eyes are lateral to the nose.
221 The terms **ipsilateral** and **contralateral** refer to structures on
222 the same side of the body or opposite sides of the body, respec-
223 tively (Table 1.2). For instance, the ascending colon and gall-
224 bladder are ipsilateral, while the ascending colon and descending
225 colon are contralateral.

226   In the human body the term **proximal** refers to a direction
227 closer to the attachment point of an extremity to the trunk;
228 thus, the femur is proximal to the body trunk as compared to
229 the ankle. In comparison, **distal** refers to a region farther from
230 the attachment of a limb to the trunk. The ankle is distal to
231 body trunk relative to the femur. The terms **superficial** and
232 **deep** refer to a location closer to the body surface or removed
233 from it; the skin is superficial to the muscles; the heart lies
234 deep to the muscles.

235 ### *PLANES*

236 The structural plan of the human body has various imaginary
237 flat surfaces called **planes**. Planes pass through the body and
238 provide reference points for the organs of the body. A **sagittal**
239 **plane**, for example, is a vertical plane dividing the body into
240 right and left sides. Such a plane may be **midsagittal** if it
241 divides the body into equal right and left halves, or **parasagittal**
242 if it divides the body into unequal right and left halves.

243   **TABLE 1.2**   *A Summary of Directional Terms*

Term	Definition	Example
244 Anterior 246 (ventral)	Nearer to or at the front of the body	Sternum is anterior to the heart
247 Posterior 248 (dorsal)	Nearer to or at the back of the body	Esophagus is posterior to the trachea
249 Superior 250 (cephalic or 251 cranial) 252	Toward the head or the upper part of a structure; generally refers to structures in the trunk	Heart is superior to the liver

TABLE 1.2 *continued*

Term	Definition	Example
Inferior (caudal)	Away from the head or toward the lower part of the structure; generally refers to structures in the trunk	Stomach is inferior to the lungs
Medial	Nearer to the midline of the body or a structure	Ulna is on the medial side of the forearm
Lateral	Away from the midline of the body	Lungs are lateral to the heart
Ipsilateral	On the same side of the body	Gallbladder and ascending colon of the large intestine are ipsilateral
Contralateral	On the opposite side of the body	Ascending and descending colons of the large intestine are contralateral
Proximal	Nearer to the attachment of an extremity to the trunk or structure	Femur is proximal to the tibia
Distal	Farther from the attachment of an extremity to the trunk of a structure	Phalanges are distal to the carpals (wrist bones)
Superficial	Toward the surface of the body	Muscles of the thoracic wall are superior to the viscera in the thoracic cavity
Deep	Away from the surface of the body	Ribs are deep to the skin of the chest

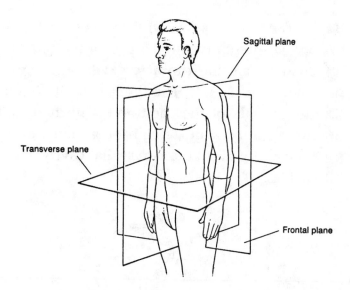

281   **FIGURE 1.3**   *The three major planes of the human body.*

282   The second important plane is the **frontal**, or **coronal**,
283   **plane**. Like the sagittal plane, the frontal plane runs longitu-
284   dinally, but it divides the body into anterior and posterior
285   portions. The frontal plane lies at a right angle to a sagittal plane
286   (Figure 1.3).

287   The third important plane is the **transverse plane**, also
288   known as the **horizontal plane**. This plane divides the body
289   into superior and inferior portions. Organs sectioned across
290   the transverse plane for study are referred to as **cross-sections**.

291   ## *BODY CAVITIES AND REGIONS*

292   The body cavities are areas within
293   the body containing its internal
294   organs. The two principal cavities
295   are the **dorsal body cavity** and the
296   **ventral body cavity**. The dorsal
297   body cavity is located along the
298   posterior (dorsal) surface of the
299   body, where it is subdivided into
300   the **cranial cavity** housing the
301   brain and the **spinal cavity**,
302   formed by the vertebral column
303   and housing the spinal cord.

Use index cards to
memorize all the bolded
vocabulary words
appearing in this and
the next section. Refer
to the diagram on
p. 304 to form your
mental images.

304   The second body cavity is the **ventral body cavity**, located
305   on the anterior (ventral) aspect of the body. Its two major sub-
306   divisions are the **thoracic cavity** and the **abdominopelvic**
307   **cavity** (Figure 1.4). The thoracic cavity is surrounded by ribs
308   and muscles of the chest and is further subdivided into the
309   two **pleural cavities**, each having a lung. In addition, there is a
310   third cavity called the **pericardial cavity**, medial to the pleural
311   cavities.

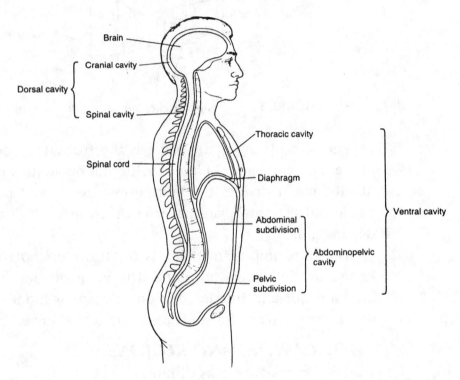

312   **FIGURE 1.4**   *The two major body cavities and their subdivisions and components.*

313   The pericardial cavity houses the heart and is located in a
314   region called the **mediastinum**. The mediastinum includes all
315   the contents of the thoracic cavity except the lungs. Within
316   the mediastinum are the heart, thymus, esophagus, trachea,
317   bronchi, and many blood and lymphatic vessels. The pericar-
318   dial cavity is actually a small space between the visceral peri-
319   cardium and parietal pericardium, which are the membranes
320   covering the heart.
321   The abdominopelvic cavity is separated from the thoracic
322   cavity by the large, dome-shaped diaphragm muscle. This cavity
323   is also known as the **peritoneal cavity**. It contains the visceral

324 organs of the abdomen and pelvis. Located within the **abdomi-**
325 **nal subdivision** are the stomach, intestines, spleen, liver, and
326 other organs. The inferior portion, called the **pelvic subdivision**,
327 contains the bladder, certain female reproductive organs, and
328 rectum.

329   Additional divisions of the abdominopelvic cavity yield nine
330 designations for various regions. The **umbilical region** is at the
331 center of the abdomen, while the **epigastric region** is imme-
332 diately superior to the umbilical region, and the **hypogastric**
333 **region** is immediately inferior. Lateral to the epigastric region
334 are the right and left **hypochondriac regions**, and lateral to
335 the umbilical region are the right and left **lumbar regions**.
336 Lateral to the hypogastric region are the right and left
337 **inguinal (iliac) regions**. In addition, four abdominopelvic
338 designations are used clinically from imaginary horizontal and
339 vertical lines intersecting at the center. These regions are the
340 **right and left upper quadrants** and the **right and left lower**
341 **quadrants** (Figure 1.5).

342 ## *MEMBRANES*

343 The walls of the ventral body cavity and its organs are covered
344 with a thin, double-layered membrane called the **serous**
345 **membrane**, so-named because it contains a lubricating fluid
346 called **serous fluid** secreted by both membranes. The fluid
347 permits organs to slide easily across cavity walls and pass by
348 one another without causing friction. Serous membranes lie
349 very close to one another.

350   The body has three major serous membranes: the **pleura**,
351 which lines the pleural cavities; the **pericardium**, which lines
352 the heart; and the **peritoneum**, which surrounds some organs
353 and covers others. The covering is peritoneal if the organs are
354 surrounded, and retroperitoneal, if the organs are covered.

355   Each of the three serous membranes has a **parietal portion**
356 and a **visceral portion**. The parietal portion lines a cavity,
357 while the visceral portion covers an organ. For example, the
358 parietal peritoneum lines the abdominal pelvic cavity, while
359 the visceral peritoneum covers the different organs within this
360 cavity. The area between the parietal peritoneum and the vis-
361 ceral peritoneum is the peritoneal cavity. The pleural cavity is
362 the space between the parietal pleura and the visceral pleura.

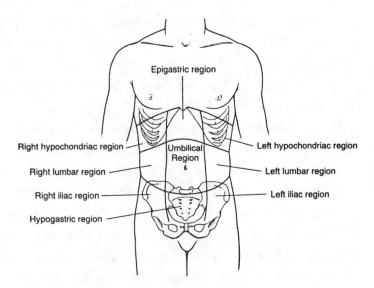

Epigastric region

Right hypochondriac region · Umbilical Region · Left hypochondriac region

Right lumbar region · Left lumbar region

Right iliac region · Left iliac region

Hypogastric region

363 **FIGURE 1.5** *The important anatomical regions of the abdominopelvic cavity.*

364   Other small cavities of the body are found in
365 the head. They include the oral cavity, the nasal
366 cavity, the middle ear cavities, and the orbital cav-
367 ities of the eyes.

368 # Review Questions

369 *PART A—Completion:* **Add the word or words**
370 **that correctly complete each of the following**
371 **statements.**

372   1. The study of the body structures without the
373   use of a microscope is known as _____.

374   2. For histologic anatomy, it is important that
375   one employ a ____.

376   3. One of the branches of physiology is cytology, which is the
377   study of _____.

378   4. The function of the excretory system is a major topic of a
379   branch of physiology known as _____.

380   5. At its most simple level of structure the body is composed
381   of _____.

> Did you remember to skim all of these questions prior to reading the material? Did you form mental movies of these questions so that you would be aware when the answers appeared in the text? Are all of these exercises necessary for you to remember and learn the chapter's important information?

382   6. Sodium chloride, proteins, lipids, and water typify the level
383   of structure of the body in which the main components
384   are _____.

385   7. The fundamental unit of all living things, including the
386   human body is _____.

387   8. A group of cells working together to perform the same
388   function represents a _____.

389   9. A type of tissue represented by the blood and bone is _____.

390   10. The organs of the body are lined with a type of tissue
391   known as _____.

392   11. Various types of tissue work together in the human body
393   to compose a _____.

394   12. The sum total of all chemical processes occurring in the
395   body is _____.
396

      13. When organic matter is built up from smaller molecules,
397   and the process usually requires an input of energy, the
398   overall process is called _____.

399   14. The metabolic process in which organic matter is broken
400   down usually with the release of energy is _____.

401   15. Two general types of movement in the body are voluntary
402   and _____.

403   16. To assist the process of movement in the body, the muscles
404   are usually attached to _____.

405   17. The body obtains materials from the environment and
406   forms more of itself in the process of _____.

407   18. The characteristic of conductivity is associated in the body
408   with muscle cells and _____.

409 19. In addition to producing an entirely new individual, new
410   cells are formed in the body for the three purposes of
411   replacement, growth, and _____.

412 20. The form of reproduction in which a fertilized egg cell
413   forms is called _____.

414 21. In the duplication of a single cell to form two identical
415   daughter cells, the reproduction is known as _____.

416 22. The steady state equilibrium existing in the body is known
417   as _____.

418 23. The cells of an organism and the organism itself remains
419   relatively constant in its chemical environment and in
420   its _____.

421 24. Part of the chemical requirements of the human body to
422   maintain homeostasis include water, nutrients, and _____.

423 25. Among the systems that contribute to the maintenance of
424   homeostasis are the nervous system and the _____.

425 26. An imbalance in the internal environment and disturbance
426   of homeostasis are both created by _____.

427 27. A system in which information decreases the system's output
428   and brings the system back to its setpoint is a _____.

429 28. The system in which information is returned in order to
430   increase the deviation from the original setpoint is a _____.

431 29. The body is erect with eyes forward, feet together, arms at
432   the side, and palms up in the _____.

433 30. In speaking of a direction toward the front of the body on
434   the belly side, one uses the term _____.

435 31. Although the term dorsal is sometimes used, the preferred
436   term when referring to the back side of a human is _____.

437
438

32. In anatomical nomenclature, the term superior refers to an aspect of the body toward the _____.

439
440

33. In anatomical terms, the abdomen is said to be inferior to the _____.

441
442

34. The anatomical term referring to a side away from the midline is _____.

443
444

35. The term proximal refers to a direction closer to the attachment point of an extremity to the body _____.

445
446

36. In the anatomical literature, the hand would be considered distal to the _____.

447
448

37. Two structures on the same side of the body such as the left arm and left leg are said to be _____.

449
450

38. A vertical plane dividing the body into right and left sides represents a _____.

451
452

39. A longitudinal plane dividing the body into anterior and posterior portions is a frontal plane, also known as a _____.

453
454

40. A horizontal plane divides the body into superior and inferior parts and is also known as a _____.

455
456
457

41. A midsagittal plane divides the body into equal right and left halves, but if the halves are unequal the plane is said to be _____.

458
459

42. The dorsal body cavity is subdivided into the spinal cavity and the _____.

460
461

43. Two major subdivisions of the ventral body cavity are the abdominopelvic cavity and the _____.

462
463

44. The heart, esophagus, trachea, and bronchi are all located in a portion of the body called the _____.

464 45. The abdominal subdivision and pelvic subdivision are por-
465   tions of the abdominopelvic cavity, which is also known as
466   the _____.

467 46. The large dome-shaped muscle separating the abdomino-
468   pelvic cavity from the thoracic cavity is the _____.

469 47. Immediately superior to the umbilical region is a region of
470   the abdominopelvic cavity known as the _____.

471 48. Lateral to the hypogastric region of the abdominopelvic
472   cavity is the iliac region, also called the _____.

473 49. Among the three major serous membranes of the body are
474   the peritoneum, the pleura, and the _____.

475 50. The three serous membranes of the body have both visceral
476   portions and _____.

477 *PART B—Multiple Choice:* **Circle the letter of the item that**
478 **correctly completes each of the following statements.**

479   1. The discipline of histologic anatomy is concerned primarily
480   with
481   (A) the development of an individual
482   (B) the study of the kidney
483   (C) the microscopic observations of cells and tissues
484   (D) the study of the brain

485   2. The fundamental unit of living things is the
486   (A) tissue
487   (B) cell
488   (C) organ
489   (D) organ system

490   3. All the following are basic types of human tissues except
491   (A) connective tissue
492   (B) nervous tissue
493   (C) epithelial tissue
494   (D) squamous tissue

4. Several organs having related functions and working together constitute
   - (A) a tissue
   - (B) an organ system
   - (C) an organism
   - (D) a cell

5. The metabolic process of catabolism involves the
   - (A) buildup of organic matter
   - (B) utilization of energy
   - (C) breakdown of organic matter
   - (D) absorption of nutrients

6. The bones of the skeletal system assist the function of movement
   - (A) by producing white blood cells
   - (B) by storing minerals
   - (C) by providing sites for the attachments of muscles
   - (D) by conducting nerve impulses

7. All of the following are characteristics of growth except
   - (A) an organism obtains materials from the environment
   - (B) an organism uses its muscles to move
   - (C) an organism forms more of itself
   - (D) the size of the body's cells increases

8. When the needs of the body's cells are met and the activities of the body are occurring smoothly, then the body is said to be in
   - (A) homeostasis
   - (B) anabolic metabolism
   - (C) growth
   - (D) ipsilateral motion

9. A feedback system operating in the body may be
   - (A) positive or negative
   - (B) lateral or contralateral
   - (C) regulatory or enabling
   - (D) proximal or distal

530 10. All the following characteristics apply to the body in the
531   anatomical position except
532   (A) the eyes are forward
533   (B) the arms are at the sides
534   (C) the feet are together
535   (D) the palms are down with the thumbs pointing to the
536   body.

537 11. Which of the following structures would be considered on
538   the anterior aspect of the body?
539   (A) the back of the head
540   (B) the navel
541   (C) the ears
542   (D) the elbows

543 12. In relationship to the stomach, the spinal cord is
544   (A) lateral
545   (B) posterior
546   (C) anterior
547   (D) ventral

548 13. The directional term referring to an area toward the lower
549   part of the body and away from the head is
550   (A) cephalic
551   (B) cranial
552   (C) superior
553   (D) inferior

554 14. If structure A lies lateral to the body, and structure B is in
555   the opposite direction, then structure B is in the direction
556   referred to as
557   (A) proximal
558   (B) medial
559   (C) ventral
560   (D) anterior

561 15. Relative to each other, the right and left arms are

562   (A) proximal

563   (B) frontal

564   (C) contralateral

565   (D) caudal

566 16. In comparison to the knee joint, the hip joint of the body is

567   said to be

568   (A) proximal

569   (B) superficial

570   (C) inferior

571   (D) dorsal

572 17. In comparison to the skin, the muscles are

573   (A) superficial

574   (B) deep

575   (C) lateral

576   (D) cephalic

577 18. Because the left arm and left leg are on the same side of the

578   body, they are said to be

579   (A) transverse

580   (B) epigastric

581   (C) ventral

582   (D) ipsilateral

583 19. Compared to the upper arm, the fingers are

584   (A) superficial

585   (B) distal

586   (C) parasagittal

587   (D) horizontal

588 20. A sagittal plane divides the body into

589   (A) right and left sides

590   (B) anterior and posterior portions

591   (C) superior and inferior portions

592   (D) lateral and contralateral portions

593   21. A cross section of an organ is made in an organ when it is
594   divided across the
595   (A) sagittal plane
596   (B) midsagittal plane
597   (C) coronal plane
598   (D) transverse plane

599   22. The cranial cavity and spinal cavity make up the
600   (A) inferior body cavity
601   (B) superior body cavity
602   (C) dorsal body cavity
603   (D) ventral body cavity

604   23. The mediastinum is located within the
605   (A) pelvic portion of the abdominopelvic cavity
606   (B) abdominal portion of the abdominopelvic cavity
607   (C) spinal cavity
608   (D) thoracic cavity

609   24. The hypogastric, iliac, and umbilical regions may all be
610   located in the
611   (A) abdominopelvic cavity
612   (B) right lower quadrant of the thoracic cavity
613   (C) upper left quadrant of the spinal cavity
614   (D) dorsal cavity

615   25. The serous fluid secreted by serous membranes
616   (A) is the site of red blood cell production
617   (B) contains digestive enzymes
618   (C) permits organs to slide easily across cavity walls
619   (D) is the medium for transport of hormones in the body

620   *PART C—True/False:* **For each of the following statements,**
621   **mark the letter "T" next to the statement if it is true. If the**
622   **statement is false, change the <u>underlined</u> word to make the**
623   **statement true.**

624   1. In the levels of structure in the body, molecules associate
625   with one another to form a <u>tissue</u>.

626   2. Two or more different kinds of tissues associate to form a
627   level of structure called an <u>organ</u>.

628   3. In the metabolic process of catabolism, organic matter is
629   broken down, usually with the <u>input</u> of energy.

630   4. In the characteristic of <u>irritability</u>, cells receive stimuli and
631   transport those stimuli from one cell part to another.

632   5. <u>Asexual</u> reproduction is that form of reproduction in which
633   a single cell duplicates to yield two identical daughter cells.

634   6. Homeostasis is associated with the relative constancy of the
635   physical and <u>chemical</u> environment in the cells of an
636   organism and in the organism itself.

637   7. The self-regulating systems that function in the body to
638   protect it against extremes are known as <u>control</u> systems.

639   8. A structure found on the belly side of the body is said to
640   exist on the <u>posterior</u> aspect.

641   9. The <u>horizontal</u> position is the reference point for all the
642   directional terms referring to the body.

643   10. A structure lying in the inferior aspect of the body may also
644   be regarded as lying in the <u>caudal</u> aspect.

645   11. The eyes are said to be <u>medial</u> to the nose.

646   12. A structure lying closer to the body surface than a second
647   structure is said to be <u>superficial</u>.

648   13. The term dorsal is similar to but not exactly the same as
649   <u>anterior</u>.

650   14. Relative to the femur, the ankle is said to be <u>deep</u>.

651   15. A <u>sagittal</u> plane is a longitudinal plane that divides the
652   body into left and right sides.

653   16. A coronal plane of the body is the same as a <u>transverse</u> plane.

654   17. A coronal plane lies at a right angle to a <u>sagittal</u> plane.

655   18. The two major subdivisions of the <u>dorsal</u> body cavity are
656   the thoracic cavity and the abdominopelvic cavity.

657   19. The esophagus, trachea, and heart lie in a region of the
658   thoracic cavity called the <u>pericardium</u>.

659   20. In the abdominopelvic cavity, the epigastric region lies
660   immediately superior to the <u>hypogastric</u> region.

661   21. Lateral to the umbilical region of the abdominopelvic cavity
662   are the right and left <u>inguinal</u> regions.

663   22. The walls of the <u>dorsal</u> body cavity and its organs are covered
664   by the serous membranes.

665   23. The abdominal organs and many pelvic organs are covered
666   by a serous membrane called the <u>pleura</u>.

667   24. Serous membranes generally lie very <u>distant</u> to one another.

668   25. The two main portions of the serous membranes are the
669   visceral portion and the <u>parietal</u> portion.

670 **ANSWERS**

671 *PART A—Completion*

672 1. gross anatomy   8. tissue
673 2. microscope   9. connective tissue
674 3. cells   10. epithelial tissue
675 4. renal physiology   11. organ
676 5. atoms   12. metabolism
677 6. molecules   13. anabolism
678 7. cell   14. catabolism

679 15. involuntary movement
680 16. bones
681 17. growth
682 18. nerve cells
683 19. repair
684 20. sexual reproduction
685 21. asexual reproduction
686 22. homeostasis
687 23. physical environment
688 24. oxygen
689 25. endocrine system
690 26. stress
691 27. negative feedback system
692 28. positive feedback system
693 29. anatomical position
694 30. anterior
695 31. posterior
696 32. head

33. thorax
34. lateral
35. trunk
36. lower arm
37. ipsilateral
38. sagittal plane
39. coronal plane
40. transverse plane
41. parasagittal
42. cranial cavity
43. thoracic cavity
44. mediastinum
45. peritoneal cavity
46. diaphragm
47. epigastric region
48. inguinal region
49. pericardium
50. parietal portions

697 *PART B—Multiple Choice*

698	1. C	6. C	11. B	16. A	21. D
699	2. B	7. B	12. B	17. B	22. C
700	3. D	8. A	13. D	18. D	23. D
701	4. B	9. A	14. B	19. B	24. A
702	5. C	10. D	15. C	20. A	25. C

703 *PART C—True/False*

704 1. cell
705 2. true
706 3. release
707 4. conductivity
708 5. true
709 6. true
710 7. feedback
711 8. anterior
712 9. anatomical
713 10. true
714 11. lateral
715 12. true
716 13. posterior

14. distal
15. vertical
16. frontal
17. true
18. ventral
19. mediastinum
20. umbilical
21. lumbar
22. ventral
23. peritoneum
24. close
25. true

PRACTICE READING 13: SOCIOLOGY

1 # SYMBOLIC INTERACTION
2 # AND EXCHANGE

> Skim the chapter and notice how the author uses boxes, italics, and tables to indicate key information. Make a mental picture of the key information.

3 # WORKS AT A GLANCE

4 **Symbolic Interactionism**

5 *Human Nature and the Social Order* by Charles Horton
6   Cooley (1902, 1922)
7 *Symbolic Interactionism: Perspective and Method*
8   by Herbert Blumer (1969)
9 *The Presentation of Self in Everyday Life* by Erving
10   Goffman (1959)

11 **Exchange Theory**
12 *Social Behavior: Its Elementary Forms* by George Caspar
13   Homans (1961, 1974)
14 *Exchange and Power in Social Life* by Peter Blau (1964)

15 We begin our survey of sociology with the individual
16 human being and the relations with other individuals that link
17 him or her to the immediate group and to the larger society.
18 This is the domain of sociological social psychology, although
19 many psychologists also claim this territory. Within sociology
20 the dominant approach to social psychology is *symbolic inter-*
21 *actionism*, which emphasizes the communications that provide
22 the individual with a personal identity and with socially-
23 scripted roles to play. *Exchange theory* is another important
24 perspective that argues that humans develop relationships
25 because of the rewards they can provide each other. Both
26 symbolic interactionism and exchange theory examine the
27 give-and-take between individuals, but the first believes that
28 symbols have great power of their own, whereas the second
29 asserts that symbols have power only to the extent that they
30 guide the person in achieving rewarding goals.
31 In 1937 Herbert Blumer coined the term *symbolic interac-*
32 *tionism*, but this perspective was created at the very beginning
33 of the century, chiefly by American writers such as Charles
34 Horton Cooley. To symbolic interactionists, a person's self-
35 image is very important, and people labor to create a good
36 impression in the minds of others. Cooley believed that humans
37 have an innate need to feel that life is meaningful and that
38 they themselves behave properly. Blumer stresses the fact that
39 human beings are constantly redefining situations and
40 actions, creating fresh meanings through social interaction.
41 Erving Goffman agreed with Blumer that individuals are active
42 creators of the world of meanings they inhabit, and he empha-
43 sized more than any other major theorist the ways that people
44 may consciously scheme to make a good impression and
45 manipulate other people's images of them. Modern symbolic
46 interactionists use a wide variety of research methods, but
47 much of the work is similar to humanistic literature, in which
48 a perceptive writer observes the world and responds with fresh
49 insights and critical arguments.
50 Sociological exchange theory draws heavily upon economics
51 and upon behaviorist psychology. Although many sociologists
52 have always been influenced by these other sciences,
53 exchange theory in sociology did not really consolidate until

54 the work of George Homans in the 1950s and the later efforts
55 of Peter Blau and James Coleman (see Coleman in Chapter 10
56 and Chapter 15). Exchange theorists argue that the desire for
57 rewards is the motivator of all behavior, including manage-
58 ment of one's public impression and conformity to the desires
59 of others. Currently, ideas from exchange theory permeate
60 much of sociology, and social psychologists have developed a
61 strong tradition of laboratory experimentation on exchange.

62 **Symbolic Interactionism**
63 Cooley, Charles Horton
64   1922 Human Nature and the Social Order. New York:
65   Scribner's.

66   At the time that Cooley wrote, many scientists and intellec-
67 tuals believed that the chief factors shaping a person's behavior
68 were individual genetic inheritance and the biological nature
69 shared by all human beings. Cooley did not disagree that these
70 were important factors, but he asserted that social influence
71 was equally significant. Although we talk about the individual
72 separately from society, and society separately from individuals,
73 really they are the same thing, what Cooley calls *Human Life*.
74 Without society, no individual human being could exist, and
75 without individuals there would be no society. It is not just
76 that each individual relies upon society for food and other
77 material necessities, but that an infant could not mature into
78 a person without the formal and informal education provided
79 by society. Society is the *collective* aspect of Human Life, and
80 individuals are the *distributive* aspect.
81   If humans are the product of biological inheritance and
82 social influence, do they have the capacity to choose, what is
83 often called "free will"? Or is human behavior essentially auto-
84 matic? True, human creativity always consists of a fresh
85 arrangement of existing ideas and memories, but when the
86 influences and alternatives are very complex, it makes sense to
87 refer to human choice and volition. For individuals, then,
88 choice is enhanced by elaborate mental processes, and for soci-
89 ety, by complex social relations. The increasing complexity of
90 modern society has magnified choice, as has the extreme
91 diversity of American democracy.

92   Cooley's theory of Human Life emphasizes the way that
93 sociability creates ideas in our minds that represent other
94 individuals, and the way that others give us impressions of
95 ourselves. A friend exists in our mind as a system of thoughts
96 and symbols, representing how that person acts, sounds,
97 looks, and responds to us. Society exists in our mind as the
98 collection of ideas we have about specific other individuals.
99 Cooley stresses that the solid facts of sociology are the imagina-
100 tions that individuals have of each other. Thus the proper
101 focus of sociological study is the thoughts that people have in
102 their minds.

103   The individual *self* is simply what a person means when he
104 or she says "I," "me," "my," or "mine." Part of it is a special
105 feeling—Cooley calls it the *my-feeling*—rooted in biological
106 instincts, which is hard to describe in words but everybody
107 understands. Although we have this feeling about our own
108 bodies, Cooley says that the social and psychological aspects
109 of self are far more important to us. The *social self* is the set of
110 ideas the individual has about himself or herself, which are
111 derived from communication with other people. An important
112 part of the social self is our impression of how other people
113 view us. Since we cannot see into their minds directly, we learn
114 about their picture of us by observing how they respond to us,
115 almost as a mirror might reflect our image back to us. Cooley
116 calls this the *looking-glass self*, a term widely quoted by later
117 sociologists. It has three main parts: (1) how we imagine we
118 appear to the other person, (2) how we think that person
119 judges us, and (3) how we react to that judgment, whether with
120 pride or shame.

121   The metaphor of a looking-glass fits when the social envi-
122 ronment is especially stable, like the solid reflecting surface of
123 a mirror. But Cooley recognizes that sometimes the social
124 environment is highly unstable, and the reflection is distorted
125 as if by rushing waters. Every human being, Cooley says, needs
126 self-expression, appreciation from others, and a reasonable
127 degree of security. When these needs are thwarted, the person
128 becomes pathological; Cooley believes this is the source of nearly
129 all social discontent. Powerless workers, exploited immigrants,
130 and members of disvalued ethnic groups are sociological

131 examples of people who are denied the chance to satisfy these
132 needs. Human beings have an instinct to demand rules, which
133 guide and reconcile their impulses, and they are comfortable
134 with habits of thought and action. Thus when a stable and
135 benign society provides ethical rules for its members, these are
136 not experienced as an imposition but as a comfortable harmony
137 between individual and group.

138   In a group, the individual develops a larger social self, using
139 words like "we," "our," and "us." Elsewhere, Cooley calls this
140 the *we-feeling*, an expanded ver-
141 sion of the my-feeling. A fan of a
142 sports team may exclaim, "We
143 won!" without ever being at the
144 game, and citizens who never
145 served in the military may feel a
146 sense of victory when "we" win
147 a war. Often, however, a person
148 develops a wider self through
149 identifying not with the group
150 but with a singular individual,
151 the hero or leader. The person
152 uses the leader as a moral guide,
153 asking what the leader would do
154 under the given circumstances
155 before taking action. Sometimes
156 that guide is a distant friend, and
157 we imagine what he or she
158 might say, or it could be our
159 fanciful image of an ideal
160 person we have never met, such
161 as a national hero or a religious
162 personage. But during unsettled times, like twentieth-century
163 America, even the face of God may be blurred, like the sun
164 reflected from troubled waters.

> What might the significance of Cooley's ideas be in modern America? Do you believe they would be widely accepted or rejected? Why? A good reader should be able to form questions like these to put information into a context, and then also be prepared to answer the questions to demonstrate an understanding of the material. Make a habit of doing this with all the important information you need to learn.

165 Blumer, Herbert
166   1969 *Symbolic Interactionism: Perspective and Method.*
167   Englewood Cliffs, New Jersey: Prentice-Hall.

168   Blumer seeks to define *symbolic interactionism* and to criticize
169 other perspectives for ignoring its key insights. Symbolic inter-
170 actionism is based on three premises:

171   1. Human beings act toward things on the basis of the mean-
172   ing those things have for them.
173   2. The meaning of things arises from social interaction.
174   3. Meanings are handled and modified through interpretation
175   by the person.

176   Thus, meanings are created socially yet interpreted actively
177 by the individual, and they are central to human action. People
178 must learn meanings from others, and an object does not simply
179 have a fixed meaning. Rather, meanings change as people
180 redefine objects. For example, the stars in the sky had very dif-
181 ferent meaning for ancient people than they have for us today,
182 now that we consider them to be distant suns. Perhaps the
183 most significant object for any person is the self, how he or
184 she understands himself or herself. The self is the key factor in
185 determining the person's actions. Like other objects, each self
186 is created through social interaction, and we see ourselves
187 from the perspective of other people. Because all objects are
188 constantly being redefined, human society and behavior are
189 constantly transformed by human creativity. Society itself is
190 the result of symbolic interaction.
191   In any society there are recurrent patterns of joint action
192 that follow somewhat stable principles, because people share
193 meanings and know what behavior is expected of them. Sociolo-
194 gists have studied many of these varied patterns, such as families,
195 boys' gangs, industrial corporations, and political parties. Some
196 sociologists say that their stability is maintained by norms and
197 values, but Blumer says the opposite is true: norms and values
198 are created and upheld by the social processes of group life.
199 Joint action consists of very complex networks of actions by
200 diverse people who are linked together. The societal institutions
201 that arise from this joint action are not stable entities in their
202 own right but result from the interrelated actions of many
203 individuals, as they define the varied situations in which they
204 find themselves. Although human beings are constantly

205 redefining objects and actions in the present, every social sit-
206 uation has a long history and cannot be understood correctly
207 without examining the processes that shaped it in the past.
208   Blumer is highly critical of sociologists who employ other
209 perspectives that assume the objectivity of such concepts as
210 *attitudes* and *variables*. The concept of attitude assumes that a
211 person has some kind of fixed tendency to act in a particular
212 way that can be distinguished from the person's other charac-
213 teristics (such as feelings, ideas, opinions, and decisions) and
214 from the actions themselves. Symbolic interactionists think
215 people do not possess a set of automatic responses but con-
216 stantly respond to new demands and possibilities in a creative
217 manner by sizing up situations and by developing fresh defin-
218 itions through social interaction. Rather than misguidedly try-
219 ing to measure a person's fixed attitudes, sociologists should
220 study the dynamic process by which the person and the group
221 define actions and mobilize for collective action.
222   In a similar manner, Blumer is critical of sociologists who
223 rely too heavily upon measurement and statistical analysis of
224 variables. A variable supposedly is a well-defined entity, like
225 the tendency to vote Republican or having a college education,
226 that varies from person to person. Blumer notes that quantita-
227 tive sociologists select variables haphazardly, and that few of
228 them represent abstract scientific concepts. Many sociologists
229 wrongly assume that a variable has a stable meaning. Rather,
230 it is constantly changing as people socially redefine it. For
231 example, the Republican Party is not the same thing today
232 that it was last year. Thus, meanings change over time, and
233 respondents to a questionnaire will interpret the questions in
234 different ways. Many sociologists claim that variations in the
235 independent variables of a research study determine variations
236 in the dependent variables. But this is wrong. For instance, a
237 research study that merely correlated the introduction of a
238 birth control program with the birth rate would be highly
239 incomplete. It would need to employ symbolic interactionism
240 to examine how birth control enters into the lives of the people,
241 through the meanings they assign to it.

242 Goffman, Erving
243   1959 *The Presentation of Self in Everyday Life.* New York:
244   Anchor.

245   Goffman analyzes the ways that people manage the public
246 impressions they make, using metaphors taken from the theater
247 and from subcultures that emphasize deception. He illustrates
248 his ideas with examples taken from some of his own research
249 in the Shetland Islands, from books about occupations and
250 settings where people are apt to deceive each other, and from
251 observations reported in unpublished dissertations and papers
252 by members of the sociology department at the University of
253 Chicago, where Goffman himself was a student. Sociologists
254 had long spoken of the roles that people play, but Goffman
255 shifted the emphasis in sociological understanding of role
256 playing in two ways. First, he described people as very active
257 shapers of their own roles, rather than merely accepting the roles
258 society scripted for them. Second, he developed a language for
259 talking about roles, partly derived from the theater, that he
260 called the *dramaturgical* approach.
261   In the theater, some people called the *actors* play roles on
262 stage that fit together into a particular drama. Other people play
263 a very different role and belong to a group called the *audience*,
264 which exists only in relationship to the actors but is excluded
265 from much inside information that the actors possess. The
266 actors on stage impose a *definition of the situation* on the audi-
267 ence, for example asserting that this is not a stage filled with
268 actors but the castle of Macbeth populated with Scottish
269 nobles and servants. Similarly, in the "real world" outside the
270 theater, people attempt to impose upon others a definition of
271 the situation that attributes to themselves characteristics that
272 they may not really possess. Goffman does not seek to test
273 whether this theory is true, or to determine statistically how
274 often it is true. Rather, using this dramaturgical perspective, he
275 identifies a number of roles, dramatic techniques, and role-
276 playing contexts, describing their dynamics and assigning
277 them names.
278   Performances vary in the degree of sincerity with which the
279 actor plays them, but insincerity is not necessarily undesirable.
280 A shoe clerk sells a customer a shoe that fits well, and lies

281 when saying that it is the size the customer requested. Carried
282 off well, this performance satisfies the customer not only with
283 physically comfortable feet but also with the pride that his or
284 her feet are not too fat. Little "white lies" commonly serve the
285 needs of the audience as well as those of the actors, but often
286 it is possible to use innuendo, strategic ambiguity, and crucial
287 omissions to achieve a successful performance without actually
288 lying. Goffman asserts that all legitimate vocations and relation-
289 ships require the performer to conceal something, and thus all
290 everyday performances are precarious. Social life is possible only
291 because all ordinary human beings have some skill as actors.
292   The part of a performance that defines the situation for the
293 audience is called *front*. This involves the setting, which includes
294 furniture, decor, physical layout, and any items that serve as
295 scenery or stage props for the performance. A doctor's office,
296 with all its strange paraphernalia, is the setting that supports the
297 role of physician. A routine performance of some importance
298 for the society becomes idealized, in the sense that everybody
299 shares standard expectations for it, and a good performance
300 upholds the moral values of the community.
301   Goffman sees much to be learned from examination of the
302 different performances that define the separate social classes,
303 especially when a person from one social class acts like a mem-
304 ber of another. In America, wealth is such a strong determi-
305 nant of social class that people struggle to buy status symbols
306 that will let them enter the next-highest class. In India, members
307 of a moderately low caste may start practicing the rituals and
308 food regulations of a higher caste to gain entry to it, despite
309 formal prohibitions against caste switching. Sometimes people
310 adopt the performances of lower classes, as when a Shetland
311 farmer simulates being poor, with ragged clothes and a house
312 in disrepair, in order to discourage the landowner from
313 increasing the rents.
314   Actors often work in teams. A *performance team* is any set of
315 people who cooperate in staging a given routine. Each teammate
316 typically has the power to ruin the performance, and because
317 the members of the team share inside knowledge about their
318 joint performance they are unable to maintain its objectivity
319 with each other. Teams are like secret societies, whose members

320 cooperate to project a particular definition of the situation on
321 their audience. They put on their performance in a *front region*,
322 where the audience observes them, and they typically need a
323 *back region* or *backstage* where the audience cannot go and
324 where they can drop their burdensome roles.
325   The example to which Goffman continually returns is the
326 hotel in the Shetland Islands where he stayed during his field
327 research. In front of the guests, especially in the dining room,
328 the staff of the hotel behaved in the dignified but respectful
329 manner of middle-class professionals serving elite clients. In
330 the backstage area of the kitchen, however, they relaxed, spoke
331 disrespectfully of the guests, and resumed their rural habits of
332 speech and manner. The presentation of food to the guests was
333 a key element of the drama, and the kitchen staff understood
334 well what the limits of play-acting were. The meat had to be
335 reasonably fresh, because the guests understood how to judge
336 it and tended to focus upon it. The soup, in contrast, could get
337 by as a mixture of yesterday's brew, plus a little left over from
338 the day before, with a few new ingredients. Perfectly good but-
339 ter would return from the dining room in odd shapes, and it
340 could be recycled simply by pressing it into nice patterns in
341 the butter molds. When the staff was very busy, it would wipe
342 the glasses rather than take the time to wash them, and the
343 guests seemed happy at prompt service and unharmed by the
344 dubious hygiene. Often, in social life, impressions count for
345 more than does reality, if, indeed, there is any reality beyond
346 the impression humans make upon each other.

347 ## Exchange Theory

348 Homans, George Caspar.
349   1974 *Social Behavior: Its Elementary Forms.* New York: Harcourt
350   Brace Jovanovich.

351   Homans seeks to set out a general theory of human social
352 behavior, but before he can do this, he needs to state what a
353 scientific theory is. Ideally, such a theory is a formal structure
354 of *propositions*, which are statements about the relationship
355 between properties of nature. Some of these propositions are
356 very general, like the axioms in classical Greek geometry. Other

357 propositions are derived from them through formal logic, like
358 the theorems and corollaries of geometry. When sociologists
359 discover a regular finding in their research, it should be stated
360 as a proposition, and that proposition should be explained. To
361 *explain* a proposition means to show that it follows as a matter
362 of pure logic from other, more general propositions.
363   Homans offers five very general propositions, which he
364 believes can explain much about human social behavior. Each
365 is very much like an axiom from geometry, except that
366 Homans believes it is rooted in human biological evolution
367 rather than in the nature of lines and planes in space, as is the
368 case for geometry. The five general propositions follow.

369 1. For all actions taken by persons, the more often a particular
370   action of a person is rewarded, the more likely the person
371   is to perform that action.
372 2. If in the past the occurrence of a particular stimulus, or set
373   of stimuli, has been the occasion on which a person's action
374   has been rewarded, then the more similar the present
375   stimuli are to the past ones, the more likely the person is
376   to perform the action, or some similar action, now.
377 3. The more valuable to a person is the result of his or her
378   action, the more likely the person is to perform the action.
379 4. The more often in the recent past a person has received a
380   particular reward, the less valuable any further unit of
381   that reward becomes for that person.
382 5. This proposition is in two parts:

383   a. When a person's action does not receive the reward he
384   expected, or receives punishment he did not expect,
385   he will be angry; he becomes more likely to perform
386   aggressive behavior, and the results of such behavior
387   will become more valuable to him.
388   b. When a person's action receives the reward he
389   expected, especially a greater reward than he expected,
390   or does not receive punishment he expected, he will be
391   pleased; he becomes more likely to perform approving
392   behavior, and the results of such behavior become
393   more valuable to him.

394   These propositions concern individual human beings,
395 rather than large-scale phenomena such as society. Homans
396 believed it would be possible to build sociological theory up
397 from the individual level. The first proposition states that an
398 individual's action is shaped by rewards. If a given action is
399 rewarded, the person becomes more likely to perform it. Imagine
400 that a fisherman has cast his line into a particular pool, and
401 has caught a fish, which is rewarding to him. He will cast his
402 line in the pool again. This proposition is taken from behavioral
403 psychology, especially from the work of Homans's colleague at
404 Harvard and close friend, B. F. Skinner.

405   The second proposition brings in stimuli, including new
406 stimuli that may be more or less similar to old ones, and new
407 actions. The fisherman may find that casting his line into dark
408 pools has been rewarding, whereas light pools have not been.
409 So he will discriminate dark pools from light ones, and be more
410 likely to cast his line into dark ones. He can also generalize
411 from the original stimuli and actions. He will try casting his
412 line into many kinds of pool, and learn which are more
413 rewarding, and he may even try hunting, which is the general-
414 ization of fishing from the water to the dry land. This proposi-
415 tion brings in the branch of psychology devoted to perception
416 and cognition. Human beings are especially capable of learning
417 complex judgments of similarity and dissimilarity compared
418 with other animals studied by psychologists, such as pigeons
419 and mice.

420   The third proposition concerns the value of results from a
421 person's actions, which may be positive (rewards) or negative
422 (punishments). Some values are innate, determined biologically
423 by the genetic inheritence shared by all human beings. For
424 example, hunger makes humans seek food. But some social
425 values may also be innate. Humans evolved as social animals,
426 living in groups that hunted and gathered food together, and
427 the desire for social contact and such intimate actions as hugging
428 may have been programmed into us by biological evolution,
429 just as horses have been programmed to roam in herds. Values
430 are not merely innate but can also be learned. For example,
431 mothers may hug their children when they perform actions
432 the mothers approve of, thus teaching children to value those

433 actions as means of obtaining hugs. Social learning—developing
434 a pattern of behavior because it is rewarded by other human
435 beings—is very important in Homans's theory, giving rise to the
436 norms of groups and to the large sets of norms we call cultures.
437   The fourth proposition concerns satiation and deprivation.
438 If we have just eaten a big meal, we are no longer hungry. Our
439 hunger has been satiated, and thus the value of food has been
440 reduced. But if we are deprived of food for a long time, our
441 hunger will increase until no reward is more important to us
442 than food. Surprisingly, this principle forms the very basis of
443 social exchange. If a person, A, has much food, A will always
444 be able to eat whenever he or she is even the least bit hungry.
445 Thus the person will not value food very much, and is willing
446 to part with it in return for some other reward that A lacks, for
447 example warm clothing. If person B is hungry but has two
448 warm coats, and the weather is cold, A may be willing to give
449 B a lot of food in return for one coat. Person B is not much
450 more satisfied by two coats than by one, so B is willing to
451 make the exchange. Thus, the fact that people have different
452 resources, and can be satisfied by a limited amount of each,
453 allows both parties to exchange to profit.
454   The fifth proposition seems complicated, but both parts of
455 it concern a person's reaction when he or she receives much
456 less or much more than expected. The first part is a standard
457 observation from psychology, that frustration often leads to
458 aggression. If unexpected loss leads to angry aggression,
459 Homans hypothesizes that unexpected gain should also lead
460 to emotional behavior, in this case approval. In an exchange
461 that frustrated one of the parties, aggression may force the
462 other party to behave better in the future. Approval tells an
463 exchange partner that some behavior was appreciated and
464 should be continued.
465   On the basis of these five fundamental theoretical proposi-
466 tions, Homans seeks to build a structure that explains much
467 human action. In office work, for example, a social relationship
468 may develop out of repeated exchanges between two people in
469 which one provides advice (the valuable reward of informa-
470 tion) in exchange for approval (a purely social reward). Norms
471 arise out of exchanges in groups. A norm defines expected

472 behavior that will receive
473 approval rather than punishing
474 aggression. Using empirical stud-
475 ies by other social scientists for his
476 illustrations, Homans develops
477 explanations of conformity, strat-
478 ification, and justice.

Summarize Homans's ideas and then imagine how they might be applied to modern thinking about social behavior.

479 Blau, Peter
480   1964 *Exchange and Power in Social Life.* New York: Wiley.

481   Blau explains that the early chapters of his book are based
482 to a great extent on Homans's *Social Behavior* (1961 edition),
483 but he goes much further than Homans in developing a theory
484 of how large-scale social structures are built out of social
485 exchange between individuals. The key task of sociology, he
486 says, is to analyze social associations, which are based on the
487 fact that both parties to an exchange can often benefit. But this
488 does not mean that the parties to an exchange benefit equally,
489 that they have complete information about the exchange, or
490 that each exchange occurs in a vacuum isolated from other
491 commitments the parties may have. Often an individual is able
492 to get more from an exchange than the other person does,
493 because he or she has more power of one kind or another.
494   People are attracted to others if they expect exchanges
495 with them to be rewarding, and they need to become attrac-
496 tive to the others in order to develop an enduring association.
497 Often a person wants something from another but has nothing
498 to give in return that the other wants. A person in this uncom-
499 fortable situation has four basic alternatives. First, it may be pos-
501 sible to force the other person to give the desired item,
502 perhaps by threat of violence or outright theft. Second, it may
503 be possible to find another person who can provide the item.
504 Third, the person who wants the item can simply learn to live
505 without it. And fourth, the person may subordinate himself or
506 herself to the person who has the item, giving that person
507 power. Thus, in the course of a large number of social
508 exchanges, some individuals come to have power over others.

509 Looking at these four alternatives from a slightly different
510 perspective, Blau examines what factors give a person indepen-
511 dence from the power of others or power over others, and how
512 these factors create large-scale social structures. He summarizes
513 his theory in a chart:

	Alternatives to Compliance	Conditions of Independence	Requirements of Power	Structural Implications
514 515				
516 517 518	1. Supply inducements	Strategic resources	Indifference to what others want	Exchange and distribution of resources
519 520	2. Obtain elsewhere	Available alternatives	Monopoly over what others need	Competition and exchange rates
521 522	3. Take by force	Coercive force	Law and order	Organization and differentiation
523 524 525	4. Do without	Ideals lessening needs	Materialistic and other relevant values	Ideology formation

526 If person *A* desires reward *X* possessed by person *B*, *A* can
527 offer some valuable resource *Y* to *B* in return for *X*. Thus, *A*
528 can be independent of *B*'s power because *A* possesses *Y*. But *B*
529 can assert power by being indifferent to *Y*. If *B* wants *Y*, then
530 *A* and *B* exchange their resources and the beginnings of a
531 distribution system for rewards emerges.

532 If alternative sources of *X* are available (people *C* and *D*, for
533 example), then *B* cannot have power over *A*, because *A* can
534 simply go to one of the other sources for *X*. However, if *B* can
535 acquire a monopoly over *X*, being the only available supplier,
536 then *B* has power. When there are multiple potential sources
537 of a reward, then there is competition, and *B*, *C*, and *D* vie with
538 each other in offering *A* favorable terms for the exchange.

539 If *A* has the capacity to exercise coercive force, then *A*
540 might take *X* from *B* against *B*'s will. Person *B* in collusion with
541 *C* and *D* can create a system of law and order that prevents the
542 use of naked force. This produces complex social organizations
543 based on law and upholding order, and a variety of such orga-
544 nizations produce a differentiated social system.

545 Person *A* may be able to do without *X*, especially if *A* can
546 adopt philosophical ideals that lessen the feeling of needing *X*.
547 Person *B* can counter these ideals with materialistic values or
548 other ideals that increase *A*'s need for *X*. The result is the forma-
549 tion of ideology. In a large collection of people having different
550 resources, many exchanges will therefore produce a complex
551 social system, consisting of institutions that distribute rewards,
552 competition between individuals and between groups, a struc-
553 ture of differentiated organizations, and ideologies.

554 Once the beginnings of such a system emerge, the dynamics
555 of power change. Collective approval legitimates power, and
556 legitimate authority forms the basis of organization. Persons *A*
557 and *B* do not merely negotiate with each other, but also turn
558 to others for support. If *B* can get *C* and *D* to agree that *B* has
559 legitimate authority, then *B*'s power over *A* is considerably
560 strengthened. A value consensus may emerge in the society,
561 convincing even poor *A* that *B*'s authority is just. Norms devel-
562 op that define the terms of fair exchange and justice. Even if
563 *A* does not agree with the con-
564 sensus, the agreement of the
565 other members of the society
566 imposes it upon *A*. Successful
567 leaders command the willing
568 compliance of many subordi-
569 nates, who in turn impose the
570 leader's power upon anyone who
571 does not comply. A successful
572 leader, therefore, cannot simply
573 be a dictator but must offer suffi-
574 cient rewards to the subordinates
575 to be socially attractive to them.
576 Thus legitimacy tends to limit an
577 individual's power, even as it cre-
578 ates a powerful social system.

How does Blau go further than Homans in developing a theory of large-scale social structures? Do you agree or disagree with his ideas? Why? These types of questions force you to think about the significance of information being read and do not permit you to merely look at the words.

Conclusion

CONGRATULATIONS ON YOUR first step toward becoming one of the top learners in the world. Speed-reading will get easier with practice and result in more benefits than you ever imagined.

Index